The Pages of History

Compiled and with

Commentaries by

DAVID CARNEY

Pen & Publish
Saint Louis, Missouri

Copyright © 2020 by David Carney

All rights exclusively reserved. No part of the commentaries in this book may be reproduced or translated into any language or utilized in any for or by any means, electronic or mechanical, including photocopying, recording, or by any information storage and retrieval system, without permission in writing from the publisher.

David Carney

The Pages of History

1st edition

ISBN: 978-1-941799-84-0 (paperback)

Published by Pen & Publish, LLC

Saint Louis, Missouri
(314) 827-6567
www.penandpublish.com

Cover Design: Pen & Publish

Contents

Foreword by Ronald Eugene Isetti 5
Preface: About these Pages 7

SECTION ONE:
AMERICAN STATESMEN 11

Patrick Henry: Address to the Second Virginia Convention 14
Thomas Jefferson: Nomination of James Monroe
    to Negotiate the Purchase of New Orleans 20
The Monroe Doctrine 25
Chief Seattle: Treaty Oration 30
Abraham Lincoln: The Gettysburg Address 35
Abraham Lincoln: Second Inaugural Address 40
Adlai Stevenson: The Cat Bill Veto 44
John F. Kennedy: Inaugural Address 48
Robert Kennedy: Eulogy for Martin Luther King 54

SECTION TWO:
FREEDOM AND THE HUMAN SPIRIT 59

The English Declaration of Rights 61
The Declaration of Independence 67
The Bill of Rights 74
The Declaration of the Rights of Man and of the Citizen 80
The Emancipation Proclamation 86
The October Manifesto 91

SECTION THREE:
THE WORLD WARS OF THE TWENTIETH CENTURY 95

The Entente Cordiale 98
The Ultimatum from Austria to Serbia 105
Kaiser Wilhelm: Address to the Reichstag 113
Woodrow Wilson: The Fourteen Points 118

The Munich Pact 124
Winston Churchill: Initial Broadcast as Prime Minister 130
The Atlantic Charter...135
Franklin Roosevelt: Address to the Nation after Pearl Harbor 139
The Japanese Instrument of Surrender 144

SECTION FOUR:
FAITH AND RELIGION   151

The Decalogue of Moses...153
Preface to the Martyrology for Christmas Day 157
Pope Urban II: The Call for a Crusade..160
The Act of Supremacy 166
The Dedication of the King James Bible 171

SECTION FIVE:
ART & SCIENCE, WISDOM & UNDERSTANDING   177

The Hippocratic Oath..180
The Abjuration of Galileo 186
Preface to the First Folio of Shakespeare..193
Johann Sebastian Bach: Two Dedications 198
Ludwig van Beethoven: The Heiligenstadt Testament 204
Franz Grillparzer: Oration at Beethoven's Funeral...209
F. T. Marinetti: The Futurist Manifesto 213
Albert Einstein: Letter to President Roosevelt..218

Afterword 223
Acknowledgments..225
Bibliography..226
Sources of Illustrations 233

Foreword

The past is darkness until we shine a light on it. Scholars have employed many different torches to illuminate what came before us. There is drum and trumpet history, bottom-up history, psycho-history, women's history, and data-driven history or cliometrics, among several other approaches.

David Carney has provided us with a novel and revealing new outlook on the past. He has chosen to reproduce and provide interesting background material on a wide variety of short documents—the "pages of history"—that have shaped the way we think and live our lives. They are as varied as the human experience: the Gettysburg Address, the Declaration of the Rights of Man and of the Citizen, the Munich Pact, the Dedication of the King James Bible, and Einstein's letter to President Roosevelt, to cite but a few examples. A lucid and sprightly writer, Carney provides illuminating background material on each of these short documents, some of which speak to each other over time.

More than ever, we need to shed light on our past. Strictly speaking, history does not repeat itself. But it can provide important lessons that we ignore at our peril. Many of the documents Carney has chosen illustrate the power of the human word to inspire and define and provoke us even today. They are the guideposts of Western Civilization, useful to ponder as we encounter the never-ending winds of change that every age must endure. How we weather those winds will rightly form the Pages of today's History that will be our legacy to the future.

Ronald Eugene Isetti, PhD
Saint Mary's College of California Emeritus

History testifies to the passing of time; it illumines reality, vitalizes memory, provides guidance in daily life and brings us tidings of antiquity.
—Cicero (106 BCE–43 BCE)

History is the version of past events that people have decided to agree upon.
—Napoleon Bonaparte (1769–1821)

History will be kind to me for I intend to write it.
—Sir Winston Churchill (1874–1965)

Preface: About these Pages

A bold premise, indeed: to present, in a single short volume, the pages of history. And that is precisely what I claim to do. Not all of the pages, surely, but enough to warrant the title. There is a catch, of course.

The premise of the book is simple. Throughout human history—at least throughout the last few millennia—there exists a number of very short documents, miniatures whose significance echoes far beyond their size. Some of these were seminal and changed the world. Others were private reflections on private matters. In some cases the documents are masterpieces of rhetoric that stir the soul; others are simple and mundane. Some are like pebbles to an avalanche and provoked great deeds. Others are simply an individual's testimony, intense and personal, but with words that still resonate for us today. These miniatures include letters, speeches, addresses, prefaces, proclamations, manifestos, declarations, and testaments. Their authors include scientists, kings, rebels, artists, the inevitable Anonymous, and perhaps even the Deity. Some of these documents are known to almost everyone, others are known only to the specialist. But all share a common trait of great economy of word while containing greatness of humanity and of spirit.

The idea for gathering together some of these miniatures into a single volume arose several summers ago in Boston, where the Boston Globe traditionally prints the Declaration of Independence as its editorial for the Fourth of July. I had not read it since school days, and I found its power amazing. It provoked me to return to some other key political documents, texts that I had read and forgotten. What struck me most in this journey of rediscovery was how short some of these texts were, and how powerful that shortness could be. The Declaration of Independence, no longer than a single newspaper editorial, was the foundation for the nation. Lincoln, in his Gettysburg Address, could describe the whole American Experiment in two dozen lines of text. Repeatedly, whether in ancient days or the recent past, we can see landmark events surrounding a remarkable economy of word. God establishes a Covenant with Moses in ten sentences.

Galileo capitulates to the Pope in five paragraphs. And Einstein leads Roosevelt into the nuclear abyss in five hundred words.

So I set out to collect some other similar works, and this volume is the result. The original idea for including each was that, in addition to being a text of some lasting significance, each work should occupy no more than a page, a characteristic that led to the book's title. But as the work began, a significant flaw soon appeared, as it became clear that the constraint of a single page might be overly restrictive—it would certainly force me, in the case of the Declaration of Independence, for instance, to present it in an unreadable tiny font, or worse, would prevent its inclusion in this volume. So I slightly relaxed my constraint. I still sought miniatures, small, compact, powerful documents. But I would allow that they spill onto a second page, and fit on two sides of a single leaf.[1]

That hurdle overcome, it still seemed that there would be few candidates that conformed to such a criterion, but the opposite turned out to be true; there were actually more selections available than could reasonably be included, and the task became more one of winnowing than of scouring. What to include and what to omit?

I decided that, for the most part, the documents should be self-contained things, and that excerpts were not in the scope of the search. In one sense, this was a very useful decision, since although the beginning concept was with the American political canon, the focus was actually the written works of the entire history of the world, with a very large number of potential selections. That so large a body of texts contains a wealth of great miniatures is obvious—but I sought those miniatures that are self-contained. The search was therefore restricted to texts that really did fit in their entirety on a single page (or two). This decision on self-containment, however, was not absolute. It turned out that there were a few occasions where an important text truly is a separate thing, yet is also embedded within a longer document. The Monroe Doctrine is a perfect example. It stands alone, both conceptually and politically. But for pragmatic reasons, Monroe chose to communicate these critical words as part of his annual message to Congress. In such cases, I tried to make reasonable decisions (and thus I did include the Monroe Doctrine).

---

[1] The Reader might, at this point, rightly accuse me of a slight fraud, since I did not change the title of the work. However, I reasoned that a title such as *The Leaves of History* left me (and several friendly reviewers) rather cold. Still worse, a title such as *The Sheets of History*, actually suggested by one reviewer, would imply a work with an entirely different focus.

But whether those decisions will be seen as reasonable is perhaps an open question: in truth, the element of personal whim cannot be denied, so stating these excuses is all just an elaborate rationalization of my choices. And since I was the one doing the choosing, I could include or omit whatever I wished. Still, I think that my adherence to my original criterion—single, short, powerful texts—has been, like a nearly perfect spouse, mostly faithful.

So, having stated these criteria, what is included herein? Things that were proclaimed. Things that were urgently imparted, usually with reference to some signal cause or condition. Things said or written by eyewitnesses that perhaps give a perspective not otherwise available in histories. And, in one or two cases, things that I stumbled upon, was very moved by, and simply wanted to include.

Of the famous documents included here, most are known to almost everyone. But as often as not, we tend to know *about* them. We discussed them in school and learned of the great events they mark. We deem them to be part of our common heritage and acknowledge their power in our lives. Yet in many, perhaps in most cases, they are not truly known, in the real sense of personal experience. While most of us can repeat a phrase or two— ". . . of the people, by the people, for the people . . ."—we seldom actually read the words for ourselves to see what they really say. So this book is an attempt to remedy that circumstance, and at the same time, to make known a few writings no less worthy, yet far less famous.

The introductions have been drawn from commonly available historical references, and are my attempts to provide, for each Page, a general summary of the circumstances of its creation. In some cases, this has resulted in commentaries that will seem to skate with dangerous glibness over very weighty and complex events, to which I plead guilty as charged. But I wanted the Pages, not my comments, to be the focus, and so I had to walk the thin tightrope between giving the depth of background that an historian might cherish, and acting simply as a guide for the nonprofessional tourist. I tried to provide the minimal amount to let the Pages speak for themselves, and others will have to judge how gracefully I managed that tightrope.

So, Reader, I think there is greatness in this book. Not mine, of course, but that of the great people, exalted or anonymous, whose words are included here. Whatever their fame, these documents are important in various and often subtle ways. If I have whetted your appetite, as I hope I have, go forward. Turn these Pages of our History, marvel at the power of brevity, and see what wonders can be found in a minimum of words. We all know that the pen is mightier than the sword. But a more interesting discovery (and the point of this book) is that the pen should need so few drops of ink.

AMERICAN STATESMEN

*Political society exists for the sake of noble actions,
and not of mere companionship (Aristotle, Politics, III,9)*

In this section I have gathered nine Pages from American history that are identified with some of our greatest statesmen. The issues that concern these Pages are various, ranging from great and mighty statements in the international arena to simple words about the domestic travails of ordinary citizens in Illinois. They span the period from the nation's birth to the mid-twentieth century. They are all very personal statements by great leaders. And for me, they somehow conjoin, like the different parts of a quilt, to make a whole, single, multicolored fabric that is quintessentially American.

That said, my choices still probably need some explanation. Some of the selections are fairly obvious candidates for a collection such as this. The Monroe Doctrine, for instance, needs no justification, nor should the selection by Thomas Jefferson (or, for that matter, almost any selection from Jefferson's pen). As for John F. Kennedy, in spite of recent reconsiderations, he is still an undisputed twentieth-century icon, having redefined the American presidency by making youth an asset and style a decisive factor. His inaugural address thrilled its hearers when he delivered it, and it is no less thrilling now, six decades later. And Patrick Henry's speech to the Virginia Assembly, though it has been reprinted often, is still an immortal text that could not be omitted from the volume.

Lincoln appears twice in this section, which befits his high place in the esteem of the nation and the world. The Gettysburg Address occupies the pinnacle of rhetorical excellence; in two hundred seventy-two words, Lincoln captures the essential tragedy of the Civil War and transcends it with perhaps the greatest vision of the nation ever voiced. And his Second Inaugural Address, coming at the end of such bitterness, is a testament to wisdom, compassion, and humanity; there are few texts anywhere that are as perfect. For contrast, there is a very human and humorous Page from Adlai Stevenson. By any definition a statesman and also a personal hero, Stevenson was far greater than is shown by this selection. But it is so winning a text that I had to include it.

Just a few years later, the assassination of Martin Luther King was a traumatic episode that had profound on American citizens of every color and creed: Robert Kennedy's words on the night of King's death capture a good deal of the sense of loss that most people felt as that news spread throughout the nation.

I have also understood the notion of "statesman" in a broader sense than is shown by the above choices. For me, the term is not confined to an individual that occupies high office, but is equally applicable to a person who speaks great words on affairs that somehow concern the nation as a whole. So Chief Seattle's famous and bittersweet oration (whoever actually wrote it) addresses a very great subject indeed, namely, the foundation of the American experience: the mere existence of the American continent was, for Europeans, justification for seizing it.

I was unhappy that I came across no selections from George Washington that could be included. The most likely possibility, his Farewell Address, was certainly a text of great importance. But it is also a text of great length, and I saw in it no justification for making an excerpt. [The beautiful photograph below will have to symbolize his contribution to American statesmanship.] I also regret that, in my view, at least, there are no occasions since 1968 when an American statesman—by anyone's definition—has uttered or written words that lay claim to greatness or immortality. This opinion may perhaps cause rebuttal from some quarters. But few would deny that a painful vacuum exists. The absence of statesmanship, manifest by the paucity of great and powerful rhetoric, is the single most evident characteristic of the Body Politic as we navigate the new millennium. From the twilight of the twentieth century until now, in the third decade of the 21st, sound bites have come to rule our public dialogue, "spin" is a word to be said without shame, the pathetic birth of "fake news" has occurred, and polls tell the candidates which truths to caress and which truths to corrupt. Hardly the nobility of action so precious to Aristotle.

The Washington Monument

Finally, since these Pages are arranged chronologically, it is easily seen that the choices I made for this section tend to be separated by a period of about a generation, except for the ninety-year gap between Lincoln and Stevenson. This gap is due to my decision to include the selections from both Wilson and Roosevelt in the section on the World War. Similarly, some of the Pages included here could easily fall into other parts of the volume; Seattle's Oration, for instance, would certainly be at home in the section on "Freedom and the Human Spirit." Mea culpa, and if putting certain Pages into the wrong category is the worst defect to be found throughout this book, then all is indeed well with the world.

Patrick Henry: Address to the Second Virginia Convention

In the 1970s, when Bicentennial fever began spreading through the country, several of the original thirteen states developed appropriate mottoes about their role in the Revolution. In Massachusetts, in recognition of the importance of the actions of the Minute Men, the slogan "Where it all began" was among those used. It is probable that any historian would agree that Massachusetts indeed played a central role in the Revolution, and that "the shot heard 'round the world" ranks high in importance. But a reading of the events leading up to the Revolution tells a fuller tale, and in any contest about "where it all began," Massachusetts would have a strong rival in her elder sister Virginia. And this is indeed apt, since there were many interesting similarities that bound the destinies of these two great colonies.

They were the sites of the earliest English settlements in North America (Virginia in 1609, Massachusetts in 1620 and 1630). Each grew and prospered around the shore of a great bay, fed by several rivers. Both were settled under the early Stuart kings, whose reigns are memorialized in such names as Jamestown, Charlestown, and the James and Charles rivers. Both became commonwealths, a status they share to this day. Together they produced a remarkably large proportion of the great leaders in the revolutionary struggle against Great Britain. Massachusetts gave us John Adams, James Otis, Samuel Adams, and Paul Revere; Virginia brought forth George Washington, Thomas Jefferson, James Madison, George Mason—and a hotheaded young lawyer named Patrick Henry. And since Patrick Henry's oration of 1775 provides the first Page of this volume, and with apologies to Massachusetts, Virginia will be, for us, at least, where it will all begin.

Patrick Henry took his place in history almost by accident. By his early 20s he had failed miserably in the business ventures he attempted, so began reading law for lack of anything better to do. With only the most meager preparation he presented himself for examination by the judges at Williamsburg. Whatever academic knowledge of the law he had, it is very likely that his gifts for dramatic and persuasive public speech helped convince the judges, for they granted him a license to practice. This skill at oratory was one of the two things that marked Henry's entire career: by all accounts he could sway his listeners like a conjurer. As described by a contemporary:

> His pauses, which for their length might sometimes be feared to dispel the attention, riveted it the more by raising the expectation.

The second important facet of Henry's personality was that from the outset, he saw the British Crown as an enemy. A constant refrain in his public utterances is the depiction of English rule as a tyrannical yoke on the Colonies. His opinion of the Crown was manifest early, when he gained his first legal fame—or rather, notoriety. It happened in a celebrated trial called the "Parson's Cause," a dispute between Virginia clergymen and the colonial government.

By a long-standing law, all Anglican clergy received a yearly salary from the colony of several thousand pounds of tobacco. When sold, this typically brought a comfortable amount to each clergyman. The 1750's however, had witnessed several crop failures, and with sharply rising prices, the tobacco payment became a substantial windfall for the clerics. Doubtless with a mind only to due fiscal responsibility, the Virginia Assembly ruled, in 1755 and 1758, that in lieu of tobacco, the salaries should be paid in cash, at the rate of two pennies per pound. The clergy, standing to lose their newfound wealth, appealed to the Crown, which overturned the Assembly's ruling. When, in 1763, the Reverend James Maury sued for payment of his salary in tobacco, a jury was named to decide the issue; Henry, a young and unseasoned lawyer, was appointed for the defense. Completely sidestepping the essential points of the case, Henry instead made a series of ringing accusations against the King. In historian John Miller's account:

> He chose, rather, to denounce the clergy as unpatriotic ingrates. . . . he pronounced the action of the British government, in disallowing the Two-Penny Act, a high-handed encroachment on Colonial liberty. Henry declared that "a King, by disallowing Acts of this salutary nature . . . has degenerated into a Tyrant and forfeits all rights to his subjects' obedience."

Though the speech horrified many, and was thought to be tantamount to treason, the result of the impassioned oration was that the jury awarded the distraught clergyman (whom Henry was supposedly defending) only one penny in damages.

His next celebrated speech, a milestone in the years before the Revolution, came in May 1765, when he electrified the Virginia House of Burgesses in a blazing denunciation of the Stamp Act. This Act had been passed by Parliament earlier that year, calling for a stamp (and thus a tax) on all commercial transactions, property exchanges, lawsuits, diplomas, and even tavern licenses. The Act was universally hated throughout the Colonies, but no one had declared any intention to violate it. Not until May, that is, when Henry took his bold and radical stand. His words again brought forth cries of "treason," this time with some justification: he compared the tyranny of King George to that of Caesar, and made a thinly-veiled reminder of the fate that tyrants like Caesar had met. At the climax of his address, he proposed seven "resolves." Five of these described the basic rights of Americans and the legal limits of Parliament to tax them. But the final two went far beyond that: they called for complete resistance to the Stamp Act and a suppression of any voice raised in its support. News of the speech spread rapidly, and protests against the Stamp Act were soon heard in every quarter. Save for a few in Georgia, no stamps were sold in the thirteen colonies, and Parliament repealed the Act the next year.

Henry's most famous words, found on the following Page, were spoken in March 1775, when Massachusetts and Virginia were both on the verge of open revolt. On March 23, at a meeting held in Richmond, Henry spoke urgently of the need to raise a militia: by this point there was no doubt in anyone's mind that fighting was close at hand (Lexington and Concord were less than a month away). Henry makes no attempt to disguise this fact. "The war is inevitable," he says, and still more strongly, "the war is begun." His speech echoed then, and still does now, with fervor and patriotism; by it alone, Henry was assured a place in the American Pantheon.

It should be noted that whatever he said on that occasion, what remains is a reconstruction, made years later, by William Wirt. How close this text is to the true one can never fully be known.[2] But presuming that the reconstruction is at all faithful, it was an oration of passion, force, and righteousness, with a closing line that is the equal of any in History.

---

[2] An exhaustive study by Stephen T. Olsen asserts that the text Wirt records was not spoken by Henry, but was by a Virginia Judge, St. George Tucker.

St. John's Church, Richmond, VA

Alfred Jones, *Patrick Henry Addressing the Second Virginia Convention*

St. John's Church, Richmond, Virginia March 23, 1775.

Mr. President: No man thinks more highly than I do of the patriotism, as well as abilities, of the very worthy gentlemen who have just addressed the House. But different men often see the same subject in different lights; and, therefore, I hope it will not be thought disrespectful to those gentlemen if, entertaining as I do, opinions of a character very opposite to theirs, I shall speak forth my sentiments freely, and without reserve. This is no time for ceremony. The question before the House is one of awful moment to this country. For my own part, I consider it as nothing less than a question of freedom or slavery; and in proportion to the magnitude of the subject ought to be the freedom of the debate. It is only in this way that we can hope to arrive at truth, and fulfil the great responsibility which we hold to God and our country. Should I keep back my opinions at such a time, through fear of giving offence, I should consider myself as guilty of treason towards my country, and of an act of disloyalty toward the majesty of heaven, which I revere above all earthly kings.

Mr. President, it is natural to man to indulge in the illusions of hope. We are apt to shut our eyes against a painful truth, and listen to the song of that siren till she transforms us into beasts. Is this the part of wise men, engaged in a great and arduous struggle for liberty? Are we disposed to be of the number of those who, having eyes, see not, and having ears, hear not, the things which so nearly concern their temporal salvation? For my part, whatever anguish of spirit it may cost, I am willing to know the whole truth; to know the worst, and to provide for it.

I have but one lamp by which my feet are guided; and that is the lamp of experience. I know of no way of judging of the future but by the past. And judging by the past, I wish to know what there has been in the conduct of the British ministry for the last ten years, to justify those hopes with which gentlemen have been pleased to solace themselves, and the House? Is it that insidious smile with which our petition has been lately received? Trust it not, sir; it will prove a snare to your feet. Suffer not yourselves to be betrayed with a kiss. Ask yourselves how this gracious reception of our petition comports with these war-like preparations which cover our waters and darken our land. Are fleets and armies necessary to a work of love and reconciliation? Have we shown ourselves so unwilling to be reconciled, that force must be called in to win back our love? Let us not deceive ourselves, sir. These are the implements of war and subjugation; the last arguments to which kings resort. I ask, gentlemen, sir, what means this martial array, if its purpose be not to force us to submission? Can gentlemen assign any other possible motive for it? Has Great Britain any enemy, in this quarter of the world, to call for all this accumulation of navies and armies? No, sir, she has none. They are meant for us; they can be meant for no other. They are sent over to bind and rivet upon us those chains which the British ministry have been so long forging. And what have we to oppose to them? Shall we try argument? Sir, we have been trying that for the last ten years. Have we anything new to offer upon the subject? Nothing. We have held the subject up in every light of which it is capable; but it has been all in vain. Shall we resort to entreaty and humble supplication? What terms shall we find which have not been already exhausted? Let us not, I beseech you, sir, deceive ourselves. Sir, we have done everything that could be done, to avert the storm which is now coming on. We have petitioned; we have remonstrated; we have supplicated; we have prostrated ourselves before the throne, and have implored its interposition to arrest the tyrannical hands of the ministry and parliament. Our petitions have been slighted; our remonstrances have produced additional violence and insult; our supplications have been disregarded; and we have been spurned, with contempt, from the foot of the throne. In vain, after these things, may we indulge the fond hope of peace and reconciliation. There is no longer any room for hope. If we wish to be free—if we mean to preserve inviolate those inestimable privileges for which we have been so long contending—if we mean not basely to abandon the noble struggle in which we have been so long engaged, and which we have pledged ourselves never to abandon until the glorious object of our contest shall be obtained, we must fight! I repeat it, sir, we must fight! An appeal to arms and to the God of Hosts is all that is left us!

They tell us, sir, that we are weak; unable to cope with so formidable an adversary. But when shall we be stronger? Will it be the next week, or the next year? Will it be when we are totally disarmed, and when a British guard shall be stationed in every house? Shall we gather strength by irresolution and inaction? Shall we acquire the means of effectual resistance, by lying supinely on our backs, and hugging the delusive phantom of hope, until our enemies shall have bound us hand and foot? Sir, we are not weak, if we make a proper use of the means which the God of nature hath placed in our power. Three millions of people, armed in the holy cause of liberty, and in such a country as that which we possess, are invincible by any force which our enemy can send against us. Besides, sir, we shall not fight our battles alone. There is a just God who presides over the destinies of nations; and who will raise up friends to fight our battles for us. The battle, sir, is not to the strong alone; it is to the vigilant, the active, the brave. Besides, sir, we have no election. If we were base enough to desire it, it is now too late to retire from the contest. There is no retreat, but in submission and slavery! Our chains are forged! Their clanking may be heard on the plains of Boston! The war is inevitable—and let it come! I repeat it, sir, let it come!

It is in vain, sir, to extenuate the matter. Gentlemen may cry, peace, peace but there is no peace. The war is actually begun! The next gale that sweeps from the north will bring to our ears the clash of resounding arms! Our brethren are already in the field! Why stand we here idle? What is it that gentlemen wish? What would they have? Is life so dear, or peace so sweet, as to be purchased at the price of chains and slavery? Forbid it, Almighty God! I know not what course others may take; but as for me, give me liberty or give me death!

Thomas Jefferson: Nomination of James Monroe to Negotiate the Purchase of New Orleans

The Mississippi River was a key factor in the economic health of the young United States. From the very beginning of the Republic, Washington considered navigation of the Mississippi as central to the nation's economic survival. By 1800, the produce from nearly half the nation passed through New Orleans on its way to the marketplace; in the words of then President Jefferson:

> There is on the globe one single spot, the possessor of which is our natural and habitual enemy. It is New Orleans...

At the end of the American Revolution in 1783, the control of the Mississippi was essentially in the hands of Spain, since the river was the eastern boundary of the Louisiana Territory, a vast tract of Spanish land stretching from the Mississippi to the Rockies, and covering some 800,000 square miles. In 1795, Thomas Pinckney had negotiated the Treaty of San Lorenzo with Spain, by which the United States obtained a "right of deposit" in New Orleans, which meant that the river could be used by America as an export passage for goods and produce. However, in 1800, Spain ceded the Louisiana Territory to France, which was then under the ever-growing domination of its new "First Consul," Napoleon Bonaparte. Napoleon was then dreaming of restoring a great colonial empire for France, and in October 1802, he ordered the American right of deposit to be rescinded.

Jefferson had long realized the danger of French ambitions in America. He had already outlined his understanding of the political realities surrounding Louisiana, the Mississippi, and Napoleon's plans in a long letter to the United States minister to Paris, Robert R. Livingston. Jefferson did not wish to alienate France, America's strongest supporter during the Revolution; but his paramount concern was to preserve American commercial rights, no matter what else may befall.

Given the need to maintain American access to New Orleans, Jefferson nominated James Monroe as "extraordinary minister" to assist Livingston in the negotiations with Napoleon for securing and maintaining a continuation of the right of deposit. If need be, Monroe and Livingston were authorized to try to purchase New Orleans itself. The following Page is Jefferson's message to Congress describing Monroe's mission.

As events turned out, Napoleon's colonial dreams were dashed by the uprising in the French colony of Haiti. Haiti was central to France's American plans, but the revolt there, led by Toussaint l'Ouverture, consumed thousands of French lives and proved to Napoleon the folly of his dream. By April of 1803, he abandoned his plan entirely, and instead instructed his Foreign Minister Talleyrand to sell the entire Louisiana Territory to the Americans. So Monroe and Livingston, who had been authorized to spend as much as $10 million for New Orleans alone, now found themselves purchasing, at a price of $15 million, enough land to double the size of the United States.

Henry Adams provides a vivid account of Napoleon's sudden turnaround. He notes that:

> Monroe arrived in sight of the French coast April 7, 1803; but while he was still on the ocean, Bonaparte, without reference to him or his mission, opened his mind to Talleyrand in regard to ceding Louisiana to the United States ... For months, [Livingston] had wearied the First Consul with written and verbal arguments, remonstrances ... that the United States cared nothing for Louisiana, but wanted only West Florida and New Orleans—'barren sands and sunken marshes'—Talleyrand had listened with his imperturbable silence ... until he suddenly looked into Livingston's face and asked 'What will you give for the whole?' Naturally Livingston for a moment lost countenance ...

As we read this Page on Monroe's nomination, Jefferson emerges as remarkably pragmatic, particularly about the shifting winds of world politics. Jefferson prudently notes, for instance, that although France was ceded the Louisiana Territory in 1800, "the possession of these provinces is still in Spain." Jefferson knew how long it took, given the Atlantic crossings, to put a new bureaucracy in place, and although the nominal *legal* owner of Louisiana was France, the actual persons that occupied state offices were still Spanish (and, in fact, it was the Spanish intendant in New Orleans who had rescinded the right of deposit, though by Napoleon's order).

But Jefferson was also well aware of how quickly conditions could change, given the volatile European situation. He clearly hedged his bets by adding a provision to empower negotiation with Spain, if events should dictate it. So Monroe would go wherever needed, and Jefferson would win, whatever happened in Europe. If Napoleon held on to power, and France continued to own Louisiana, Livingston would negotiate with Napoleon (with Monroe's assistance). If for some unforeseen reason Spain got Louisiana back, well and good: Pinckney would negotiate with Spain (again, with Monroe's support).

Ironically, though he lost everything in the end, Napoleon was not without his own perceptions about world events. For instance, the Louisiana Purchase was illegal both under the French Constitution and also under the the terms by which Spain had ceded the territory to France. But Napoleon ignored the legal niceties, and went ahead with the sale in any case. When challenged about pursuing this course, he gave the following prescient response:

> I have just given England a maritime rival that sooner or later will lay low her pride.

January 11, 1803

Gentlemen of the Senate:

The cession of the Spanish Province of Louisiana to France, and perhaps of the Floridas, and the late suspension of our right of deposit at New Orleans are events of primary interest to the United States. On both occasions such measures were promptly taken as were thought most likely amicably to remove the present and to prevent future causes of inquietude. The objects of these measures were to obtain the territory on the left bank of the Mississippi and eastward of that, if practicable, on conditions to which the proper authorities of our country would agree, or at least to prevent any changes which might lessen the secure exercise of our rights. While my confidence in our minister plenipotentiary at Paris is entire and undiminished, I still think that these objects might be promoted by joining with him a person sent from hence directly, carrying with him the feelings and sentiments of the nation excited on the late occurrence, impressed by full communications of all the views we entertain on this interesting subject, and thus prepared to meet and to improve to an useful result the counter propositions of the other contracting party, whatsoever form their interests may give to them, and to secure to us the ultimate accomplishment of our object.

I therefore nominate Robert R. Livingston to be minister plenipotentiary and James Monroe to be minister extraordinary and plenipotentiary, with full powers to both jointly, or to either on the death of the other, to enter into a treaty or convention with the First Consul of France for the purpose of enlarging and more effectually securing our rights and interests in the river Mississippi and in the Territories eastward thereof.

But as the possession of these provinces is still in Spain, and the course of events may retard or prevent the cession to France being carried into effect, to secure our object it will be expedient to address equal powers to the Government of Spain also, to be used only in the event of its being necessary.

I therefore nominate Charles Pinckney to be minister plenipotentiary, and James Monroe, of Virginia, to be minister extraordinary and plenipotentiary, with full powers to both jointly, or to either on the death of the other, to enter into a treaty or convention with His Catholic Majesty for the purposes of enlarging and more effectually securing our rights and interests in the river Mississippi and in the Territories eastward thereof.

Th: Jefferson

Rembrandt Peale, ***Thomas Jefferson***

Jacques-Louis David, ***Napoleon Crossing the Alps***

The Monroe Doctrine

In December 1823, the nation was nearly half a century old. It had withstood the rigors of another war with Britain, had grown enormously in size, and was starting to assert itself in world affairs. That December, President James Monroe enunciated his famous Doctrine in his annual message to Congress. Historian Richard Morris singles out this address as the cornerstone of this emergent assertiveness:

> The Monroe Doctrine was really a commitment to leadership in world politics, a bold and far-reaching commitment, modified in the course of time and extended to meet changing circumstances. Constituting the classic definition of the role of the United States in international affairs, it has been with considerable justice called the "most significant of all American state papers."

There were three major (and overlapping) political currents that provoked Monroe's statement. The first was bound up with the legacy of the Napoleonic wars. At the Congress of Vienna that met after Napoleon's defeat, the major European rulers concurred that the leading threat to the legitimate established order (and the factor that had led to Napoleon) lay in the revolutions that were cropping up in Europe and the Americas. The major outcome of the Congress, therefore, was an agreement among the Great Powers to suppress, under the guise of "legitimacy," all republican or revolutionary activity. So when, in 1820, a rebellion against King Ferdinand VII of Spain resulted in victory for the rebels and a great reduction in power of the Spanish monarchy, an alliance of Russia, Prussia, Austria, and France (called the "Holy Alliance") chose to intervene in Spain. There were two goals for this intervention: the foremost was restoration of Ferdinand's authority, but of nearly equal importance was the restoration of Spanish authority over her Latin American colonies, most of which were in some state of revolutionary activity.

The second political current lay in Great Britain's opposition to this action by the Holy Alliance. In political sympathy, she was no ardent supporter of revolution, nor did she applaud the notion of any imperial power losing its colonies to rebellion. But the decreased French and Spanish presence in South America had brought with it a corresponding increase of commercial possibilities for Britain. Given such a vacuum, and the lucrative potential for Britain to fill it, she had no desire for a return of Spanish hegemony in Latin America. This led Britain to the unusual posture of opposing any further European involvement in the Americas, a position of unexpected harmony with the United States. Britain even went so far as to propose a joint declaration, by Britain and America, against the Alliance, a proposal that was eventually rejected by Monroe.

The third political current was Russia's eastern outlook. In addition to her European activities, Russia was also a Pacific power and maintained a sizable colonial presence on the west coast of North America. This presence included Alaska, but also extended as far south as California. When in 1821 Tsar Alexander declared that Russian traders had exclusive authority from the 51st parallel north (slightly above present-day Vancouver), his words provoked an immediate and negative reaction in the United States.

The political concepts that underlie the Monroe Doctrine were not new to Monroe or his time; they were embedded in Washington's Farewell Address given almost three decades earlier in 1796. Washington had distinguished between an "American system" and a "European system," with an obvious preference for the former:

> Europe has a set of interests which to us have none or a very remote relation. Hence. she must be engaged in frequent controversies, the causes of which are essentially foreign to our concerns ... Our detached and distant situation invites and enables us to pursue a different course ... the period is not far off when we may defy material injury from external annoyance ... It is our true policy to steer clear of permanent alliances with any part of the foreign world.

Secretary of State John Quincy Adams was one of the major influences that led to the formulation of the Doctrine. When Russia made its pronouncement about the 51st parallel, Adams declared to the Russian ambassador that:

> We should contest the right of Russia to any territorial establishment on this continent ... The American continents are no longer subjects for any new European colonial establishments ...

Adams, in effect, thought that the time had come when Washington's prediction had come true: America could now "defy material injury from external annoyance ..." and the occasion was ripe for the United States to declare herself among the Great Powers. In Adams' own words, we should "take our stand against the Holy Alliance, and at the same time decline the overture from Great Britain [to jointly oppose the Holy Alliance]."

Adams had also wanted the text to be expressed in the form of a diplomatic correspondence between the President and the European ministries. If Monroe had followed Adams' advice, my task would have been slightly easier, since the Doctrine would then easily have met my confines of a single Page. But instead, Monroe overruled Adams, and the actual words of the Monroe Doctrine are found in two widely separated parts of the longer message to Congress, So, as with a few other of the Pages in this book, I plead guilty of breaking my own rules, claiming in this case that if Morris is right, then "the most significant of all American state papers" deserves an exception.

Samuel Morse, *James Monroe*

... At the proposal of the Russian Imperial Government, made through the minister of the Emperor residing here, a full power and instructions have been transmitted to the minister of the United States at St. Petersburg to arrange by amicable negotiation the respective rights and interests of the two nations on the northwest coast of this continent. A similar proposal has been made by His Imperial Majesty to the Government of Great Britain, which has likewise been acceded to. The Government of the United States has been desirous by this friendly proceeding of manifesting the great value which they have invariably attached to the friendship of the Emperor and their solicitude to cultivate the best understanding with his Government. In the discussions to which this interest has given rise and in the arrangements by which they may terminate the occasion has been judged proper for asserting, as a principle in which the rights and interests of the United States are involved, that the American continents, by the free and independent condition which they have assumed and maintain, are henceforth not to be considered as subjects for future colonization by any European powers...

It was stated at the commencement of the last session that a great effort was then making in Spain and Portugal to improve the condition of the people of those countries, and that it appeared to be conducted with extraordinary moderation. It need scarcely be remarked that the results have been so far very different from what was then anticipated. Of events in that quarter of the globe, with which we have so much intercourse and from which we derive our origin, we have always been anxious and interested spectators. The citizens of the United States cherish sentiments the most friendly in favor of the liberty and happiness of their fellow-men on that side of the Atlantic. In the wars of the European powers in matters relating to themselves we have never taken any part, nor does it comport with our policy to do so. It is only when our rights are invaded or seriously menaced that we resent injuries or make preparation for our defense. With the movements in this hemisphere we are of necessity more immediately connected, and by causes which must be obvious to all enlightened and impartial observers. The political system of the allied powers is essentially different in this respect from that of America. This difference proceeds from that which exists in their respective Governments; and to the defense of our own, which has been achieved by the loss of so much blood and treasure, and matured by the wisdom of their most enlightened citizens, and under which we have enjoyed unexampled felicity, this whole nation is devoted. We owe it, therefore, to candor and to the amicable relations existing between the United States and those powers to declare that we should consider any attempt on their part to extend their system to any portion of this hemisphere as dangerous to our peace and safety. With the existing colonies or dependencies of any European power we have not interfered and shall not interfere. But with the Governments who have declared their independence and maintain it, and whose independence we have, on great consideration and on just principles, acknowledged, we could not view any interposition for the purpose of oppressing them, or controlling in any other manner their destiny, by any European power in any other light than as the manifestation of an unfriendly disposition toward the United States. In the war between those new Governments and Spain we declared our neutrality at the time of their recognition, and to this we have adhered, and shall continue to adhere, provided no change shall occur which, in the judgement of the competent authorities of this Government, shall make a corresponding change on the part of the United States indispensable to their security.

The late events in Spain and Portugal shew that Europe is still unsettled. Of this important fact no stronger proof can be adduced than that the allied powers should have thought it proper, on any principle satisfactory to themselves, to have interposed by force in the internal concerns of Spain. To what extent such interposition may be carried, on the same principle, is a question in which all independent powers whose governments differ from theirs are interested, even those most remote, and surely none of them more so than the United States. Our policy in regard to Europe, which was adopted at an early stage of the wars which have so long agitated that quarter of the globe, nevertheless remains the same, which is, not to interfere in the internal concerns of any of its powers; to consider the government de facto as the legitimate government for us; to cultivate friendly relations with it, and to preserve those relations by a frank, firm, and manly policy, meeting in all instances the just claims of every power, submitting to injuries from none. But in regard to those continents circumstances are eminently and conspicuously different. It is impossible that the allied powers should extend their political system to any portion of either continent without endangering our peace and happiness; nor can anyone believe that our southern brethren, if left to themselves, would adopt it of their own accord. It is equally impossible, therefore, that we should behold such interposition in any form with indifference. If we look to the comparative strength and resources of Spain and those new Governments, and their distance from each other, it must be obvious that she can never subdue them. It is still the true policy of the United States to leave the parties to themselves, in hope that other powers will pursue the same course. . . .

Chief Seattle: Treaty Oration

There have been many misunderstandings about this famous text. The first issue concerns its essential veracity: it is very possible that Chief Seattle[3] never said these words.

The historical facts upon which we can rely are thin. A Chief Seattle did exist, the city did take its name from him, and he did participate in negotiations to sell Indian land in the Puget Sound area to the White settlers. But aside from those few details, the record grows less clear. This oration is generally thought to date from the occasion of the signing of the Point Elliott Treaty in 1855. However, the source for this ascription is one "Dr. Henry Smith." Smith was a recent arrival in the area, his command of Seattle's native language was probably less than perfect, and he did not publish his account of it until more than thirty years later (in the Seattle Sunday Star, October 29, 1887). So Smith's rendering of Seattle's words is almost certainly a paraphrase, and was conceivably only Smith's notion of what Seattle would be saying, or should have said.

The second controversial issue concerns variant texts. A reprint of the Smith text in 1931 was essentially faithful to the 1887 text, but added three short sentences to the end, an addition that has been maintained in most subsequent versions. Then Smith's version was updated by William Arrowsmith in 1969 (to "translate" it from its Victorian ornateness); this version also preserves the essential shape and meaning of the 1887 text.

However two other variants appeared in 1972 and 1974 (the latter for the Spokane Expo), both of which were substantial revisions. The 1972 revision, prepared for use in an environmental television documentary, was heavily flavored with pro-ecological sentiment, and inventions of things that the real Seattle could never have said. The additions include condemnation of the white man's greed ("I have seen a thousand rotting buffaloes on the prairie, left by the white man who shot them from a passing train") mixed with unlikely sentimentality. The 1974 revision had the same bias as the 1972 version, but was drastically shortened.

Regardless of its authenticity, the revised text of 1972—clearly a different text, but still ascribed to Chief Seattle—gained a wide following. It made its way into

---

[3] Chief Seattle's proper name is Sealth (Seathle, Seathl, or See-ahth). This original name is preserved through the name of Chief Sealth International High School, as well as the well-known bronze statue of Chief Sealth raising his right arm in greeting, found at Tilikum Place in Seattle.

documentaries and books, and spread not only throughout the country but throughout the world; in short order, the revision had supplanted Smith's "real" 1887 text. Several attempts were made to rectify the misattribution. Finally, in 1987, Rudolph Kaiser, a West German historian, published a fully documented article entitled "Chief Seattle's Speech(es): American Origins and European Reception" that told the full tale, and from which I have borrowed this brief literary history.

Variants aside, the 1887 text, which is the one presented here, still poses the question as to how much is Seattle's and how much is Smith's, and the inevitable question of the text's real value. Jerry Clark, of the National Archive and Records Administration, firmly comes down as opposing its value:

> Does it really make any difference today whether the oration in question actually originated with Chief Seattle in 1855 or with Dr. Smith in 1887? Of course it matters, because this memorable statement loses its moral force and validity if it is the literary creation of a frontier physician rather than the thinking of an articulate and wise Indian leader. Noble thoughts based on a lie lose their nobility. The dubious and murky origins of Chief Seattle's alleged "Unanswered Challenge" renders it useless as supporting evidence. The historical record suggests that the compliant and passive individual named Seattle is not recognizable in the image of the defiant and angry man whose words reverberate in our time.

The truth will probably never be known. But Clark's statement notwithstanding, the text is still a commanding statement about the Native American sensibility and the loss of his continent to the white man. It is by turns sad, bitter, poignant, and hopeful, the latter when it speaks of a common destiny for all men. And these words, from whomever's hand, need no spurious or sentimental additions to resonate powerfully in our own confusing and uncertain age.

Some notes about the text itself. Many of the sentences are long, and contemporary style would probably suggest breaking some of them. I have not done so, however, for the last thing needed in this case is yet another variant. The mention of "great chief Washington" is a reference to President Franklin Pierce; for Seattle, the president's name was always "Washington." The reference to "his son" is to Governor Stevens, who was the Commissioner for Indian Affairs in the Territory. Similarly, when Seattle speaks of "George," he is speaking of the British monarch (who was, at that time, Queen Victoria). And the mention of "George's boundary moving North" refers to the division of the Oregon Territory between the United States and Great Britain in 1846. As a result of this boundary shift,

Seattle's people were no longer British subjects, but became United States citizens.

Finally, the text includes the word "tamanamus," a word that I could find in no dictionary. Arrowsmith's version of the text (i.e., the one that was "translated from the Victorian") renders this as a "prayer to the great Spirit."

Chief Seattle, photographed in 1864

Yonder sky has wept tears of compassion on our fathers for centuries untold, and which, to us looks eternal, may change. Today is fair, tomorrow it may be overcast with clouds. My words are like the stars that never set. What Seattle says, the great chief Washington, can rely upon, with as much certainty as our pale-face brothers can rely upon the return of the seasons. The son of the white chief says that his father sends us greetings of friendship and goodwill. This is kind, for we know he has little need of our friendship in return, because his people are many. They are like the grass that covers the vast prairies, while my people are few, and resemble the scattering trees of a wind-swept plain.

The great, and I presume good, white chief sends us word that he wants to buy our lands but is willing to allow us to reserve enough to live on comfortably. This indeed appears generous, for the red man no longer has rights that he need respect, and the offer may be wise, also, for we are no longer in need of a great country. There was a time when our people covered the whole land as the waves of a wind-ruffled sea cover its shell-paved floor. But that time long since passed away with the greatness of tribes almost forgotten. I will not mourn over our untimely decay, nor reproach my pale-face brothers with hastening it, for we too may have been somewhat to blame.

When our young men grow angry at some real or imaginary wrong and disfigure their faces with black paint, their hearts also are disfigured and turn black, and then their cruelty is relentless and knows no bounds, and our old men are unable to restrain them.

But let us hope that the hostilities between the red man and his paleface brothers may never return. We would have everything to lose and nothing to gain. True it is that revenge, with our young braves, is considered gain, even at the cost of their own lives, but old men who stay at home in times of war, and mothers who have sons to lose, know better.

Our great father Washington, for I presume he is now our father as well as yours, since George has moved his boundaries to the north; our great and good father, I say, sends us word by his son who, no doubt, is a great chief among his people, that if we do as he desires, he will protect us. His brave armies will be to us a bristling wall of strength, and his great ships of war will fill our harbors so that our ancient enemies far to the northward, the Simsiams and Hydas, will no longer frighten our women and old men. Then he will be our father and we will be his children. But can this ever be? Your God loves your people and hates mine; he folds his strong arms lovingly around the white man and leads him as a father leads his infant son, but he has forsaken his red children; he makes your people wax strong every day, and soon they will fill the land; while our people are ebbing away like a fast-receding tide, that will never flow again. The white man's God cannot love his red children or he would protect them. They seem to be orphans and can look nowhere for help. How then can we become brothers? How can your father become our father and bring us prosperity and awaken in us dreams of returning greatness?

Your God seems to be partial. He came to the white man. We never saw Him; never even heard His voice; He gave the white man laws but He had no word for His red children whose teeming millions filled this vast continent as the stars fill the firmament. No, we are two distinct races and must ever remain so. There is little in common between us. The ashes of our ancestors are sacred and their final resting place is hallowed ground, while you wander away from the tombs of your fathers seemingly without regret.

Your religion was written upon tables of stone by the iron finger of an angry God, lest you might forget it. The red man could never remember nor comprehend it. Our religion is the traditions of our ancestors, the dreams of our old men, given them by the great Spirit, and the visions of our sachems, and is written in the hearts of our people.

Your dead cease to love you and the homes of their nativity as soon as they pass the portals of the tomb. They wander off beyond the stars, and are soon forgotten and never return. Our dead never forget the beautiful world that gave them being. They still love its winding rivers, its great mountains, and its sequestered vales, and they ever yearn in tenderest affection over the lonely hearted living and often return to visit and comfort them. Day and night cannot dwell together. The red man has ever fled the approach of the white man, as the changing mists on the mountain flee before the blazing morning sun.

However, your proposition seems a just one, and I think that my people will accept it and will retire to the reservation you offer them, and we will dwell apart and in peace, for the words of the great white chief seem to be the voice of nature speaking to my people out of the thick darkness that is fast gathering around them like a dense fog floating inward from a midnight sea.

It matters but little where we pass the remainder of our days. They are not many. The Indian's night promises to be dark. No bright star hovers about the horizon. Sad-voiced winds moan in the distance. Some grim Nemesis of our race is on the red man's trail, and wherever he goes he will still hear the sure approaching footsteps of the fell destroyer and prepare to meet his doom, as does the wounded doe that hears the approaching footsteps of the hunter. A few more moons, a few more winters and not one of all the mighty hosts that once filled this broad land or that now roam in fragmentary bands through these vast solitudes will remain to weep over the tombs of a people once as powerful and as hopeful as your own.

But why should we repine? Why should I murmur at the fate of my people? Tribes are made up of individuals and are no better than they. Men come and go like the waves of the sea. A tear, a tamanamus, a dirge, and they are gone from our longing eyes forever. Even the white man, whose God walked and talked with him, as friend to friend, is not exempt from the common destiny. We *may* be brothers after all. We shall see.

We will ponder your proposition, and when we decide we will tell you. But should we accept it, I here and now make this the first condition: That we will not be denied the privilege, without molestation, of visiting at will the graves of our ancestors and friends. Every part of this country is sacred to my people. Every hillside, every valley, every plain and grove has been hallowed by some fond memory or some sad experience of my tribe. Even the rocks that seem to lie dumb as they swelter in the sun along the silent seashore in solemn grandeur thrill with memories of past events connected with the fate of my people, and the very dust upon your feet responds more lovingly to our footsteps than to yours, because it is the ashes of our ancestors, and our bare feet are conscious of the sympathetic touch, for the soil is rich with the life of our kindred.

The sable braves, and fond mothers, and glad-hearted maidens, and the little children who lived and rejoiced here, and whose very names are now forgotten, still love these solitudes, and their deep fastnesses at eventide grow shadowy with the presence of dusky spirits. And when the last red man shall have perished from the earth and his memory among white men shall have become a myth, these shores shall swarm with the invisible dead of my tribe, and when your children's children shall think themselves alone in the field, the shop, upon the highway, or in the silence of the woods they will not be alone. In all the earth there is no place dedicated to solitude. At night when the streets of your cities and villages shall be silent, and you think them deserted, they will throng with the returning hosts that once filled them and still love this beautiful land. The White Man will never be alone. Let him be just and deal kindly with my people, for the dead are not altogether powerless.

Abraham Lincoln: The Gettysburg Address

On July 1, 1863, at Gettysburg, Pennsylvania, near the Blue Ridge mountains, a battle began between a Union army under General George Meade and a Confederate army under General Robert E. Lee. The battle was one of the few Civil War battles fought in the North, and came at a crucial moment for both sides. The South had enjoyed remarkable military success until that point, and Lee had moved into Pennsylvania filled with confidence after his victory at Chancellorsville. He was hoping to replenish his dwindling supplies, but also to keep the Union forces occupied in the North, thus preventing any reinforcements from going to Vicksburg, where the Confederate cause was in great danger. Meade, having taken command of the Union army only days before, was intent on keeping Lee from threatening Baltimore or Washington.

Though the two armies had been stalking each other for some days, the battle in Gettysburg began almost by accident, with an unexpected skirmish. But it swiftly escalated into a full-scale confrontation and continued for three days of devastation, with moments of unparalleled carnage. The first day of battle saw staggering losses; one company that numbered 10,000 men at the start of the day had less than 3,000 by nightfall. On the third day of fighting, a deafening artillery exchange lasting over an hour prefaced the worst of the battle's mayhem, the infamous "Pickett's charge." In this hopeless encounter, 15,000 Confederate soldiers marched directly into a withering fire by Union rifles and cannon; fully half were slaughtered by the time the Confederate advance was turned back. At the end of the three days, with some 50,000 from both sides dead or wounded, Lee retreated south toward Virginia.[4]

The battle's immediate aftermath was, by all accounts, a scene from Hell itself, as bodies rotted unburied in the summer heat. Bruce Catton cites an eyewitness account of the Union dead littering the bloody countryside:

> As far as the eye could reach on both sides of the Cashtown road you could see blue-coated boys, swollen up to look as giants, quite black in the face, but nearly all on their backs, looking into the clear blue with open eyes, with their clothes torn open. It is strange that dying men tear their clothes in this manner. You see them lying in platoons of infantry

---

[4] Although the Confederate retreat was halted at Williamsport by the rain-swollen Potomac, Meade ignored the opportunity to attack the remnant of Lee's army, choosing to delay pursuit until Lee had safely crossed the river.

with officers and arms exactly as they stood or ran—artillery men with caisson blown up and four horses, each in position, dead.

Sometimes horrible battles are decisive and have lasting consequences. Other times such battles are meaningless, and have no other outcome than to prove the senselessness of war. In military terms, Gettysburg was certainly not the former; Vicksburg and Chattanooga were far more significant victories for the North. In the words of historian Richard McMurry:

> If the word "decisive" has any meaning when applied to a military engagement, it must denote a battle that determined the outcome of a war—or a battle that at least put the conflict irrevocably on the path of its final outcome. The Battle of Gettysburg did neither . . . Nor did it hasten the ultimate Northern triumph.

Its military importance notwithstanding, however, Gettysburg had a lasting consequence of a far different kind, for it brought into existence one of the most memorable works of political rhetoric ever written, and surely one of the greatest of the Pages of History. The occasion was the dedication of a cemetery.

The town of Gettysburg at that time numbered only a few thousand inhabitants, and there was little room in the existing town cemetery for the large number of corpses that needed burial. By autumn, a national cemetery had been created at the battle site; the Union soldiers who had died would be buried therein, each state having a separate section for its fallen sons. On November 19, the cemetery was dedicated, with the principal address (lasting two hours) given by the renowned orator Edward Everett. Also invited, almost as an afterthought, was President Abraham Lincoln, who spoke briefly, his speech listed in the program simply as "Dedicatory Remarks." Those remarks were Lincoln's Gettysburg Address.

This short speech—272 words— is among the most familiar texts in our history. Students memorize it, scholars analyze its variants, and writers ponder its brilliance. In it, Lincoln scales the heights of rhetorical excellence, using words with such economy and yet with such power that there are few of any era—whether writers or politicians or orators or dramatists—that can be claimed his better. It looms large in the consideration of historians of every perspective. Dwight G. Anderson, analyzing its religious implications, calls the Gettysburg Address "the best-known speech in American history." For Glen E. Thurow, discussing its role in American politics:

> It is not an exaggeration to say that the Gettysburg Address pictures everything of importance, including the meaning of life and death itself,

as being dependent on the continued existence of an America dedicated to human equality.

Statue of Lincoln at the Lincoln Memorial

The relation of the Declaration of Independence to the Gettysburg Address is central. Garry Wills' lengthy examination of the Address is a telling explication of how the Address brought about a fundamental change in the American political system. In brief, through this brief three-minute "remark," Lincoln managed to place the Declaration of Independence on the same level as the Constitution as a founding document of the nation. The principle of equality, critical to the Declaration but ignored in the Constitution, was therefore foundational for the nation, as much as were any of the other principles defined in the Constitution. Lincoln's insistence on the importance of the Declaration underlies even the very start of his Address: the "four score and seven years" point back to 1776, the date of the Declaration; for Lincoln this was the true formation of the United States. Wills notes how Lincoln's position on this point echoes one that Daniel Webster had made years earlier:

> [For Lincoln,] the Declaration of Independence was closer to being <u>the</u> founding document of the United States than was the Constitution . . . He not only put the Declaration in a new light as a founding <u>law</u>, but put its central proposition, equality, in a newly favored position as a principle of the Constitution . . . [because of the] Address, its concept of a single people dedicated to a proposition, we have been changed.

Indeed we have. The Constitution was amended, slavery was broken, and the spirit of the Gettysburg Address has resonated throughout the succeeding fifteen decades of our history. And its significance continues: with the full promise of this text still not kept, these great words are no less imperative today than they were then, at the bloody field that gave this Page its name.

One note on the text: There are numerous versions of the Gettysburg Address. Some are from variant drafts, others from newspaper accounts. The text on the following Page is that of the "Bliss Copy," which was made several months later; this was the last copy that Lincoln himself made.

Lincoln's handwritten text of the Address

Four score and seven years ago our fathers brought forth on this continent, a new nation, conceived in Liberty and dedicated to the proposition that all men are created equal.

Now we are engaged in a great civil war, testing whether that nation, or any nation so conceived and so dedicated, can long endure. We are met on a great battle-field of that war. We have come to dedicate a portion of that field, as a final resting-place for those who here gave their lives that that nation might live. It is altogether fitting and proper that we should do this.

But in a larger sense, we cannot dedicate—we cannot consecrate—we cannot hallow—this ground. The brave men, living and dead, who struggled here, have consecrated it, far above our poor power to add or detract. The world will little note, nor long remember what we say here, but it can never forget what they did here. It is for us the living rather to be dedicated here to the unfinished work which they who fought here have thus far so nobly advanced. It is rather for us to be here dedicated to the great task remaining before us—that from these honored dead we take increased devotion to that cause for which they gave the last full measure of devotion—that we here highly resolve that these dead shall not have died in vain— that this nation, under God, shall have a new birth of freedom—and that government of the people, by the people, for the people, shall not perish from the earth.

Abraham Lincoln: Second Inaugural Address

Given human nature, it is probably inevitable that the more painful and bitter a war, the more the winning side seeks to humble the loser, exacting retribution and reparation. Seldom does the victor express compassion for his defeated foe, nor admit that the time for enmity is past. The former approach is the easier, and is certainly the more popular; it takes wisdom and great statesmanship to choose the latter course.[5]

Of all the examples that history offers, Lincoln's brilliant and moving address at his second Inauguration, on March 4, 1865, is possibly the greatest statement of generosity and magnanimity from a conqueror to a vanquished enemy. In seven hundred impeccable words, Lincoln gazes at the causes and tragedy of the Civil War from its beginnings, and invokes the aid of Heaven to bring it to a full and charitable end. He is meticulous about avoiding recrimination; the South is not called evil nor the North good. As Garry Wills points out, the entire nation is accused of guilt:

> It is this counter-rhetoric of joint responsibility for the historical sin of slavery that gives Lincoln's last great statement on the war its tortured radiance ... In this last speech, war is made to pay history's dues in a prophet's ledger, where scales balance precisely the blood drawn by the lash and by the bayonet ... Lincoln speaks of "American Slavery" as a single offence ascribed to the whole nation.

There was no doubt that Lincoln meant to translate the sentiments expressed in the Inaugural Address into national policy. A month later, in April 1865, he made public his plan for reconstruction. Henry Steele Commager calls that plan:

> ... the most magnanimous terms toward a helpless opponent ever offered by a victor. For Lincoln did not consider himself a conqueror. He was, and had been since 1861, the President of the United States. The rebellion must be forgotten; and every Southern state readmitted to her full privilege in the Union.

It is interesting to see how Lincoln's desire to avoid bitterness and rancor was shared by Robert E. Lee (who seems, much moreso than Jefferson Davis, to be Lincoln's real opposite number). Lee was a man of great personal stature. He rejected the institution of slavery, and had freed the slaves that he had inherited.

---

[5] We have ample evidence in the twentieth century, in the armistice of 1918 and that of 1945, concerning these different approaches and the different results that each can bring about.

He had vainly hoped to preserve the Union: "I can contemplate no greater calamity for the country than a dissolution of the Union," he wrote just before the start of the war. Like Lincoln, he sought for healing at the war's end:

> I have since the cessation of the hostilities advised all with whom I have conversed ... to take the oath of allegiance and accept in good faith the amnesty offered ... I believe it to be the duty of everyone to unite in the restoration of the country and the re-establishment of peace and harmony ... I have too exalted an opinion of the American people to believe that they will consent to injustice ... I know of no surer way to eliciting the truth than by burying contention with the war.

Would that this hope, shared by Lincoln, Lee, and some few others of vision and wisdom, had been fulfilled. Instead, Lincoln was killed, and his plan for healing and generosity was overthrown by petty and mean men; the North embarked on a "reconstruction" based on punishment and revenge. The pain of that error has not yet disappeared; in the words of theologian Reinhold Niebuhr:

> [We today] encounter resentments in the South which are not so much the fruits of the terrible conflict as of the vindictiveness of Reconstruction ... that is, of the harsh years when the North proved that, without humility, idealism can be easily transmuted into a cruel vindictiveness.

But that sad outcome was still in the future when Lincoln spoke these great and healing words. The Second Inaugural Address, arguably among the greatest speeches ever given, still stands as a monument to what might have been, These lines are over one hundred and fifty years old, but are no less stirring, or moving, or true for us as we brave the first quarter of this fevered century. And Lincoln's wisdom is a beacon to all future victors—since there are, without doubt, wars still unfought—that shows the only rational way to define a Peace.

At this second appearing to take the oath of the Presidential office there is less occasion for an extended address than there was at the first. Then, a statement somewhat in detail of a course to be pursued seemed fitting and proper. Now, at the expiration of four years, during which public declarations have been constantly called forth on every point and phase of the great contest which still absorbs the attention and engrosses the energies of the nation, little that is new would be presented. The progress of our arms, upon which all else chiefly depends, is as well known to the public as to myself, and it is, I trust, reasonably satisfactory and encouraging to all. With high hope for the future, no prediction in regard to it is ventured.

On the occasion corresponding to this, four years ago all thoughts were anxiously directed to an impending civil war. All dreaded it, all sought to avert it. While the inaugural address was being delivered from this place, devoted altogether to saving the Union without war, insurgent agents were in the city seeking to destroy it without war, seeking to dissolve the Union and divide effects, by negotiation. Both parties deprecated war, but one of them would make war rather than let the nation survive, and the other would accept war rather than let it perish, and the war came.

President Harding at the Dedication of the Lincoln Memorial

One-eighth of the whole population were colored slaves, not distributed generally over the Union, but localized in the southern part of it. These slaves constituted a peculiar and powerful interest. All knew that this interest was somehow the cause of the war. To strengthen, perpetuate, and extend this interest was the object for which the insurgents would rend the Union, even by war; while the Government claimed no right to do more than to restrict the territorial enlargement of it. Neither party expected for the war the magnitude or the duration which it has already attained. Neither anticipated that the cause of the conflict might cease with, or even before, the conflict itself should cease. Each looked for an easier triumph, and a result less fundamental and astounding. Both read the same Bible and pray to the same God, and each invoked His aid against the other. It may seem strange that any men should dare to ask a just God's assistance in wringing their bread from the sweat of other men's faces, but let us judge not, that we be not judged. The prayers of both could not be answered. That of neither has been answered fully. The Almighty has His own purposes. "Woe unto the world because of offenses; for it must needs be that offenses come, but woe to that man by whom the offense cometh." If we shall suppose that American slavery is one of those offenses which, in the providence of God, must needs come, but which, having continued through His appointed time, He now wills to remove, and that He gives to both North and South this terrible war as the woe due to those by whom the offense came, shall we discern therein any departure from those divine attributes which the believers in a living God always ascribe to Him? Fondly do we hope, fervently do we pray, that this mighty scourge of war may speedily pass away. Yet, if God wills that it continue until all the wealth piled by the bondsman's two hundred and fifty years of unrequited toil shall be sunk, and until every drop of blood drawn with the lash shall be paid by another drawn with the sword, as was said three thousand years ago, so still it must be said "the judgments of the Lord are true and righteous altogether."

With malice toward none, with charity for all, with firmness in the right as God gives us to see the right, let us strive on to finish the work we are in, to bind up the nation's wounds, to care for him who shall have borne the battle and for his widow and his orphan, to do all which may achieve and cherish a just and lasting peace among ourselves and with all nations.

Adlai Stevenson: The "Cat Bill" Veto

During the election campaign of 1952, a volume of speeches by Adlai Stevenson was published that included a candid and compelling foreword by John Steinbeck. There, Steinbeck identifies the sole reason why he switched his political support away from Eisenhower: the quality of Stevenson's speeches. Using deceptively casual words, he says:

> There are four approaches in knowing a man. What does he look like? What has he done? What does he say—in other words think—and, last and most important, as a conditioner— what has he done to or for me?
>
> I know Mr. Stevenson only from pictures of him . . . I did not switch to Stevenson because of physical appearance, surely. Neither candidate is any great shucks in that department. I could not have changed on a basis of past achievements because Eisenhower's contribution is second to none in the world and certainly overshadows the record of the Governor of Illinois, no matter how good it may have been. I have switched entirely because of the speeches.
>
> A man cannot think muddled and write clear. Day by day it has seemed to me that Eisenhower's speeches have become more formless and mixed up and uncertain . . . Stevenson, on the other hand, has touched no political, economic, or moral subject on which he has not taken a clear and open stand . . .
>
> In a word I think Stevenson is more durable, socially, politically, and morally. Neither candidate has or is likely to do anything to or for me personally. And I can't hurt or help either of them. As a writer I love the clear, clean writing of Stevenson. As a man I like his intelligent, humorous, logical, civilized mind.

This is high praise indeed, especially striking for us today, perhaps, given the current poverty of leadership abroad in the land. And it somehow helps us understand the lasting influence that Stevenson exerts in American political thought.

It was a foregone conclusion that Adlai Stevenson would enter public life. His grandfather (also an Adlai) was Grover Cleveland's vice-president, and had been William Jennings Bryan's running mate in 1900, the year that the second Adlai was born. He came of age politically during the long Roosevelt era, and during the Second war was an assistant to the Secretary of the Navy. In 1945, he was one of the architects that defined the United Nations, participating in its earliest meetings in 1946 and 1947. Stevenson's first electoral attempt made him Governor of Illinois in 1948, and he enjoyed reasonable success in that office. He was an early opponent of McCarthyism and the anti-communist fear that percolated through the nation. He countered hysteria with common sense; when a bill to require loyalty oaths arrived on his desk, he vetoed it with: "Does anyone seriously think that a real traitor will hesitate to sign a loyalty oath?"

By 1950, and for the entire decade thereafter, Stevenson was the principal standard-bearer for the Democratic Party. He was the presidential candidate in 1952 and 1956, losing both times to Dwight Eisenhower. And he was interested, at least to some degree, in being the candidate again in 1960, though he eventually deferred to John F. Kennedy's determined pursuit of the nomination.

Though Stevenson never became president, he was nevertheless regarded, then and now, as a highly important persona in the political life of the mid-twentieth century. He was generally considered a champion of the liberal perspective. And though some later observers have contested that view, I believe that Herbert Muller's assessment remains an accurate one:

> Stevenson illumines the liberal tradition. . . . He was a moderate, never so militant as were the traditional liberals, crusaders for social and political reform. Hence, he is criticized by some contemporary liberals. . . . As I read American history, however, Stevenson spoke out of the tradition [that came] down from Jefferson and Jackson ... To my mind he represented the maturity of the liberal tradition. . . . He carried on in a temper more genuinely, philosophically liberal than the [doctrinaire] crusaders. . . .

Stevenson's influence on the Democratic Party continued to be felt until his death in 1965. He was Kennedy's Ambassador to the United Nations, and the essential outlines of Kennedy's "New Frontier" as well as of Johnson's "Great Society" echo positions taken by Stevenson a decade earlier. Jeff Broadwater, in his excellent study of Stevenson's legacy, explains Stevenson's ongoing impact:

> Stevenson endured, finally, because he refused to go quietly into oblivion. He worked hard, even after his second defeat, to retain his voice in public affairs.

True enough. And even now, three-quarters of a century later, Stevenson still refuses to go into oblivion. New studies, analyses, and commentaries continue to appear and he retains an appeal far greater than would be supposed for a twice-defeated candidate. At bottom, my own guess for Stevenson's gaining and holding such a high place in the political esteem of his fellows was that he was a statesman of perception, principle, integrity, and courage, qualities that are rare at any time, and seem to be in ever-diminishing supply. Whether he would have been a great American President is unknown; but that he was a great American is unquestionable.

The following Page is a veto message, written early in his tenure as Governor of Illinois, of a rather curious bill called the "Cat Bill." This oddity had surfaced in the Illinois Legislature at varying times in previous years, finally winning passage in 1949; it gave the new Governor an interesting test of political acumen and finesse. I intend no disservice to Stevenson by including this, and not any of his more serious writings. On the contrary, this miniature masterpiece not only gives us a wonderful insight into his wit, but also shows his deft political skill in a very unusual circumstance. After reading this gentle Page, we feel very much as though we know the man that wrote it, and want to hear more from him; this Page tells us that its author is worthy of our trust. Clear, clean writing, as Steinbeck says; hallmarks of intelligence, humour, and logic. Above all, evidence of a civilized man.

Adlai Stevenson

To the Honorable, the Members of the Senate of the Sixty-sixth General Assembly

April 23, 1949

I herewith return, without my approval, Senate Bill No. 93 entitled, "An Act to Provide Protection to Insectivorous Birds by Restraining Cats." This is the so-called "Cat Bill." I veto and withhold my approval from this Bill for the following reasons:

It would impose fines on owners or keepers who permitted their cats to run at large off their premises. It would permit any person to capture, or call upon the police to pick up and imprison, cats at large. It would permit the use of traps. The bill would have statewide application—on farms, in villages, and in metropolitan areas.

This legislation has been introduced in the past several sessions of the Legislature, and it has, over the years, been the source of much comment—not all of which has been in a serious vein. It may be that the General Assembly has now seen fit to refer it to one who can view it with a fresh outlook. Whatever the reasons for passage at this session, I cannot believe there is a widespread public demand for this law or that it could, as a practical matter, be enforced.

Furthermore, I cannot agree that it should be the declared public policy of Illinois that a cat visiting a neighbor's yard or crossing the highways is a public nuisance. It is in the nature of cats to do a certain amount of unescorted roaming. Many live with their owners in apartments or other restricted premises, and I doubt if we want to make their every brief foray an opportunity for a small game hunt by zealous citizens—with traps or otherwise. I am afraid this Bill could only create discord, recrimination, and enmity. Also consider the owner's dilemma: To escort a cat abroad on a leash is against the nature of the cat, and to permit it to venture forth for exercise unattended into a night of new dangers is against the nature of the owner. Moreover, cats perform useful service, particularly in rural areas, in combatting rodents—work they necessarily perform alone and without regard for property lines.

We are all interested in protecting certain species of birds. That cats destroy some birds, I well know, but I believe this legislation would further but little the worthy cause to which its proponents give such unselfish effort. The problem of cat versus bird is as old as time. If we attempt to resolve it by legislation who knows but what we may be called upon to take sides as well in the age old problems of dog versus cat, bird versus bird, or even bird versus worm. In my opinion, the State of Illinois and its local governing bodies already have enough to do without trying to control feline delinquency.

For these reasons, and not because I love birds the less or cats the more, I veto and withhold my approval from Senate Bill No. 93.

John F. Kennedy: Inaugural Address

During the six decades since his election, the popular standing of John Fitzgerald Kennedy has fluctuated widely, abetted by an intriguing share of mystery. Lionized during his presidency, brought almost to sainthood by his assasination, his memory unavoidably affected by his family's later misfortunes, his widow's remarriage, and finally by revelations of his foibles and humanness, Kennedy has become a study in contradiction and a symbol of the distinction between image and reality.

There are several modifiers, of course. For one thing, the very idea that an historical assessment of Kennedy should be colored by the subsequent actions of his relations is absurd. Far more important is that any assessment of Kennedy (as president, at least) must comprehend the world as it was on November 8, 1960, when Kennedy was elected; it is a world that we no longer know. That period was entirely dominated by the ongoing antagonism, military rivalry, and vast arms competition between the United States and the Soviet Union called the Cold War. The boundary between the two superpowers, first described as an "Iron Curtain" by Winston Churchill in 1946, was quite real to America in 1960, and it would soon become tangible when Berlin was bisected by an ugly stone wall in 1961.

That world seems very far away now, with the Soviet Union dismembered and Communism a word that has grown dusty. But in 1960, the Cold War was the central fact of politics, and was the defining issue in the electoral contest between Kennedy and Richard Nixon. The Soviet Union was a huge, menacing presence in the world. Its leader, Nikita Khrushchev, had promised, in 1956, to bury the West.[6] The politics of the 50s, symbolized by the U-2 debacle, appeared aimless and ineffective. Russia was apparently on the leading edge of the "missile gap," and the West seemed to be on the brink of a perilous chasm.

This was how the world felt at the time, and for a leader intending to confront such a dangerous world, an aggressive and militant posture was an asset. So although, a decade later, Viet Nam would make the term "hawk" a term of derision, hawkishness was not yet a liability in 1960. And while Kennedy has often been assumed to be a "dove" by a later generation (because he was a

---

[6] In truth, the English version of his speech misrepresented Khrushchev's real meaning, which was considerably less provocative; a more accurate translation might have been "We will outlast you." A Russian friend suggested that a more idiomatic translation might be "We will dance at your funeral."

Democrat, hence he must have been a liberal, and thus anti-war), we sometimes overlook how much of a hawk he really was.

For instance, in the 1960 presidential debates on television, it was Kennedy, far more than Nixon, that raised the spectre of the Communist menace. In analyzing one of those debates, Garry Wills remarks how informative it is to read the words abstracted from the two candidates' images. Warning of the threat of Communism, one man says:

> We should support ... the laws which the United States has passed in order to protect us from those who would destroy us from within. We should sustain ... the Department of Justice and the FBI, and we should be continually alert.

And the other retorts:

> It is also essential to being alert that we be fair; fair because by being fair we uphold the very freedoms that the Communists would destroy ... We also fight Communism at home by moving against those various injustices ... which the Communists feed upon.

Surprising to some is that the first of these excerpts is Kennedy, the second Nixon. It is even more surprising to see the assessment of Kennedy as hawk echoed from a most unexpected source, the Soviet Foreign Minister. Writing ten years after Kennedy's death, Andrei Gromyko made the following appraisal:

> The Kennedy presidency exemplifies the extent to which the reactionary rightist forces exert power in the United States ... Only during the third year of his presidency did Kennedy attempt to step out of the vicious circle of "old war diplomacy" [that is, to] stop the practice of taking extremely provocative actions on a number of fronts.

Curious indeed, and yet not that different from Wills' analysis.

While not as visible as the Cold War, the major domestic issue of the 1960 election was civil rights. And here, though Kennedy is widely regarded as a hero, the triumph of style over substance is very apparent. Again, the presidential debates are revealing. Will notes how, in the debate intended to focus on domestic issues, Kennedy forced the internal civil rights question into a global perspective:

> In the election of 1860, Abraham Lincoln said that the question was whether this nation could exist half-slave or half-free. In the election of 1960, and with the world around us, the question is whether the world can exist half-slave or half-free ... We discuss tonight domestic issues,

> but I would not want . . . any implication that this does not involve directly our struggle with Mr. Khrushchev

For Kennedy, domestic questions were always second to foreign affairs during the campaign and remained so after the election. It is sometimes forgotten that the major legislation that marked the victory of the civil rights movement came under Lyndon Johnson, not Kennedy. And, as will be described below, even the inclusion of civil rights into Kennedy's Inaugural Address was almost an afterthought.

Whatever its failings, the Inaugural Address is a masterful speech. It was delivered during the first flowering of the Television Age, when the nation as a whole was learning how closely it could witness the political process, from the conventions through the inauguration. And Kennedy well understood the power of television to transform. He was a thrilling presence: young, vital, heroic, bearing all of the graces needed for the task at hand. Wisdom hovered nearby as Robert Frost dignified the proceedings with his poetry. Nor was it all show: Kennedy's Address, with the bold strokes of its rhetoric, and its sequence of "let us . . . let us not . . ." clauses, can still move the listener who hears it for the first time, with Kennedy's ringing affirmations of our need for vigilance, courage, and honor.

Yet in dealing only with foreign affairs and the Cold War, Kennedy overlooked the burning question of the African American, the painful and central domestic concern of that day and one that is still with us. Harris Wofford, later to be a Senator from Pennsylvania, was then an advisor to Kennedy. He claims that the civil rights question is, in fact, included in the Address:

> Kennedy . . . sent the word forth "that the torch has been passed to a new generation of Americans . . . unwilling to witness or permit the slow undoing of those rights to which this nation has always been committed today at home and around the world . . ."

But Wofford is perhaps being too modest, and hides his own role in getting the issue included. Writing many years later, Richard Reeves is far more critical:

> [While listening to the Inaugural Address] Wofford . . . was listening for two words . . . Wofford was straining to hear the new President say something about civil rights. "You can't do this," he [Wofford] had told Kennedy the day before, when he had seen the final draft of the Inaugural Address . . . There was not a single word on civil rights in the speech . . . or any domestic concern at all . . . "Okay," Kennedy said, and wrote in two words ["today <u>at home</u> and around the world"]. That was it. Two words . . .

Still, it is easy today to criticize, or imagine what should have been. There can be no doubt that the threat of Communism and fear of nuclear war was a pervasive concern of the nation; the burgeoning struggle for civil rights was still finding its way. Kennedy might be faulted for overlooking that young movement, but he cannot be faulted for making the subject of his Address the topic that the nation cared most about.

So on to the Address itself. (And, borrowing Kennedy's rhetorical style: Let us not concern ourselves with what he might have said; let us concern ourselves with what he said.)

John F. Kennedy

We observe today not a victory of party, but a celebration of freedom—symbolizing an end, as well as a beginning—signifying renewal, as well as change. For I have sworn before you and Almighty God the same solemn oath our forebears prescribed nearly a century and three quarters ago.

The world is very different now. For man holds in his mortal hands the power to abolish all forms of human poverty and all forms of human life. And yet the same revolutionary beliefs for which our forebears fought are still at issue around the globe—the belief that the rights of man come not from the generosity of the state, but from the hand of God.

We dare not forget today that we are the heirs of that first revolution. Let the word go forth from this time and place, to friend and foe alike, that the torch has been passed to a new generation of Americans—born in this century, tempered by war, disciplined by a hard and bitter peace, proud of our ancient heritage—and unwilling to witness or permit the slow undoing of those human rights to which this Nation has always been committed, and to which we are committed today at home and around the world.

Let every nation know, whether it wishes us well or ill, that we shall pay any price, bear any burden, meet any hardship, support any friend, oppose any foe, in order to assure the survival and the success of liberty. This much we pledge—and more.

To those old allies whose cultural and spiritual origins we share, we pledge the loyalty of faithful friends. United, there is little we cannot do in a host of cooperative ventures. Divided, there is little we can do—for we dare not meet a powerful challenge at odds and split asunder.

To those new States whom we welcome to the ranks of the free, we pledge our word that one form of colonial control shall not have passed away merely to be replaced by a far more iron tyranny. We shall not always expect to find them supporting our view. But we shall always hope to find them strongly supporting their own freedom—and to remember that, in the past, those who foolishly sought power by riding the back of the tiger ended up inside.

To those peoples in the huts and villages across the globe struggling to break the bonds of mass misery, we pledge our best efforts to help them help themselves, for whatever period is required—not because the Communists may be doing it, not because we seek their votes, but because it is right. If a free society cannot help the many who are poor, it cannot save the few who are rich.

To our sister republics south of our border, we offer a special pledge—to convert our good words into good deeds—in a new alliance for progress—to assist free men and free governments in casting off the chains of poverty. But this peaceful revolution of hope cannot become the prey of hostile powers. Let all our neighbors know that we shall join with them to oppose aggression or subversion anywhere in the Americas. And let every other power know that this Hemisphere intends to remain the master of its own house.

To that world assembly of sovereign states, the United Nations, our last best hope in an age where the instruments of war have far outpaced the instruments of peace, we renew our pledge of support—to prevent it from becoming merely a forum for invective—to strengthen its shield of the new and the weak—and to enlarge the area in which its writ may run.

Finally, to those nations who would make themselves our adversary, we offer not a pledge but a request: that both sides begin anew the quest for peace, before the dark powers of destruction unleashed by science engulf all humanity in planned or accidental self-destruction. We dare not tempt them with weakness. For only when our arms are sufficient beyond doubt can we be certain beyond doubt that they will never be employed. But neither can two great and powerful groups of nations take comfort from our present course—both sides overburdened by the cost of modern weapons, both rightly alarmed by the steady spread of the deadly atom, yet both racing to alter that uncertain balance of terror that stays the hand of mankind's final war.

So let us begin anew—remembering on both sides that civility is not a sign of weakness, and sincerity is always subject to proof. Let us never negotiate out of fear. But let us never fear to negotiate.

Let both sides explore what problems unite us instead of belaboring those problems which divide us. Let both sides, for the first time, formulate serious and precise proposals for the inspection and control of arms—and bring the absolute power to destroy other nations under the absolute control of all nations. Let both sides seek to invoke the wonders of science instead of its terrors. Together let us explore the stars, conquer the deserts, eradicate disease, tap the ocean depths, and encourage the arts and commerce. Let both sides unite to heed in all corners of the earth the command of Isaiah—to "undo the heavy burdens . . . and to let the oppressed go free."

And if a beachhead of cooperation may push back the jungle of suspicion, let both sides join in creating a new endeavor, not a new balance of power, but a new world of law, where the strong are just and the weak secure and the peace preserved.

All this will not be finished in the first 100 days. Nor will it be finished in the first 1,000 days, nor in the life of this Administration, nor even perhaps in our lifetime on this planet. But let us begin.

In your hands, my fellow citizens, more than in mine, will rest the final success or failure of our course. Since this country was founded, each generation of Americans has been summoned to give testimony to its national loyalty. The graves of young Americans who answered the call to service surround the globe.

Now the trumpet summons us again—not as a call to bear arms, though arms we need; not as a call to battle, though embattled we are—but a call to bear the burden of a long twilight struggle, year in and year out, "rejoicing in hope, patient in tribulation"—a struggle against the common enemies of man: tyranny, poverty, disease, and war itself.

Can we forge against these enemies a grand and global alliance, North and South, East and West, that can assure a more fruitful life for all mankind? Will you join in that historic effort?

In the long history of the world, only a few generations have been granted the role of defending freedom in its hour of maximum danger. I do not shrink from this responsibility—I welcome it. I do not believe that any of us would exchange places with any other people or any other generation. The energy, the faith, the devotion which we bring to this endeavor will light our country and all who serve it—and the glow from that fire can truly light the world.

And so, my fellow Americans: ask not what your country can do for you—ask what you can do for your country.

My fellow citizens of the world: ask not what America will do for you, but what together we can do for the freedom of man.

Finally, whether you are citizens of America or citizens of the world, ask of us the same high standards of strength and sacrifice which we ask of you. With a good conscience our only sure reward, with history the final judge of our deeds, let us go forth to lead the land we love, asking His blessing and His help, but knowing that here on earth God's work must truly be our own.

Robert Kennedy: Eulogy for Martin Luther King

This Page marks the event that intertwined the lives of two men who were central in American political events during the mid-1960s: Robert Kennedy, and Martin Luther King, Jr. Both of them achieved their greatest prominence as the American political order began to unravel following the assassination of John F. Kennedy in 1963; both played major roles in the American civil rights movement as well as the opposition to the Vietnam War; and both were themselves assassinated in 1968.

At that time in America, politics had become a fiery furnace of discontent and civil disorder, with a constant threat of violence that occasionally neared revolutionary fervor. The civil rights movement was marked by bombings, murders, and other violence against marchers and protesters. The anti-war movement saw larger and more heated rallies and demonstrations, while students burned their draft cards and fled to Canada.

The relationship between Robert Kennedy and Martin Luther King actually began before the election of John Kennedy in 1960. John Kennedy was a moderate supporter of the civil rights movement, but was aware, as every politician was, of the huge gulf that existed between the changes demanded by the black community and the changes that were socially possible. And as a Roman Catholic candidate for President, he was not likely to take positions that would be unpopular to a large percentage of Southern voters.

So the Kennedys' support of King was necessarily cautious, a fact that King was well aware of. In October 1960, just weeks before the election, King was arrested in Georgia and sentenced to four months in jail on an old traffic charge. Soon thereafter, John Kennedy called King's wife Coretta offering his support, and Robert subsequently called the judge in the case, thus winning King's release.

In January 2014, an old tape recording made by Dr. King was made public that discusses those phone calls; it reveals the way that King kept both Kennedys at a distance. On the recording, King says:

> Now it is true that Sen. Kennedy did take a specific step, [i.e., to assist King at that time] . . . He was in contact with officials in Georgia during my arrest, and he called my wife, made a personal call and expressed his concern and said to her that he was working and trying to do something to make my release possible. His brother [Robert Kennedy], who at that time was his campaign manager, also made direct contact

with officials and even a judge in Georgia, so the Kennedy family did have some part, at least they expressed a concern and they did have some part in the release, but I must make it clear that many other forces worked to bring it about also . . .

The relationship between King and Robert Kennedy continued after John's assassination, though little of it was public, as attested in a recent study of those men by Robert Margolick:

> The story of Martin Luther King and Robert Kennedy is hard to tell because they left so few fragments of it behind. For two such famous men whose lives and fates were so closely intertwined, there was only a scant paper trail. Lots of what happened between them happened privately, mostly in unrecorded phone calls, beyond the reach of journalists and historians.

After John's assassination in 1963, Robert left his post as Attorney General, and ran for Senator from New York, winning that seat in 1964. During this period, King continued his civil rights activities, but at the same time, his opposition to the Vietnam War grew as well; in 1967 he delivered a blistering speech condemning the war that alienated even several of his colleagues in the civil rights community.

By 1968, Kennedy had decided to run for President, and was aware that the support of the African American community for him would be useful. So for him, an alliance with King would be valuable, but it would necessarily need to be a cautious one; and King seemingly agreed. As Margolick points out:

> Politically, Kennedy typically took care not to cozy up to King, [whose] views on Vietnam—he favored immediate withdrawal—were far too extreme for Kennedy to embrace, as was his larger critique of American foreign policy and culture . . . For his part, King never got in bed with politicians, even the most promising, and sympathetic: invariably, they'd disappoint him. Unless he kept them guessing, and bidding for his support, they'd take him for granted.

In April 1968, Kennedy planned to deliver a speech to an African American rally in Indianapolis. Before he was to deliver his speech, however, he was informed that Martin Luther King Jr. had been assassinated earlier that day. The city authorities strongly recommended that he not deliver the speech, fearing that a riot was possible. He nevertheless went to the rally, where he found the people upbeat in anticipation of his appearance. Realizing that they were unaware of the tragic event, he began his speech by announcing King's death.

What he subsequently said was largely spontaneous; he had rejected notes made up for him by aides. But its effect on the crowd was profound: while dozens of other cities exploded into riots, Indianapolis did not. Many observers praised the speech highly, and the website "American Rhetoric" considers it to rank 17th in the 100 best American speeches of the twentieth century.

Whatever else may be true, his comments were moving and heartfelt, as can be seen by watching the film of it available in many places on the web. It calls to mind a painful and tragic time in the life of the country, a time that is useful to recall at the present moment.

Martin Luther King

Robert Kennedy

I have bad news for you, for all of our fellow citizens, and people who love peace all over the world, and that is that Martin Luther King was shot and killed tonight. Martin Luther King dedicated his life to love and to justice for his fellow human beings, and he died because of that effort.

In this difficult day, in this difficult time for the United States, it is perhaps well to ask what kind of a nation we are and what direction we want to move in. For those of you who are black—considering the evidence there evidently is that there were white people who were responsible—you can be filled with bitterness, with hatred, and a desire for revenge. We can move in that direction as a country, in great polarization—black people amongst black, white people amongst white, filled with hatred toward one another.

Or we can make an effort, as Martin Luther King did, to understand and to comprehend, and to replace that violence, that stain of bloodshed that has spread across our land, with an effort to understand with compassion and love.

For those of you who are black and are tempted to be filled with hatred and distrust at the injustice of such an act, against all white people, I can only say that I feel in my own heart the same kind of feeling. I had a member of my family killed, but he was killed by a white man. But we have to make an effort in the United States, we have to make an effort to understand, to go beyond these rather difficult times.

My favorite poet was Aeschylus. He wrote: "In our sleep, pain which cannot forget falls drop by drop upon the heart until, in our own despair, against our will, comes wisdom through the awful grace of God."

What we need in the United States is not division; what we need in the United States is not hatred; what we need in the United States is not violence or lawlessness; but love and wisdom, and compassion toward one another, and a feeling of justice toward those who still suffer within our country, whether they be white or they be black.

So I shall ask you tonight to return home, to say a prayer for the family of Martin Luther King, that's true, but more importantly to say a prayer for our own country, which all of us love—a prayer for understanding and that compassion of which I spoke.

We can do well in this country. We will have difficult times; we've had difficult times in the past; we will have difficult times in the future. It is not the end of violence; it is not the end of lawlessness; it is not the end of disorder.

But the vast majority of white people and the vast majority of black people in this country want to live together, want to improve the quality of our life, and want justice for all human beings who abide in our land.

Let us dedicate ourselves to what the Greeks wrote so many years ago: to tame the savageness of man and make gentle the life of this world. Let us dedicate ourselves to that, and say a prayer for our country and for our people.

FREEDOM AND THE HUMAN SPIRIT

Freedom all solace to man gives;
He lives at ease who freely lives. (John Barbour, The Bruce)

The Pages in this section are milestones in the unceasing search for personal freedom, a quest that has engaged the political, moral, and social energies of mankind. These selections all contribute in some way to that quest, since each establishes, for some group of people, at some particular time, a foundation upon which their basic rights are guaranteed, whether by fiat, by covenant, or by legislation. Taken individually, each Page is no more than a snapshot, a document that culminates some particular series of historical events. But taken together, these Pages attest to the unquenchable desire by human beings to gain individual control over their own destiny.

Selecting these Pages proved an interesting journey. One part of that journey was most unhappy: As I noted in the Preface, the Magna Carta, from which all of the other Pages in this Section are in some way descended, is not here. In spite of its singular importance, and in spite of its original form (a single Page, as shown overleaf), it was simply too long to include. But reading it—and reading about it—is a revelation. It is one thing to have a vague instinct that our legal system is based on ancient principles; it is quite another to see these words nearly a millennium old:

> *No freeman shall be taken or imprisoned, or disseised of any freehold, or liberties, or free customs, or outlawed, or banished, or in any other way destroyed, nor will we go upon him, nor send upon him, except by the legal judgement of his peers or by the law of the land. To no one will we sell, to no one will we deny, or delay right or justice.*

This is the actual and specific basis for the right that we call "due process," a right that we assume, and largely take for granted. (And thus by airing this revelation, at least a part of this great Page has made its way into this book.)

So on with my journey. The original impetus for this book emerged from a reading of the Declaration of Independence, and that Page, together with the Bill of Rights, are the anchors of this section. These works need neither introduction nor justification; they are the very soul of our nation. But it was interesting to realize how close their kinship was with their English and French cousins, the Declaration of Rights, and the Declaration of the Rights of Man. These four Pages have many cross currents among them, and they form a close-knit quartet, a fact that is pointed out by many writers. Yet they are cousins, not brothers; each arose from different circumstances, and each has its own unique qualities. I took pains, therefore (and I hope successfully), that the introductory comments for each one indicate their individuality as well as their family resemblances.

The remaining two Pages are quite different from those four and from each other. The Emancipation Proclamation deals with the less savory side of the national experience, its two centuries of slavery. This stain on American history has been the subject of commentary from de Tocqueville to the present. The pain of its heritage continues to this day, even though many men of good will have tried to find its cure. But whatever the evils that were done during those centuries, and whatever evils still remain, the Emancipation Proclamation marks the point at which the country changed its fundamental posture. Through his brief proclamation, Lincoln spoke on behalf of the whole nation, and rejected the practice that had brought us to such a calamitous state.

Finally, the October Manifesto marks the beginning of the end of the Russian monarchy. Russia was the last of the Great Powers to move toward democratic or constitutional principles; the movement toward personal freedom was arrested by the Bolsheviks almost as soon it began. And as if to repeat that sad history, democracy once again emerged on the Russian littoral in this century, only to slowly seep away once more. The Manifesto had only a short lifetime at the start of the century, but its seed is still living. It may, yet again, grow strong.

The Magna Carta

The Declaration of Rights

The English Declaration of Rights was the culmination of the Revolution of 1688, often called the "Glorious Revolution." This revolution marked the end of the Stuart dynasty, which had ruled since 1603 when James I united the crowns of England and Scotland. The Stuarts did not have the happiest time on the English throne. Charles I was executed in 1649, the succession was interrupted by the sad and puritanical Commonwealth of Oliver Cromwell, and James II, after reigning only three tempestuous years, was forced to flee to France, the crown then passing to William of Orange and his wife Mary (James' daughter). This Page marks the events by which James lost the throne.

In reading of those events, it is useful to recall that the Revolution of 1688 was also of singular importance for the American Revolution a century later, and that the English Bill of Rights has a striking resonance not only with our own Bill of Rights, but with our Declaration of Independence as well. So even if this tale is new to some readers, its details may seem very familiar. It is also sadly true that the passions that brought about this revolution three centuries ago are not entirely quenched in the British Isles of today, and are occasionally no less bitter than they were then.

The principal focus of the Glorious Revolution was religion. England throughout the 1600s was continually shaken by relentless struggles between Protestants and Catholics. The country had been made Protestant in name by Henry VIII's decrees in 1534, and by the middle of the seventeenth century, it was Protestant in fact. But there was still a substantial Catholic minority, and the future of Protestant Anglicanism as the dominant religion was by no means definite.

The country had also been wracked by the ongoing civil disorder that accompanied the last years of Cromwell; with the restoration of the monarchy in 1660, no one wanted more fighting. However, when Charles II died in 1685, the rightful heir to the throne was his brother James, a staunch Catholic, and this brought back the spectre of renewed religious strife. To ease fears on all sides, James quickly announced his intention to maintain the status quo and to leave the Anglican faith in place as the state religion. Further, both of James' daughters, Mary and Anne were Protestant. So a Protestant succession seemed assured, and it appeared that a peaceful solution—maintaining the rightful sovereign, yet also maintaining the legal religion—was at hand.

Almost immediately, James went back on his word. He tried to populate the army with Catholic officers, he suspended Parliament when it protested his actions, he dismissed judges who disagreed with his commands. Finally, when a son was born to James in 1688, suggesting the possibility of a Catholic succession to the throne, open rebellion began. A group of nobles appealed to William of Orange, ruler of the Netherlands, to lead an uprising against James. William of Orange was the husband of James' daughter Mary, which lent some slender authority to his right to the throne; more important, he was Protestant. William arrived in England in November 1688, and King James' few remaining followers quickly deserted him. James fled to France, leaving the country without a King.

William convened the insurgents to discuss how to proceed. There was an immediate question of legitimacy: the gathering could not legally be considered a formal Parliament, since it had not been called by the King. However, the convention decided that since James had fled the country, he had, for all practical purposes, abdicated. They therefore offered the crown to William and Mary, and the Stuart reign was over. The convention also prepared a "Declaration of Rights and Liberties of the Subject." This declaration contains some dozen statements that guarantee the British citizen specific liberties, and that limit the monarch from impinging on these liberties. (These statements subsequently had a large impact on the formation of the American Bill of Rights that amends the Constitution; some of the wording in the American text borrows heavily from the English.)

The rights agreed to by the February convention were later formally included in an Act passed by Parliament ten months later. This Act, which is often called the "Bill of Rights," is a much longer document that also contains a lengthy description of the misdeeds of James and the specific conditions of the succession of William and Mary.[7]

It is significant that the major importance of the Declaration of Rights was not that any particular liberties were proclaimed. In actual fact, most of these rights had been in force for a long time, some even going back to the Magna Carta. Historian J. R. Jones points out that:

> Essentially, [the Declaration of Rights] was declaratory of ancient rights, which it re-established and secured; it did not create new rights.

But what did happen was that the source of the ruling power in England was forever changed. The Glorious Revolution reversed in a stroke the concept that the King was empowered through divine right; the revolution placed the ultimate ruling power squarely in the hands of Parliament. Lunt, in his "History of England," states that:

---

[7] There is thereby a common confusion for Americans. The shorter list of specific rights is the "Declaration of Rights" and the longer document that contains them is called the "Bill of Rights."

The revolution of 1688 settled finally the contest between the King and parliament for sovereignty. Since parliament had made a King, it could unmake one. Henceforth there could be no doubt of the superiority of Parliament . . . Thereafter no King who so far transgressed the limitations placed upon him by law . . . could hope to retain the throne. The theory of divine right as a working principle of government in England was dead.

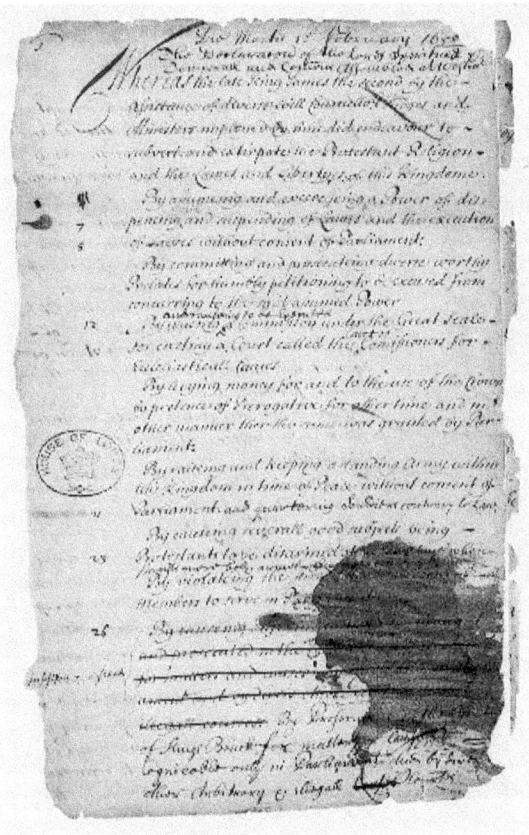

The Declaration of Rights

Now, having taken this little journey, it is time to read the actual Page, an excerpt from the full document whose title is "An Act Declaring the Rights and Liberties of the Subject and Settling the Succession of the Crown." (As noted in the Preface, this was one of the occasions where I felt justified in using an excerpt.) I had originally planned to include here only the Declaration of Rights section, i.e., the statement made at the convention. However, after delving through the full Bill, I also decided to include the long preamble, where James is blamed for almost every imaginable ill. There was a marked tonal similarity between the way that James is censured and condemned here in this Bill of Rights, and the way that Thomas Jefferson censured George III in the American Declaration of

Independence a century later: an interesting occurrence, perhaps, of "what's good for the goose . . ." This preamble occupies most of the text on the first side of the Page. The list of rights, as commonly cited, starts toward the bottom, with the text "And whereas the said late King James. . . ."

Samuel Wale, *The Bill of Rights Ratified at the Revolution by King William, and Queen Mary*

Whereas the Lords Spiritual and Temporal and Commons assembled at Westminster, lawfully, fully and freely representing all the estates of the people of this realm, did upon the thirteenth day of February in the year of our Lord one thousand six hundred eighty-eight present to their Majesties, then called and known by the names and style of William and Mary, prince and princess of Orange, being present in their proper persons, a certain declaration in writing made by the said Lords and Commons in the words following, viz.:

Whereas the late King James the Second, by the assistance of divers evil counsellors, judges and ministers employed by him, did endeavor to subvert and extirpate the Protestant religion and the laws and liberties of this kingdom;

By assuming and exercising a power of dispensing with the suspending of laws and the execution of laws without consent of Parliament;

By committing and prosecuting divers worthy prelates for humbly petitioning to be excused from concurring to the said assumed power;

By issuing and causing to be executed a commission under the great seal for erecting a court called the Court of Commissioners for Ecclesiastical Causes;

By levying money for and to the use of the Crown by pretence of prerogative for other time and in other manner than the same was granted by Parliament;

By raising and keeping a standing army within this kingdom in time of peace without consent of Parliament, and quartering soldiers contrary to law;

By causing several good subjects being Protestants to be disarmed at the same time when papists were both armed and employed contrary to law;

By violating the freedom of election of members to serve in Parliament;

By prosecutions in the Court of King's Bench for matters and causes cognizable only in Parliament, and by divers other arbitrary and illegal courses;

And whereas of late years partial corrupt and unqualified persons have been returned and served on juries in trials, and particularly divers jurors in trials for high treason which were not freeholders;

And excessive bail hath been required of persons committed in criminal cases to elude the benefit of the laws made for the liberty of the subjects;

And excessive fines have been imposed;

And illegal and cruel punishments inflicted;

And several grants and promises made of fines and forfeitures before any conviction of judgement against the persons upon whom the same were to be levied;

All which are utterly and directly contrary to the known laws and statutes and freedom of this realm;

And whereas the said late King James the Second having abdicated the government and the throne being thereby vacant, his Highness the prince of Orange (whom it hath pleased Almighty God to make the glorious instrument of delivering this kingdom from popery and arbitrary power) did (by the advice of the Lords Spiritual and Temporal and divers principal persons of the Commons) cause letters to be written to the Lords Spiritual and Temporal being Protestants, and other letters to the several counties, cities, universities, boroughs and cinque ports, for the choosing of such persons to represent them as were of right to be sent to Parliament, to meet and sit at Westminster upon the two and twentieth day of January in this year one thousand six hundred eighty and eight [old style date], in order to such an establishment as that their religion, laws and liberties might not again be in danger of being subverted, upon which letters elections having been accordingly made;

And thereupon the said Lords Spiritual and Temporal and Commons, pursuant to their respective letters and elections, being now assembled in a full and free representative of this nation, taking into their most serious consideration the best means for attaining the ends aforesaid, do in the first place (as their ancestors in like case have usually done) for the vindicating and asserting their ancient rights and liberties declare

That the pretended power of suspending the laws or the execution of laws by regal authority without consent of Parliament is illegal;

That the pretended power of dispensing with laws or the execution of laws by regal authority, as it hath been assumed and exercised of late, is illegal;

That the commission for erecting the late Court of Commissioners for Ecclesiastical Causes, and all other commissions and courts of like nature, are illegal and pernicious;

That levying money for or to the use of the Crown by pretence of prerogative, without grant of Parliament, for longer time, or in other manner than the same is or shall be granted, is illegal;

That it is the right of the subjects to petition the king, and all commitments and prosecutions for such petitioning are illegal;

That the raising or keeping a standing army within the kingdom in time of peace, unless it be with consent of Parliament, is against law;

That the subjects which are Protestants may have arms for their defence suitable to their conditions and as allowed by law;

That election of members of Parliament ought to be free;

That the freedom of speech and debates or proceedings in Parliament ought not to be impeached or questioned in any court or place out of Parliament;

That excessive bail ought not to be required, nor excessive fines imposed, nor cruel and unusual punishments inflicted;

That jurors ought to be duly impanelled and returned, and jurors which pass upon men in trials for high treason ought to be freeholders;

That all grants and promises of fines and forfeitures of particular persons before conviction are illegal and void;

And that for redress of all grievances, and for the amending, strengthening and preserving of the laws, Parliaments ought to be held frequently.

The Declaration of Independence

This Page, a text so familiar that it almost defies introduction, is Thomas Jefferson's greatest offspring, the document that we honor as the foundation of the nation. (And speaking quite selfishly, it was also the trigger that began my search for other single Pages that were, like the Declaration, short yet significant milestones of History.)

Though the Declaration might need no introduction in a general sense, there are, as with all close friends, some sides of its history that are not universally remembered, and that bear repeating. The first one, commonplace to scholars but perhaps not to everyone, is how much Jefferson relied on earlier texts in writing the Declaration. He was deeply in debt to the work of John Locke, the brilliant seventeenth-century philosopher, and particularly to Locke's two "Treatises on Civil Government." These were powerful essays, made in the aftermath of the Glorious Revolution of 1688, that contained careful and reasoned arguments about the origins of political power, the nature and limitations of Government, and the essential equality of men:

> To understand political power aright . . . we must consider what estate all men are naturally in, and that is a state of perfect freedom to order their actions and dispose of their possessions and persons as they think fit, within the bounds of the law of Nature, without asking leave or depending upon the will of any other man.

As did all political thinkers of the time, Jefferson knew Locke's treatises well; it should only be expected that there are some resonances of Locke in Jefferson's work. Hence, when the Declaration says that:

> . . . all men are created equal, that they are endowed by their Creator with certain unalienable rights, that among these are life, liberty, and the pursuit of happiness . . .

it has unmistakable echoes of Locke:

> Man, being born . . . with a title to perfect freedom and an uncontrolled enjoyment of all the rights and privileges of the law of Nature . . . that is, his life, liberty, and estate . . .

Acknowledging the debt to Locke (as well as other political forebears) in no way denigrates Jefferson; any criticism of the Declaration for such borrowings misses a critical point. As Carl Becker notes:

> The strength of the Declaration was precisely that it said what everyone was thinking. Nothing could have been more futile than an attempt to justify a revolution on principles that no one had ever heard of before,

And Jefferson himself, writing four decades later, addresses this criticism:

> Neither aiming at originality of principles or sentiments, nor yet copied from any particular or previous writing, it [the Declaration] was intended to be an expression of the American mind. . . . All its authority rests then on the harmonizing sentiments of the day, whether expressed in conversation, in letters, printed essays, or the elementary books of public right, as Aristotle, Cicero, Locke, Sidney, etc.

A second interesting and sometimes forgotten point about the Declaration is what its real place in the Revolution was. The fighting between the Colonists and Britain had begun the year before, yet until well into 1776 the goal of the rebellion was not entirely clear. Thomas Paine, in his pamphlet "Common Sense" argued passionately for independence—"A Government of our own is our natural right"— but the goal of independence was not fully shared by all of the colonists. By June 1776, however, the Continental Congress began considering a resolution submitted by Richard Henry Lee of Virginia, that declared:

> ... these United Colonies are, and of right ought to be, free and independent states ...

This resolution was approved by the Congress on July 2, 1776, and that is the real date on which the Colonies declared their independence; the role of the document read on July 4 was to explain the vote taken two days earlier. Quoting Benjamin Fletcher Wright:

> We call it the Declaration of Independence, but independence had already been voted. This was a declaration stating the reasons and the justification for the vote.

A third point about the Declaration, and a most unhappy one, concerns what it does not say. The writing of the text had begun in mid-June, when the Congress appointed a committee (Jefferson, John Adams, Benjamin Franklin, Roger Sherman, and Robert Livingston) to prepare a formal statement about independence; Jefferson was named the principal author. He produced an initial draft that was revised and amended by the committee before being presented to the Congress; it then underwent further insertions and deletions before the final text as we know it was approved. One of the deletions was to have profound implications for the nation's future.

The paragraph in question was a passionate denunciation of slavery. According to Becker, John Adams thought it one of the best parts of the Declaration. Jefferson speaks quite bluntly, referring to slavery as "an assemblage of horrors." But the passage was deleted by the Congress. Forty years later, Jefferson described that deletion:

> Severe strictures [regarding] the importation of slaves were disapproved by some Southern gentlemen, whose reflections were not yet matured to the full abhorrence of that traffic.[8]

A brief, low-key recollection, behind which lay a terrible portent for the future (and which shows that even then, the slavery question was a North-South issue). Though sidestepped for a time, the issue could not be ignored; it was inevitable that it would become more and more central for the nation until four score and seven years later when, with blood and many tears, the question of equality for all Americans reached its painful apotheosis in the cemetery at Gettysburg.

Any failings notwithstanding, the Declaration is the fount of the American experiment. Today, two and one-half centuries later, it continues to hold its promise and to guide the fortunes of the Republic. In the words of Ralph Barton Perry:

> The history of American democracy is a gradual realization, too slow for some and too rapid for others, of the implications of the Declaration of Independence.

Some notes on the text. There has been considerable effort expended by scholars in finding the accurate text of the Declaration, since numerous versions exist. Of considerable interest is Carl Becker's study of three of these versions (the "Rough Draft," the "Lee copy,' and the "Parchment copy"); he includes all of the insertions and deletions made between Jefferson's original draft from late June and the text that was proclaimed on July 4. The "Parchment copy," borrowed from Becker, is the source of the text on the following Page.

Finally, there was an issue that arose when the Declaration was completed in 1775, and it seemed wise to disseminate it throughout the land as quickly as possible. In that era, one of the most useful ways to accomplish this was called a "broadside," a single large sheet of paper on which some announcement or advertisement would be printed. But in order to fit the full Declaration onto one single large sheet, the text would have to be diddled a bit. What they did was to eliminate all spaces that we today would find necessary. For example, in enumerating the sins of King George as a list of separate items:

---

[8] The deleted text actually aims at Britain, condemning the King for refusing to permit any anti-slave legislation to be passed in the Colonies. In any case, the net effect of deleting it was to remove the topic of slavery from appearing in the Declaration.

> He has refused his Assent to Laws . . .
>
> He has forbidden his Governors to pass Laws . . .
>
> He has refused to pass other Laws . . .

The Fathers compressed them thus:

> He has refused his Assent to Laws . . . —He has forbidden his Governors to pass Laws . . . —He has refused to pass other Laws

thereby permitting the entire text to squeeze onto a single, large page. Now, this trick might work for a huge sheet of broadside, but in the 10-point font of the present volume, this approach taxes the eyes a bit much. And since this document is the cornerstone of the volume, and notwithstanding my respect for Tom Jefferson and his chums, I chose that the Declaration should be read without constraint. So I allowed myself to waive the self-imposed constraint of two sides, and let the text spill out onto a third page.

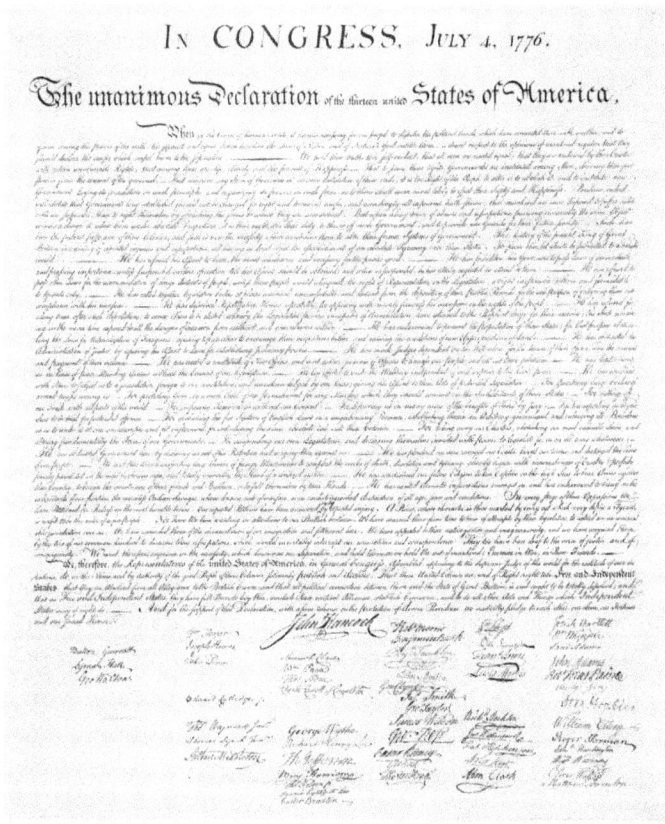

The Declaration of Independence

When in the Course of human events, it becomes necessary for one people to dissolve the political bands which have connected them with another, and to assume among the Powers of the earth, the separate and equal station to which the Laws of Nature and of Nature's God entitle them, a decent respect to the opinions of mankind requires that they should declare the causes which impel them to the separation.

We hold these truths to be self-evident, that all men are created equal, that they are endowed by their Creator with certain unalienable Rights, that among these are Life, Liberty, and the pursuit of Happiness. That to secure these rights, Governments are instituted among Men, deriving their just powers from the consent of the governed. That whenever any Form of Government becomes destructive of these ends, it is the Right of the People to alter or to abolish it, and to institute new Government, laying its foundation on such principles and organizing its powers in such form, as to them shall seem most likely to effect their Safety and Happiness. Prudence, indeed, will dictate that Governments long established should not be changed for light and transient causes; and accordingly all experience hath shown, that mankind are more disposed to suffer, while evils are sufferable, than to right themselves by abolishing the forms to which they are accustomed. But when a long train of abuses and usurpations, pursuing invariably the same Object, evinces a design to reduce them under absolute Despotism, it is their right, it is their duty, to throw off such Government, and to provide new Guards for their future security. Such has been the patient sufferance of these Colonies; and such is now the necessity which constrains them to alter their former Systems of Government. The history of the present King of Great Britain is a history of repeated injuries and usurpations, all having in direct object the establishment of an absolute Tyranny over these States. To prove this, let Facts be submitted to a candid world.

He has refused his Assent to Laws, the most wholesome and necessary for the public good.

He has forbidden his Governors to pass Laws of immediate and pressing importance, unless suspended in their operation till his Assent should be obtained; and when so suspended, he has utterly neglected to attend to them.

He has refused to pass other Laws for the accommodation of large districts of people, unless those people would relinquish the right of Representation in the Legislature, a right inestimable to them and formidable to tyrants only.

He has called together legislative bodies at places unusual, uncomfortable, and distant from the depository of their public Records, for the sole purpose of fatiguing them into compliance with his measures.

He has dissolved Representative Houses repeatedly, for opposing with manly firmness his invasions on the rights of the people.

He has refused for a long time, after such dissolutions, to cause others to be elected; whereby the Legislative powers, incapable of Annihilation, have returned to the People at large for their exercise; the State remaining in the mean time exposed to all the dangers of invasion from without, and convulsions within.

He has endeavoured to prevent the population of these States; for that purpose obstructing the Laws of Naturalization of Foreigners; refusing to pass others to encourage their migrations hither, and raising the conditions of new Appropriations of Lands.

He has obstructed the Administration of Justice, by refusing his Assent to Laws for establishing Judiciary powers

He has made Judges dependent on his Will alone, for the tenure of their offices, and the amount and payment of their salaries.

He has erected a multitude of New Offices, and sent hither swarms of Officers to harass our People, and eat out their substance.

He has kept among us, in times of peace, Standing Armies without the Consent of our legislatures.

He has affected to render the Military independent of and superior to the Civil power.

He has combined with others to subject us to a jurisdiction foreign to our constitution, and unacknowledged by our laws; giving his Assent to their Acts of pretended Legislation:

For quartering large bodies of armed troops among us:

For protecting them, by a mock Trial, from Punishment for any Murders which they should commit on the Inhabitants of these States:

For cutting off our Trade with all parts of the world:

For imposing Taxes on us without our Consent:

For depriving us in many cases, of the benefits of Trial by Jury:

For transporting us beyond Seas to be tried for pretended offences: For abolishing the free System of English Laws in a neighbouring Province, establishing therein an Arbitrary government, and enlarging its Boundaries so as to render it at once an example and fit instrument for introducing the same absolute rule into these Colonies:

For taking away our Charters, abolishing our most valuable Laws, and altering fundamentally the Forms of our Governments:

For suspending our own Legislatures, and declaring themselves invested with power to legislate for us in all cases whatsoever.

He has abdicated Government here, by declaring us out of his Protection and waging War against us. He has plundered our seas, ravaged our Coasts, burnt our towns, and destroyed the Lives of our people. He is at this time transporting large armies of foreign mercenaries to compleat the works of death, desolation and tyranny, already begun with circumstances of Cruelty & perfidy scarcely paralleled in the most barbarous ages, and totally unworthy the Head of a civilized nation. He has constrained our fellow Citizens taken Captive on the high Seas to bear Arms against their Country, to become the executioners of their friends and Brethren, or to fall themselves by their Hands. He has excited domestic insurrections amongst us, and has endeavoured to bring on the inhabitants of our frontiers, the merciless Indian Savages, whose known rule of warfare is an undistinguished destruction of all ages, sexes and conditions.

In every stage of these Oppressions We have Petitioned for Redress in the most humble terms: Our repeated Petitions have been answered only by repeated injury. A Prince, whose character is thus marked by every act which may define a Tyrant, is unfit to be the ruler of a free people. Nor have We been wanting in attention to our British brethren. We have warned them from time to time of attempts by their legislature to extend an unwarrantable jurisdiction over us. We have reminded them of the circumstances of our emigration and settlement here. We have appealed to their native justice and magnanimity, and we have conjured them by the ties of our common kindred to disavow these usurpations, which would inevitably interrupt our connections and correspondence. They too have been deaf to the voice of justice and of consanguinity. We must, therefore, acquiesce in the necessity, which denounces our Separation, and hold them, as we hold the rest of mankind, Enemies in War, in Peace Friends.

We, therefore, the Representatives of the united States of America, in General Congress, Assembled, appealing to the Supreme Judge of the world for the rectitude of our intentions, do, in the Name, and by Authority of the good People of these Colonies, solemnly publish and declare, That these United Colonies are, and of Right ought to be Free and Independent States; that they are Absolved from all Allegiance to the British Crown, and that all political connection between them and the State of Great Britain, is and ought to be totally dissolved; and that as Free and Independent States, they have full Power to levy War, conclude Peace, contract Alliances, establish Commerce, and to do all other Acts and Things which Independent States may of right do. And for the support of this Declaration, with a firm reliance on the Protection of Divine Providence, we mutually pledge to each other our Lives, our Fortunes and our sacred Honor.

The Bill of Rights

The popular media sometimes present a rather mythic view of the early years of the Republic. With independence won, so the myth goes, the political affairs of America became peaceful, and entered a time of quiet deliberation. The framers of the Constitution carefully and calmly worked together with a collective and harmonious wisdom, and bequeathed the majestic document that governs the life of the country. With temperate solemnity, later men made equally careful and thoughtful revisions, while the nation came of age.

What is wrong in this picture is that it portrays the process as quiet and peaceful: nothing could be further from the truth. As Daniel T. Rodgers wryly puts it:

> From the closely fought struggle over the Constitution's ratification . . . the past has been far messier. . . . From [the creation of the Bill of Rights] to the present day, the rights of Americans have never been out of the teeth of controversy . . . the current angry clamor over abortion rights is no aberration; it is one of the basic noises of our history.

Between the signing of the Declaration of Independence in 1776 and the ratification of the Bill of Rights in 1791, fifteen years passed, a stretch of time that can be very long in the course of human events. In the twentieth century, for instance, the same number of years spanned 1956—when Eisenhower started his second term, before Sputnik was launched—and 1971, long after Kennedy's assassination, Johnson's tragic presidency, the morass of Viet Nam, and Nixon's first election.

Then as now, a lot can happen in one-and-a-half decades. Between 1776 and 1791, during which France fell toward revolution and chaos, the American colonists fought the British Empire and won, the young nation adopted and then rejected the Articles of Confederation, a group of political geniuses created the American Constitution, the Federal Capital wandered between New York and Philadelphia, and the fledgling nation quelled its first rebellion. And throughout that whole period, the issue of rights, and bills of rights, was a perennial, contentious, and unresolved topic.

The root of the matter was that the American colonists were Englishmen at heart, and the legacy of the Glorious Revolution, when the English nobility imposed a Declaration of Rights on William and Mary, was as strong in the Colonies as it was in England. So as the frictions between the colonists and the Crown grew into rebellion, the basis of the colonists' anger at the King was that he had trampled on their natural and inalienable rights.

In 1776, for instance, even before the Declaration of Independence was signed, the colony of Virginia had passed its own Declaration of Rights as the initial chapter of the colony's new constitution. The rights that it described echo the general political sentiment of the eighteenth century:

> ... That all men are by nature equally free and independent, and have certain inherent rights.... That all power is vested in, and consequently derived from, the people ...

Virginia was the first, but several other states soon added declarations of rights to their individual Constitutions. A decade later, therefore, when the Federal Constitution was being debated in Philadelphia, it was a natural question whether a similar declaration of rights should be included. George Mason, author of the Virginia Declaration, made such a proposal, but he was supported only by Elbridge Gerry of Massachusetts; the remaining members of the Constitutional Convention were against it.

Many of those who opposed a bill of rights did so on the grounds that the individual states' bills of rights would be a sufficient mechanism for insuring peoples' rights. Alexander Hamilton was even more emphatic:

> I go further and affirm that bills of rights, in the sense and to the extent in which they are contended for, are not only unnecessary in the proposed Constitution, but would even be dangerous.

One danger would lie in exclusion: by listing any set of rights, however broad that set might be, it could logically be argued these were the only rights that were guaranteed, and any others could be excluded. Thus, no list could ever be sufficient. More to the point, Hamilton argued, all rights were already implicit in the Constitution as it stood:

> Why declare that things shall not be done which there is no power to do?

So the Convention approved the Constitution as it stood, and sent it to the thirteen states for their consideration. But Mason and Gerry had been correct: the lack of a bill of rights was greeted with dismay in every quarter. The majority of Americans were clearly unhappy, so much so that ratification of the Constitution, for most of the thirteen states, was predicated on the demand for its immediate amendment. By March 1789, when the first Federal Congress met, nearly two hundred separate amendments had been proposed.

It fell to James Madison to draw up the Federal Bill of Rights. Madison was lukewarm in his support for a rights declaration, but agreed to the task as a necessary expedient. By September he had created a set of twelve proposed amendments. His intention was to sprinkle these amendments throughout the Constitution's text, but that was not to be. Citing Helen Veit:

> Madison had to accept Roger Sherman of Connecticut's insistence that all amendments be placed at the end of the Constitution and not be woven into it. Thus, America owes to Sherman, who was actually an opponent of amending the Constitution, the existence of a separate group of amendments known as the Bill of Rights.

For the next two years these twelve amendments were considered, debated, and contested throughout the young nation. The first two received no general support, but by December 1791, the remaining amendments were ratified as Virginia became the eleventh state to accept them.[9] Thus the Bill of Rights joined the Constitution as the law of the land.

The relationship of the American Bill of Rights to its English and French cousins is worth noting. Unquestionably, its debt to the English Declaration of Rights is strong, even to reusing some of its text almost verbatim:

> (English:) That excessive bail ought not to be required, nor excessive fines imposed, nor cruel and unusual punishment inflicted.

> (American): Excessive bail shall not be required, nor excessive fines imposed, nor cruel and unusual punishments inflicted.

These similarities notwithstanding, the two documents were born out of very different needs. John H. Krout describes this essential difference:

> Its parallelism with the English Bill of Rights tends to obscure the fact that the two documents rest on somewhat different assumptions. Both, to be sure, are concerned with specific threats to liberty, and with the practical means of thwarting them. For the English, however, the source of danger was the unrestrained prerogative of the Crown; and the defense was sought in the power exercised by a majority in the Parliament. For Americans, the danger seemed to lie in the will of the majority, as expressed through its representatives in Congress assembled.

Likewise, the French Declaration of Rights, which was being created at almost precisely the same time, answered very different needs from the American Bill. The French Declaration is a strong affirmation of absolute democracy; it almost revels in the supremacy of majority rule that the French rebels sought, but which the Americans feared:

---

[9] By then Vermont had entered the Union, so a three-quarters majority consisted of eleven states.

> (French:) The source of all sovereignty lies essentially in the Nation. No corporate body, no individual may exercise any authority that does not expressly emanate from it ... The Law is an expression of the general will ...

To be sure, the concept of the absolute power of the majority did have a certain appeal to those in America who opposed a strong Federal government. But many others viewed that principle as unacceptable. Writing in 1791, John Quincy Adams asserted:

> This principle, that a whole nation has a right to do whatever it pleases, cannot in any sense whatever be admitted as true. The eternal and immutable laws of justice and of morality are paramount to all human legislation ... If, therefore, a majority ... are bound by no law human or divine, and have no other rule but their sovereign will and pleasure to direct them, what possible security can any citizen of the nation have for the protection of his inalienable rights?

To this day, such hotly debated questions about our individual rights, and their basis in the Bill of Rights, play a central role in our lives. They figure, one way or another, in a large percentage of judicial decisions, from abortion to flag burning, from our rights about birth and marriage to our right to die. And it will probably always be so. Daniel Rogers sums it up neatly:

> In time, the amendments were to become, as Madison grudgingly admitted they might, "a good ground for an appeal to the sense of the community." Unlike the Constitution, drafted in secret convention, the Bill of Rights was born as a demand from below. It was not a speaking of the framers' mind, as the current partisans of "original intent" have imagined. but a document born in debate, dissension, compromise, and politics—in short, out of the usual processes of democracy.

Article One

Congress shall make no law respecting an establishment of religion, or prohibiting the free exercise thereof; or abridging the freedom of speech, or of the press; or the right of the people peaceably to assemble, and to petition the government for a redress of grievances.

Article Two

A well regulated militia, being necessary to the security of a free state, the right of the people to keep and bear arms, shall not be infringed.

Article Three

No soldier shall, in time of peace be quartered in any house, without the consent of the owner, nor in time of war, but in a manner to be prescribed by law.

Article Four

The right of the people to be secure in their persons, houses, papers, and effects, against unreasonable searches and seizures, shall not be violated, and no warrants shall issue, but upon probable cause, supported by oath or affirmation, and particularly describing the place to be searched, and the persons or things to be seized.

Article Five

No person shall be held to answer for a capital, or otherwise infamous crime, unless on a presentment or indictment of a grand jury, except in cases arising in the land or naval forces, or in the militia, when in actual service in time of war or public danger; nor shall any person be subject for the same offense to be twice put in jeopardy of life or limb; nor shall be compelled in any criminal case to be a witness against himself, nor be deprived of life, liberty, or property, without due process of law; nor shall private property be taken for public use, without just compensation.

Article Six

In all criminal prosecutions, the accused shall enjoy the right to a speedy and public trial, by an impartial jury of the state and district wherein the crime shall have been committed, which district shall have been previously ascertained by law, and to be informed of the nature and cause of the accusation; to be confronted with the witnesses against him; to have compulsory process for obtaining witnesses in his favor, and to have the assistance of counsel for his defense.

Article Seven

In suits at common law, where the value in controversy shall exceed twenty dollars, the right of trial by jury shall be preserved, and no fact tried by a jury, shall be otherwise reexamined in any court of the United States, than according to the rules of the common law.

Article Eight

Excessive bail shall not be required, nor excessive fines imposed, nor cruel and unusual punishments inflicted.

Article Nine

The enumeration in the Constitution, of certain rights, shall not be construed to deny or disparage others retained by the people.

Article Ten

The powers not delegated to the United States by the Constitution, nor prohibited by it to the states, are reserved to the states respectively, or to the people.

The twelve amendments originally proposed by James Madison

The Declaration of the Rights of Man and of the Citizen

Of the immortal lines from the pen of Charles Dickens, his description of the late eighteenth century as "the best of times . . . the worst of times" is among the most famous. As a description of the French Revolution, it is probably the most accurate. During the years between 1789, when the Bastille fell, and 1800, when Napoleon named himself the "First Consul," France witnessed a dizzying parade of extremes, a roller coaster ride through heroism and horror, glory and gore. And whether best or worst, it was definitely a stunning time, both for France and for her neighbors: the French Revolution brought to the heart of Europe, in a way that the American Revolution never could, the harsh reality of the republican age that was dawning. And it was painful, far more brutal, and far, far bloodier than the American struggle had been. Yet there were moments of triumph as well, and high among them was the creation of the great charter of liberties found on the following Page.

This charter, the Declaration of the Rights of Man and of the Citizen[10] was the godchild of the Marquis de Lafayette, the wealthy French nobleman who, before his 30th birthday, had become the hero of the New World. When he resumed his life in France in 1783, Lafayette was wearing the laurels that he had won in the American Revolution. He was an intimate of Washington, and a close friend of Jefferson; he also had impeccable credentials both as a soldier of skill and as a zealous champion of freedom, human rights, and liberation from tyranny. The France he found on his return was in great need of heroism; it was beset by staggering financial woes and seething with social unrest. Under the rule of the hapless Louis XVI, the country was battered by disastrous fiscal policies, the nobility refusing to share the cost of maintaining the state, the peasants crushed by an ever-increasing tax burden. The treasury was approaching bankruptcy and the people of Paris were approaching starvation. Finding his homeland in this perilous condition, Lafayette proved himself a hero of the Old World as well as the New. He served France doubly, during the chaotic days between the Revolution and the Terror, as both a skillful statesman and as a soldier of distinction.

By 1788, King Louis had finally realized the depth of the crisis and, with no other solution at hand, convened the Estates General. This body was France's closest

---

[10] The document had several names, all very similar. After its original appearance in 1789, it became the "Declaration of the Rights of Man" in the Constitution of 1793, and subsequently the "Declaration of the Rights and Duties of Man and the Citizen" in the Constitution of 1795.

equivalent to a Parliament, and consisted of three "estates" representing the clergy (the First Estate), the nobles (the Second Estate), and the commoners (the Third Estate). It was an ancient institution, dating from 1302. But it was the shell of a Parliament, not a real one—the Estates General had not met for nearly two centuries, and had no power except to advise the King. Further, each Estate had a single vote, which meant that the Third Estate, the commoners and peasants, were usually outvoted by the other two estates, regardless either of the number of delegates present or of the huge populace that the Third Estate represented.

When the Estates General met in May 1789, though the crisis was grave, there were widespread hopes (at least among the commoners) for change and reform. The American experiences were well known, as were the political and philosophical writings of Locke, Rousseau, and Voltaire, that argued for natural rights and individual liberties. Sadly, it became immediately apparent that Louis intended to keep the stranglehold of the old order in place in France. But those times were not like other times, and the Third Estate refused the King's will. In June, they declared themselves a "National Assembly" and announced their intention to prepare a constitution that would remake the French political structure. The convening of the National Assembly was effectively the start of the Revolution.

The rebels (though they did not yet see themselves as such) had many different ideas about what the Constitution should be. But by near-universal consent, they wanted it to begin with a declaration of rights, and this was the occasion for Lafayette the statesman to appear. Lafayette had long desired to introduce into France some of the great principles of liberty that he had seen in America. In January of that year he had completed drafting such a declaration. He had shown it to Thomas Jefferson, then the American ambassador to France, and Jefferson offered suggestions for improvement.[11] In early July, therefore, as the Assembly began its search for a Declaration of Rights, Lafayette submitted his text to them; in its essential concepts, and in much of its wording, it provided the basis for the Declaration that was finally approved.

In truth, Lafayette had company: there were over a dozen drafts by other authors of "declarations of rights" that were submitted. None of the proposed texts, neither Lafayette's nor any other, was accepted in its entirety. Each portion of the final Declaration was debated and revised by exhaustive compromise. Still, Lafayette's contribution to the final result was great. Historian Louis Gottschalk says:

---

[11] Jefferson also sent a finished copy of Lafayette's Declaration back to James Madison, who was at that very time preparing the American Bill of Rights.

In sum, as Lafayette claimed about forty years later, the "Declaration of the Rights of Man and of the Citizen" was based more upon his [submission] than upon any one other, and the greater part of his was incorporated in it.

Between August 20 and August 26, the Assembly agreed to the final text of the Declaration, the following Page. This document has been the essential guiding principle of French political life to the present day.

By then, however, the social circumstances had changed drastically. When the National Assembly had established itself two months earlier, most people hoped for a reformation of the French state and of its government; few were then envisioning France without a King. Something like the British model, a constitutional monarchy, with the royal power held in check by the elected Parliament, was a reasonable aim. But in July, events began to spin out of control. Riots began in Paris, and on July 14, a mob stormed the royal prison called the Bastille; its garrison was killed by the raging crowd. The spectre of civil collapse provided Lafayette the second opportunity to prove his heroism to France. He was named Commander of the "National Guard," and he worked valiantly to maintain order, and to keep military discipline over a collection of citizens that daily became less an army and more a rabble.

He quickly calmed much of the unrest following the fall of the Bastille, and in October, he subdued a huge throng that threatened the King in Versailles. Lafayette prevented a violent encounter, and persuaded the King to return to Paris under his guard. For several months, Lafayette was virtually the single source of moderation in the country. He mediated between royalists and republicans (earning the hatred of each) and kept the slow-burning powder of insurrection from exploding. Throughout this period, Lafayette maintained his allegiance to the King: "We must all rally around the King to establish a Constitution," he wrote in 1790. But as the turbulent months passed, the royalist support was withering. By 1792, with the forces of the radical Robespierre in the ascendant (and the royal family only months away from execution), Lafayette left France, not to return until Napoleon was in power seven years later.

The remainder of Lafayette's career, and his place in French history, are topics beyond the scope of this volume. It is sufficient to realize that Lafayette's contribution to the Declaration of Rights is central, as it was in his own thoughts. And he was quite correct: the role of this document in political history cannot be overestimated. Notwithstanding its debt to the American models, it was the French Declaration that sparked much of the revolutionary fever that spread throughout Europe in the nineteenth century. Sherman Kent, in his essay on the Declaration, notes that:

> The importance of its impact upon the people of the West ... was and still is profound ... What effects the idea of a declaration of rights had upon the Old World ... must be largely ascribed to [the French Declaration of Rights] ... It destroyed the groundwork on which divine right or patriarchal monarchy rested, upon which the superiority of certain men rested, upon which the economic discrimination and privilege of feudal and mercantile economics were based ... It closed out the old pattern of values which had long dominated in French politics, society, and economic life.

A weighty Page indeed, to do so much. It is, therefore, a good idea to read it and let it now speak for itself.

Charles Willson Peale, *The Marquis de Lafayette*

Preamble

The representatives of the French people, formed into a National Assembly, considering ignorance, forgetfulness, or contempt of the rights of man to be the only causes of public misfortunes and the corruption of Governments, have resolved to set forth, in a solemn Declaration, the natural, unalienable and sacred rights of man, to the end that this Declaration, constantly present to all members of the body politic, may remind them unceasingly of their rights and their duties; to the end that the acts of the legislative power and those of the executive power, since they may be continually compared with the aim of every political institution, may thereby be the more respected; to the end that the demands of the citizens, founded henceforth on simple and uncontestable principles, may always be directed toward the maintenance of the Constitution and the happiness of all.

In consequence whereof, the National Assembly recognizes and declares, in the presence and under the auspices of the Supreme Being, the following Rights of Man and of the Citizen.

Article first—Men are born and remain free and equal in rights. Social distinctions may be based only on considerations of the common good.

Article 2—The aim of every political association is the preservation of the natural and imprescribable rights of man. These rights are Liberty, Property, Safety, and Resistance to Oppression.

Article 3—The source of all sovereignty lies essentially in the Nation. No corporate body, no individual may exercise any authority that does not expressly emanate from it.

Article 4—Liberty consists in being able to do anything that does not harm others; thus, the exercise of the natural rights of every man has no bounds other than those that ensure to the other members of society the enjoyment of those same rights. These bounds may be determined only by Law.

Article 5—The Law has the right to forbid only those actions that are injurious to society. Nothing that is not forbidden by Law may be hindered, and no one may be compelled to do what the Law does not ordain.

Article 6—The Law is the expression of the general will. All citizens have the right to take part, personally or through their representatives, in its making. It must be the same for all, whether it protects or punishes. All citizens, being equal in its eyes, shall be equally eligible to all high offices, public positions, and employments, according to their ability and without other distinction than that of their virtues and talents.

Article 7—No man may be accused, arrested, or detained except in the cases determined by the Law, and following the procedure that it has prescribed. Those who solicit, expedite, carry out, or cause to be carried out arbitrary orders must be punished; but any citizen summoned or apprehended by virtue of the Law, must give instant obedience; resistance makes him guilty.

Article 8—The Law must prescribe only the punishments that are strictly and evidently necessary; and no one may be punished except by virtue of a Law drawn up and promulgated before the offence is committed, and legally applied.

Article 9—As every man is presumed innocent until he has been declared guilty, if it should be considered necessary to arrest him, any undue harshness that is not required to secure his person must be severely curbed by Law.

Article 10—No one may be disturbed on account of his opinions, even religious ones, as long as the manifestation of such opinions does not interfere with the established Law and Order.

Article 11—The free communication of ideas and of opinions is one of the most precious rights of man. Any citizen may therefore speak, write, and publish freely, except what is tantamount to the abuse of this liberty in the cases determined by Law.

Article 12—To guarantee the Rights of Man and of the Citizen a public force is necessary; this force is therefore established for the benefit of all, and not for the particular use of those to whom it is entrusted.

Article 13—For the maintenance of the public force, and for administrative expenses, a general tax is indispensable; it must be equally distributed among all citizens, in proportion to their ability to pay.

Article 14—All citizens have the right to ascertain, by themselves, or through their representatives, the need for a public tax, to consent to it freely, to watch over its use, and to determine its proportion, basis, collection, and duration.

Article 15—Society has the right to ask a public official for an accounting of his administration.

Article 16—Any society in which no provision is made for guaranteeing rights or for the separation of powers has no Constitution.

Article 17—Since the right to Property is inviolable and sacred, no one may be deprived thereof, unless public necessity, legally ascertained, obviously requires it, and just and prior indemnity has been paid.

The Emancipation Proclamation

Some observers have noted a supposed disconnect between Abraham Lincoln's private beliefs and his public actions. On one hand, he espoused an unmistakable condemnation of slavery:

> We think it is a moral, a social, and a political wrong . . . it is a wrong [that] affects the existence of the whole nation . . .

And yet, in a letter to Horace Greeley, Lincoln could say:

> My paramount object in this struggle is to save the Union, and is not either to save or destroy slavery. If I could save the Union without freeing any slaves I would do it; and if I could save the Union by freeing all the slaves I would do it; and if I could save the Union by freeing some and leaving others alone, I would also do that.

Thus the claim of ambiguity: to those who view the Civil War in absolute terms, as did the Abolitionists of the time, Lincoln might even appear hypocritical. But this view is naive, as many other commentators have pointed out. Lincoln was dealing with several problems simultaneously, and there were competing constraints that each brought. Historian Allan Nevins notes that the ability to grapple with contradictory aims was in fact one of Lincoln's greatest traits:

> He had qualities far more valuable . . . one was his accurate and penetrating insight; his power of clear logical thought in complicated situations where wisdom and expediency come into conflict and right and wrong seem blurred.

Another commentator, the great Protestant theologian Reinhold Niebuhr, analyzes this perceived disconnect in a brilliant essay "The Religion of Abraham Lincoln." Niebuhr, himself a writer of historical works, first notes that some ambivalence about significant issues is unavoidable:

> The drama of history is shot through with moral meaning; but the meaning is never exact. Sin and punishment, virtue and reward are never precisely proportioned.

Then more strongly, Niebuhr argues that Lincoln was well aware of this ambiguity. While he certainly shared the essential goal of the Abolitionists—

eradication of the institution of slavery—he was neither an idealist nor a zealot. And though surrounded by fierce partisans on either side:

> Lincoln alone had a sense of historical meaning so high as to cast doubts on the intentions of both sides ... Lincoln had a Jeffersonian belief in the new nation ... thus, not only national survival but the survival of democracy was involved in the fortunes of the Civil War ... In short, Lincoln's opposition to slavery cannot be questioned. If there is moral ambiguity in his position, it is an ambiguity which he shared with the founding fathers ... He exhibited not his own ambiguity but the moral ambiguity of the political order itself.

That statement certainly characterizes the attitude of the founding fathers towards slavery; it is manifest in almost all of the constitutions, the national one and those of the individual states, that were written between 1776 and 1783. Benjamin Fletcher Wright notes that:

> Nearly all of the constitutions contained some statement about equality ... [but] in no bill of rights ... is the equality provision accompanied by an abolition of slavery ... It is far from clear just what most of the men of '76 meant by equality.

It is against this backdrop that the Emancipation Proclamation must be read. Though it was profoundly important—Henry Steele Commager called it "potentially more revolutionary in human relationships than any event in American history since 1776"—it was born in the shadow of the wildly dangerous political currents that Lincoln was then trying to navigate. So it too reflects that same "ambiguity" of which Lincoln was accused.

Its timing, for one thing, shows how Lincoln judged that emancipation should be gained by politics, not idealism. He had been considering the notion of general emancipation since 1861. But the wavering loyalty of the Border States, and more, the lack of Northern successes on the battlefield, made it highly inadvisable to take such an action, no matter how it might placate the Abolitionists. Losing one or two more states to the Confederacy would have had a disastrous effect on the morale and stability of the Union. So although Lincoln had prepared a first draft of the Emancipation Proclamation by July 1862, not until September 22, and only after the decisive battle at Antietam, was the Proclamation made public.

Nor was the Proclamation truly general. It freed slaves just in the rebellious states and even then, it exempted those parts of Virginia and Louisiana presently under Union control. Thus, those states that had remained loyal to the Union but where slavery was still widespread were not bound by the Proclamation of 1862.

Some of those states made individual acts of emancipation—West Virginia in 1863, Maryland and Missouri in 1864, Tennessee in 1865—but slavery was not abolished in Delaware and Kentucky until the passage of the Thirteenth Amendment.

And the Proclamation was worded, probably intentionally, in almost dull terms. Though Lincoln was demonstrably a master of rhetoric, there are no poetic images, no stirring or high-minded calls to the human spirit; we look in vain for the same glorious language that we find in the Gettysburg Address or the Second Inaugural Address. Citing historian Richard Hofstadter, it had "all the moral grandeur of a bill of lading."

Yet the centrality of the Emancipation Proclamation cannot be denied. It was a decisive turning point both for the war and for the history of America. In Commager's words:

> [The Proclamation] lifted the Civil War to the dignity of a crusade ... the cause of American union had been definitely fused with that of human liberty.

And though full and general emancipation would only occur through the amendments to the Constitution (and implicitly, the Gettysburg Address), it is the Proclamation that symbolizes for posterity the breaking of slavery in America. It is the source of the common portrayal of Lincoln as "the Great Emancipator." And it is the Page to which we now turn.

By the President of the United States of America:

A Proclamation.

Whereas on the 22nd day of September, A.D. 1862, a proclamation was issued by the President of the United States, containing, among other things, the following, to wit:

That on the 1st day of January, A.D. 1863, all persons held as slaves within any State or designated part of a State the people whereof shall then be in rebellion against the United States shall be then, thenceforward, and forever free; and the executive government of the United States, including the military and naval authority thereof, will recognize and maintain the freedom of such persons and will do no act or acts to repress such persons, or any of them, in any efforts they may make for their actual freedom.

That the executive will on the 1st day of January aforesaid, by proclamation, designate the States and parts of States, if any, in which the people thereof, respectively, shall then be in rebellion against the United States; and the fact that any State or the people thereof shall on that day be in good faith represented in the Congress of the United States by members chosen thereto at elections wherein a majority of the qualified voters of such States shall have participated shall, in the absence of strong countervailing testimony, be deemed conclusive evidence that such State and the people thereof are not then in rebellion against the United States.

Now, therefore, I, Abraham Lincoln, President of the United States, by virtue of the power in me vested as Commander-In-Chief of the Army and Navy of the United States in time of actual armed rebellion against the authority and government of the United States, and as a fit and necessary war measure for suppressing said rebellion, do, on this 1st day of January, A.D. 1863, and in accordance with my purpose so to do, publicly proclaimed for the full period of one hundred days from the first day above mentioned, order and designate as the States and parts of States wherein the people thereof, respectively, are this day in rebellion against the United States the following, to wit:

Arkansas, Texas, Louisiana, (except the Parishes of St. Bernard, Plaquemines, Jefferson, St. John, St. Charles, St. James Ascension, Assumption, Terrebonne, Lafourche, St. Mary, St. Martin, and Orleans, including the City of New Orleans) Mississippi, Alabama, Florida, Georgia, South Carolina, North Carolina, and Virginia, (except the forty-eight counties designated as West Virginia, and also the counties of Berkley, Accomac, Northampton, Elizabeth City, York, Princess Ann, and Norfolk, including the cities of Norfolk and Portsmouth), and which excepted parts, are for the present, left precisely as if this proclamation were not issued.

And by virtue of the power and for the purpose aforesaid, I do order and declare that all persons held as slaves within said designated States and parts of States are, and henceforward shall be, free; and that the Executive Government of the United States, including the military and naval authorities thereof, will recognize and maintain the freedom of said persons.

And I hereby enjoin upon the people so declared to be free to abstain from all violence, unless in necessary self-defense; and I recommend to them that, in all case when allowed, they labor faithfully for reasonable wages.

And I further declare and make known that such persons of suitable condition will be received into the armed service of the United States to garrison forts, positions, stations, and other places, and to man vessels of all sorts in said service.

And upon this act, sincerely believed to be an act of justice, warranted by the Constitution upon military necessity, I invoke the considerate judgment of mankind and the gracious favor of Almighty God.

In witness whereof, I have hereunto set my hand and caused the seal of the United States to be affixed

Done at the city of Washington, the first day of January, in the year of our Lord one thousand eight hundred and sixty-three, and of the independence of the United States of America the eighty-seventh.

By the President: Abraham Lincoln

William H. Seward, Secretary of State

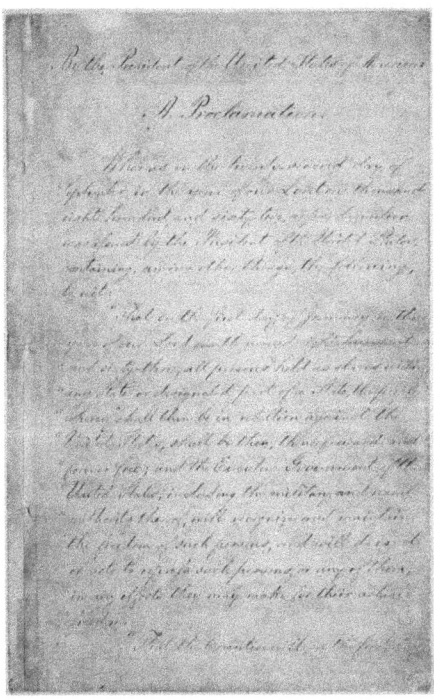

Lincoln's handwritten draft of the Proclamation

The October Manifesto

Like several other Pages in this section, the October Manifesto of Tsar Nicholas II marks the emergence of democracy in a country ruled for centuries by an autocratic monarch. Coming at the end of the long Romanov dynasty, this brief document was a milestone in the complex metamorphosis whereby the antiquated Russian Empire became the Communist superstate that defined much of the twentieth century's history. Unlike many of the other documents that it resembles, however, the October Manifesto was issued not by rebels or radicals, but by the reigning emperor against whom the radicals were agitating. The occasion that brought the Page about, however, was very familiar.

The end of the nineteenth century had witnessed vast changes in the social fabric of Russia. The growth of industrialization and capitalism, even in limited doses, had remade much of the nation, producing a large middle class and an emergent labor movement. Both of these clamored for reform of the autocratic government of the Tsarist regime. Their clamoring was very vocal. In the words of historian Nicholas Riasanovsky:

> As the twentieth century opened, Russia was in turmoil. Strikes spread throughout the country. Student protests and disturbances became more frequent.... [The agitation and unrest] offered increased opportunities to the Socialist Revolutionaries, just as the growth of the labor movement encouraged the Social Democrats

Then Russia fought a disastrous war against Japan in 1904-05. The Japanese had attacked Port Arthur without warning in February 1904, then inflicted several defeats of Russian armies and crushed a large Russian fleet in the Tsushima Strait. The war ended with the Treaty of Portsmouth in early 1905. From the outset, the war was unpopular; with the humiliating defeat, the prestige of the Tsar plummeted.

While this disaster was occurring in the international arena, a greater one was coming to a boil domestically. A Russian Orthodox priest named Georgy Gapon had been organizing laborers in St. Petersburg to protest for better working conditions and higher wages. In January 1905, Gapon led a march on the Winter Palace to present a petition to the Tsar. The demonstration was orderly but very large and, at least to some of the watching police, was growing out of control. As the marchers entered the square in front of the palace, the police opened fire. One hundred and thirty people were killed in a tragedy that was quickly named "Bloody Sunday." Riasanovsky points out the horrible ironies that attended the massacre:

> The workers were converging on the Winter Palace—ignorant of the fact that Nicholas II was not there—with icons and the Tsar's portraits, as faithful subjects ... of their sovereign, begging him for redress and help. [The massacre] meant a bloody break between the Tsar and those numerous workers who had until that "Bloody Sunday" remained loyal to him.

This tragedy, coming on the heels of the humiliating war, led to widespread fury. The Tsar's uncle was assassinated in Moscow in February. Sailors aboard the battleship Potemkin mutinied. Strikes and violence grew throughout the year, and the country was in genuine crisis by the autumn. A large general strike was held in October that paralyzed the nation. The word "soviet" first appeared on the Russian political horizon as a group of workers in St. Petersburg organized a council—a soviet—of laborers in opposition to the Government.

Finally, at the urging of Sergei Witte, the Russian Finance Minister (and one of the few people of the period who saw the danger ahead), the Tsar issued this Manifesto for the purpose of granting civil rights and establishing a constitutional monarchy. In particular, the Manifesto created a legislative body, the Duma, and promised (though with little specificity) the universal franchise in the near future.

The October Manifesto served its purpose. The widespread agitation was calmed, the liberal movement was defused, and order was restored. In the larger perspective, however, the Tsar had no genuine interest in diminishing the autocratic power of the Russian Imperial state, and thus the Manifesto contained noble ambitions but little of real substance. When the Duma actually met, in 1906, the Tsar's notion of a "constitutional monarchy" became apparent: he retained the majority of his authority, he maintained personal control of half the state budget, and he held veto power over all legislation enacted by the Duma. The first two sessions of the Duma, in 1906 and 1907, proved useless, and Nicholas unilaterally revised the electoral laws. The new Duma that was created was essentially a body that would concur with his decisions.

But the events of October 1905, were not without effect. They showed that even the Tsar could be forced to heed the will of the people, if the people were loud enough. The revolutionary movement, though temporarily silenced, did not disappear, but went underground, and remained active in the years preceding the Great War (the Prime Minister, Peter Stolypin, was assassinated in 1911.) And by enacting the October Manifesto, the Tsar himself contributed to the chain of events that eventuated in the cataclysm of 1917, the rise of the Bolshevik state under Lenin, and the foundation of the Soviet Union.

Earnest Lipgart, ***Tsar Nicholas II***

Fr. Gapon and the marchers

On the improvement of order in the state

The disturbances and unrest in St. Petersburg, Moscow and in many other parts of our Empire have filled Our heart with great and profound sorrow. The welfare of the Russian Sovereign and His people is inseparable and national sorrow is His too. The present disturbances could give rise to national instability and present a threat to the unity of Our State. The oath which We took as Tsar compels Us to use all Our strength, intelligence and power to put a speedy end to this unrest which is so dangerous for the State. The relevant authorities have been ordered to take measures to deal with direct outbreaks of disorder and violence and to protect people who only want to go about their daily business in peace. However, in view of the need to speedily implement earlier measures to pacify the country, we have decided that the work of the government must be unified. We have therefore ordered the government to take the following measures in fulfillment of Our unbending will:

1. Fundamental civil freedoms will be granted to the population, including real personal inviolability, freedom of conscience, speech, assembly and association.

2. Participation in the Duma will be granted to those classes of the population which are at present deprived of voting powers, insofar as is possible in the short period before the convocation of the Duma, and this will lead to the development of a universal franchise. There will be no delay to the Duma elect already been organized.

3. It is established as an unshakable rule that no law can come into force without its approval by the State Duma and representatives of the people will be given the opportunity to take real part in the supervision of the legality of government bodies.

We call on all true sons of Russia to remember the homeland, to help put a stop to this unprecedented unrest and, together with this, to devote all their strength to the restoration of peace to their native land.

THE WORLD WARS OF THE TWENTIETH CENTURY

You shall hear of wars, and rumours of wars (Matthew 24:6)

The Pages in this section are all related to the protracted conflict that dominated the twentieth century's first half, a conflict that is commonly divided into the First and Second World Wars. In its beginnings it was a European war. But as it grew in intensity and complexity it spread across both the Atlantic and Pacific oceans, and became truly global. As with all real history, its chronological boundaries are not easily defined. The years of actual combat are precise, to be sure: 1914-1918 and 1939-1945. But the two decades between 1918 and 1939 were more a hiatus than a genuine peace, with the seeds of the Second war sown by the termination of the First. And the conflict's complex beginnings go back well into the nineteenth century, long before the outbreak of fighting in 1914.

The war had many origins: colonial frictions, emergent nationalism in Eastern Europe, and age-old rivalries hallowed by centuries of hatred. When it came, the war was one of the most brutal ever fought, a fact that was especially stunning after so quiescent a period in European history. Following Napoleon's defeat in 1815, the nineteenth century had been comparatively peaceful. Most of the Great Powers were engaged in stifling internal dissent and socialist uprising; they had little time or occasion to wage war on their neighbors. War did happen, to be sure—the Crimean War was a nasty, useless war, Prussia taught brief and painful lessons to Denmark, Austria, and France, and the powder keg of the Balkans sputtered into occasional minor eruptions. But in terms of major conflicts, nineteenth-century Europe somehow managed to avoid the frequent and costly outbreaks of fighting among the Great Powers that had occurred regularly throughout the seventeenth and eighteenth centuries.

But even as major war was avoided, preparation for it went on at a furious pace. Arms races with new and very destructive weapons, secret treaties, constant jostling to be on the heavier side of the balance of power: by the century's end, Europe was in an ominous state, and almost everyone expected that some significant bout of war was imminent. In 1891, Bismark said to a friend: "I shall not live to see the world war, but you will. And it will start in the East." Nor was it only the leaders who had this awareness; the public at large was quite cognizant of the political situation. Writing for that public in 1904, Sir Arthur Conan Doyle painted an accurate picture of the time in "The Adventure of the Second Stain," when his fictional Prime Minister says:

> Mr. Holmes, you take me into regions of high international politics. But if you consider the European situation you will have no difficulty in perceiving the motive. The whole of Europe is an armed camp. There is

a double league which makes a fair balance of military power. Great Britain holds the scales. If Britain were driven into war with one confederacy, it would assure the supremacy of the other confederacy, whether they joined in the war or not.

The double league Doyle speaks of was, on one hand, the central powers: Germany and the Austro-Hungarian Empire, and on the other, the two major powers that flanked them, France and Russia. At the turn of the twentieth century, Britain had ties of varying strength with all of these powers, but was not the declared ally of any.

Europe at the start of the Great War

This is the point that we join these complex events, with an important and interesting Page: the pact that ended finally the ancient hostility between Britain and France. This document, known as the "Entente Cordiale," brought accord where there had been enmity for almost a millennium. But this rapprochement had an unavoidable effect on the rest of the European landscape. As Doyle's Prime Minister had foreseen, an England allied with France eventually led to an England opposed to Germany and Austria. The result— England, France, and Russia all facing the German center—was a posture that was maintained through decades of war, carnage, and suffering.

The remaining Pages of the section chronologically trace the war through its two terrible parts. Austria's Ultimatum to Serbia and the Kaiser's Address to the

Reichstag signaled the start of the fighting in 1914; Wilson's enunciation of the Fourteen Points had a large part in promoting the Armistice of 1918, which endured for over two decades. But the Versailles Treaty could never succeed, and Hitler and the Nazis arose in the 1930s, just as some had predicted. The Munich Pact marked the last-ditch effort to preserve the hopeless peace. The mood it reflects, one of desperate appeasement, is sharply contrasted by the forceful opposition to Hitler that Churchill voiced a year later in his initial address to the British nation.

The final three pages reflect America's growing participation in the war. The Atlantic Charter shows America on the verge of joining the Allies, a step she took only after the Japanese attack on Pearl Harbor. Roosevelt's address to Congress marks not only America's entry into the war, but also, in the fullest sense, the war's expansion into a global conflict. The final Page is the last action of the war, Japan's surrender to the Allies on September 2, 1945, thirty-one years and one month after the fighting began.

The Entente Cordiale between France and Great Britain

On April 8, 1904, Great Britain and France signed an agreement to settle their colonial disagreements in Egypt and Morocco. This agreement, called the "Entente Cordiale," essentially granted Great Britain hegemony in Egypt and France a free hand in Morocco.[12] While the events that led to its signing—in truth, a summary of the entire European political currents at the turn of the century—are far more complex than can be fully discussed in the scope of this book, we can at least look at a few of the major causes. Of these, the most interesting by far is the part played by King Edward VII of England, a remarkable person and an even more remarkable monarch.

"Cordial" is a term seldom applied to relations between France and Britain. Even granting that European History is little more than a sad tale of never-ending national hatreds, the perpetually unpleasant antagonism between these two nations stands out in special relief. Ever since William and his Normans defeated Harold and his Saxons in 1066, the flames of bitterness on both sides of the Channel have waxed more or less bright, but have seldom waned. Throughout the century of the Hundred Years' War, through the costly contest for colonial domination in the New World, up to the rise of Napoleon in 1800, England and France were usually at odds, and frequently at war.

Though open conflict was avoided after Waterloo, the two nations carried out their rivalry through the proxies of their colonial empires. The most recent friction (a crisis that nearly provoked the two nations into war) had occurred in September 1898, when French and English military units met at a remote Egyptian locale called Fashoda. The French military force was part of a move by France to strengthen its claim on part of Egypt. But it met a much stronger English force intent on securing British possession of the Suez Canal. Negotiations were delicate, since no way out of the impasse was acceptable for both sides, and fighting would have catapulted the two nations into war. England would accept nothing except complete control of the Canal. Eventually, France backed down, and withdrew. But the result was that French public opinion was even more strongly anti-British than ever: the following year, when the Boers humbled the British in South Africa, the French public cheered.

---

[12] There were actually three documents signed on that date. The first two dealt with colonial issues in Newfoundland, Africa, and the Far East. The third, which concerned the Mediterranean locales, was by far the most important, and is what drove several subsequent political developments before the Great War.

It is against this backdrop that Edward, in 1901, became king after the long and glorious Victorian era. Eldest son of Albert and Victoria, Edward was 62 years old when he ascended the throne. He had been Prince of Wales from the period soon after the death of Napoleon until the turn of the twentieth century, all of that time excluded from any active role in government by his mother's disdain of his abilities. At his accession, most observers supposed that his reign would be a continuation of his lifelong predilection for women and social pleasure: there was little expectation that he would take any interest in governing the nation as had his mother. Edward was, however, a far more able diplomat and politician than Victoria (or anyone else, for that matter) realized. His political skill was evidenced by the very major role he played for the present Page, the Entente Cordiale and the events that led to it. Of paramount importance was that in his personal disposition, Edward was a confirmed francophile. He had suffered a painful childhood under the stern Teutonic rule of his father Albert, and whether for this or for other causes, Edward loved everything French even as he loathed the German temperament.

At the time of Edward's accession, relations between Britain, France, and Germany were in a highly fluid state. On one hand, Britain had tried several times to define a formal alliance with Germany. But these attempts had failed and instead, Britain watched with growing discomfort as Germany underwent an enormous naval buildup that threatened British supremacy at sea. At the same time, France was still smarting from her defeat by Germany in 1871. To offset German dominance on the Continent, the French foreign Minister, Théophile Delcassé, began a deliberate course toward smoothing relations with England. The political situation came to a very public climax in the Spring of 1903. King Edward was on a protracted cruise of the Mediterranean when, on his own initiative, he suddenly planned a visit to Paris. Against the wishes of his own Government, he demanded that it be a state visit with as much formality as the French would permit.

On his arrival, he was loudly booed. His procession down the Champs-Elysees was met with silence, except for a few shouts of "Vive les Boers." The entire visit threatened to be a disaster. Edward, however, parried insults with charm. While at the theatre that same evening, he made no attempt at anonymity, but sauntered boldly through the lobby at intermission. He happened upon Mme. Jeanne Granier, an actress whom he had admired in London some time previously. In conversation with her he spoke glowingly and admiringly, and his words of praise were overheard by the crowd (as they were meant to be). The following day he loudly affirmed his love of Paris to the city's mayor. By the end of his four-day visit he left the city with crowds cheering "Vive le Roi" loudly and often.

Delcassé moved quickly to capitalize on Edward's personal triumph. The French President, Loubet, made an official visit to London two months later, where Edward received him with great pomp. During the visit, Delcassé approached Lord Lansdowne, the British Foreign Minister, with a formal proposal about an alliance. Lansdowne agreed, and Paul Cambon, the French ambassador to London, was entrusted to conduct the negotiations. Nine months later the Entente Cordiale was signed.

The Entente was not a treaty, nor did it promise any future military or diplomatic activities. Nevertheless, it was a profoundly important document that had critical consequences for all of Europe. By establishing harmony with France, it brought the Anglo-German naval rivalry into sharp relief. It paved the way for the subsequent Triple Entente between England, France, and Russia. And though it initially was regarded as insignificant, it soon threw the German Foreign Office into dismay: up until early 1904, Prince Von Bulow, the German Chancellor, had based much of his foreign policy assumptions on the fact that an Anglo-French accord was unthinkable. When the Entente was signed, it invalidated all of those assumptions. In V.R. Berghans's words:

> The forming of the Entente Cordiale threw the German foreign office into a mood of deep depression, and was widely considered to be one of the worst defeats for German policy since the conclusion of the Franco-Russian Alliance.

This depression was justified a decade later, when the Continent erupted into the Great War.

One final note. In the treaties, alliances, and covenants written around the turn of the century, it was almost a certainty that there would be some sort of secret appendix or addendum. So it was with the Entente Cordiale, which had five secret articles. Three of these pertained to Spain, who had long since ceased to be one of the European Great Powers. It was the existence of these secret portions of treaties that led Woodrow Wilson to begin the Fourteen Points with a forceful plea for "open covenants, openly arrived at." In the interest of such openness, I have appended the secret articles as an additional Page. There is little that we today would find particularly in need of secrecy. But Cambon and Lansdowne obviously felt so, and these articles were not revealed until 1911, when the drums of war were much louder and very close.

Luke Fildes, *Portrait of King Edward VII, 1902*

Théophile Delcassé

DECLARATION BETWEEN THE UNITED KINGDOM AND FRANCE RESPECTING EGYPT AND MOROCCO.

ARTICLE I. His Britannic Majesty's Government declare that they have no intention of altering the political status of Egypt.

The Government of the French Republic, for their part, declare that they will not obstruct the action of Great Britain in that country by asking that a limit of time be fixed for the British occupation or in any other manner, and that they give their assent to the draft Khedivial Decree annexed to the present Arrangement, containing the guarantees considered necessary for the protection of the interests of the Egyptian bondholders, on the condition that, after its promulgation, it cannot be modified in any way without the consent of the Powers Signatory of the Convention of London of 1885.

It is agreed that the post of Director-General of Antiquities in Egypt shall continue, as in the past, to be entrusted to a French savant.

The French schools in Egypt shall continue to enjoy the same liberty as in the past.

ARTICLE II The Government of the French Republic declare that they have no intention of altering the political status of Morocco.

His Britannic Majesty's Government, for their part, recognise that it appertains to France, more particularly as a Power whose dominions are conterminous for a great distance with those of Morocco, to preserve order in that country, and to provide assistance for the purpose of all administrative, economic, financial, and military reforms which it may require.

They declare that they will not obstruct the action taken by France for this purpose, provided that such action shall leave intact the rights which Great Britain, in virtue of Treaties, Conventions, and usage, enjoys in Morocco, including the right of coasting trade between the ports of Morocco, enjoyed by British vessels since 1901.

ARTICLE III His Britannic Majesty's Government, for their part, will respect the rights which France, in virtue of Treaties, Conventions, and usage, enjoys in Egypt, including the right of coasting trade between Egyptian ports accorded to French vessels.

ARTICLE IV The two Governments, being equally attached to the principle of commercial liberty both in Egypt and Morocco, declare that they will not, in those countries, countenance any inequality either in the imposition of customs duties or other taxer, or of railway transport charges.

The trade of both nations with Morocco and with Egypt shall enjoy the same treatment in transit through the French and British possessions in Africa. An Agreement between the two Governments shall settle the conditions of such transit and shall determine the points of entry. This mutual engagement shall be binding for a period of thirty years. Unless this stipulation is expressly denounced at least one year in advance, the period shall be extended for five years at a time.

Nevertheless, the Government of the French Republic reserve to themselves in Morocco, and His Britannic Majesty's Government reserve to themselves in Egypt, the right to see that the concessions for roads, railways, ports, etc., are only granted on such conditions as will maintain intact the authority of the State over these great undertakings of public interest.

ARTICLE V His Britannic Majesty's Government declare that they will use their influence in order that the French officials now in the Egyptian service may not be placed under conditions less advantageous than those applying to the British officials in the same service.

The Government of the French Republic, for their part, would make no objection to the application of analogous conditions to British officials now in the Moorish service.

ARTICLE VI In order to insure the free passage of the Suez Canal, His Britannic Majesty's Government declare that they adhere to the stipulations of the Treaty of the 29th October, 1888; and that they agree to their being put in force. The free passage of the Canal being thus guaranteed, the execution of the last sentence of paragraph 1 as well as of paragraph 2 of Article VIII of that Treaty will remain in abeyance.

ARTICLE VII. In order to secure the free passage of the Straits of Gibraltar, the two Governments agree not to permit the erection of any fortifications or strategic works on that portion of the coast of Morocco comprised between, but not including, Melilla and the heights which command the right bank of the River Sebou.

This condition does not, however, apply to the places at present in the occupation of Spain on the Moorish coast of the Mediterranean.

ARTICLE VIII. The two Governments, inspired by their feeling of sincere friendship for Spain, take into special consideration the interests which that country derives from her geographical position and from her territorial possessions on the Moorish coast of the Mediterranean. In regard to these interests the French Government will come to an understanding with the Spanish Government. The agreement which may be come to on the subject between France and Spain shall be communicated to His Britannic Majesty's Government.

ARTICLE IX. The two Governments agree to afford to one another their diplomatic support, in order to obtain the execution of the clauses of the present Declaration regarding Egypt and Morocco.

In witness whereof his Excellency the Ambassador of the French Republic at the Court of His Majesty the King of the United Kingdom of Great Britain and Ireland and of the British Dominions beyond the Seas, Emperor of India, and His Majesty's Principal Secretary of State for Foreign Affairs, duly authorised for that purpose, have signed the present Declaration and have affixed thereto their seals.

Done at London, in duplicate, the 8th day of April, 1904.

(L.S.) LANSDOWNE   (L.S.) PAUL CAMBON

Secret Articles

ARTICLE 1. In the event of either Government finding themselves constrained, by the force of circumstances, to modify their policy in respect to Egypt or Morocco, the engagements which they have undertaken towards each other by Articles 4, 6, and 7 of the Declaration of today's date would remain intact.

ARTICLE 2. His Britannic Majesty's Government have no present intention of proposing to the Powers any changes in the system of the Capitulations, or in the judicial organisation of Egypt.

In the event of their considering it desirable to introduce in Egypt reforms tending to assimilate the Egyptian legislative system to that in force in other civilised Countries, the Government of the French Republic will not refuse to entertain any such proposals, on the understanding that His Britannic Majesty's Government will agree to entertain the suggestions that the Government of the French Republic may have to make to them with a view of introducing similar reforms in Morocco.

ARTICLE 3. The two Governments agree that a certain extent of Moorish territory adjacent to Melilla, Ceuta, and other presides should, whenever the Sultan ceases to exercise authority over it, come within the sphere of influence of Spain, and that the administration of the coast from Melilla as far as, but not including, the heights on the right bank of the Sebou shall be entrusted to Spain.

Nevertheless, Spain would previously have to give her formal assent to the provisions of Articles 4 and 7 of the Declaration of today's date, and undertake to carry them out.

She would also have to undertake not to alienate the whole, or a part, of the territories placed under her authority or in her sphere of influence.

ARTICLE 4. If Spain, when invited to assent to the provisions of the preceding article, should think proper to decline, the arrangement between France and Great Britain, as embodied in the Declaration of today's date, would be none the less at once applicable.

ARTICLE 5. Should the consent of the other Powers to the draft Decree mentioned in Article I of the Declaration of today's date not be obtained, the Government of the French Republic will not oppose the repayment at par of the Guaranteed, Privileged, and Unified Debts after the 15th July, 1910.

Done at London, in duplicate, the 8th day of April, 1904.

(L.S.) LANSDOWNE (L.S.)PAUL CAMBON

Ultimatum from Austria to Serbia

It is difficult to say precisely when in 1914 the World War really began. Historian A.J.P. Taylor notes, for instance, that

> In the minds of Englishmen, 4 August is unshakably fixed as the date when the first World war began; yet by then France and Germany had been at war for twenty-four hours, Russia and Germany for three days, Serbia and Austria-Hungary for almost a week.

Nor is it easy to locate any one source for the war. The jockeying for power and influence among the Great and near-Great Powers had been unceasing since long before the turn of the century, and the flash points in the Balkans had already flared into active warfare repeatedly in 1912 and 1913. But high among the proximate causes, and certainly the most important in the public eye, was the assassination of the Austrian Archduke, Franz Ferdinand, in Sarajevo, Bosnia, on June 28, 1914.

While the assassination was only the last straw of many (and while a war of major dimensions would likely have erupted in any case), Sarajevo was a particularly explosive event. In his "Diplomatic History of Europe," René Albrecht-Carrié states, with some justification, that:

> "The shot heard round the world" fits Sarajevo rather better than the original occasion of the phrase.

The assassin who fired that shot was Gavrilo Princip, a nineteen-year old student from Belgrade and a member of a Serbian revolutionary cabal. The tale of that cabal is bound up with the complex story of Serbia's gradual emergence as an independent state, a long story that is impossible reasonably to tell in brief. Suffice to say that the Serbs, along with many other Balkan peoples—Croats, Bulgars, Rumanians—were striving throughout the nineteenth century to free themselves from an imperial yoke, whether Ottoman, Russian, or Austrian. By 1878, several Balkan states, Serbia among them, had emerged from the dying Ottoman Empire. But many Slavic populations still lived under the rule of either Turkey or Austria; Serbia, though still a small state, was in the throes of nationalistic zeal. The dream of a "southern Slav empire" fired the imagination of the young Slavs within and without Serbia's borders.[13]

The Austrians were wary of their new neighbor. They had ostensibly welcomed the new Kingdom of Serbia at its birth, and by the Treaty of 1881, Austria expressed the desire to "second the interests of Serbia" among the other Great

---

[13] This dream was eventually realized as the Yugoslavian federation that existed roughly between 1920 and 1990.

Powers. But the prospect of a large and powerful pan-Slavic state on her southeastern border soon grew less welcome, and Austria (and behind her, Germany) began viewing an expanding Serbia as a threat rather than a neighbor. In truth, the Serbs were only one of many restive groups in Central Europe: Slovenes, Ruthenians, Albanians, and a dozen other peoples living in three great empires were jockeying to gain independence while the rulers of those empires were striving to withhold it. But of all of these, Austria saw Serbia, with some justification, as the most likely source of an emergent military and political rivalry.

Bosnia, then as now, was a particularly contentious issue. Though inhabited largely by a Slavic population, its administrative control had been taken over by Austria in 1879, when the Turks were driven from the Balkans. The Serbs—and, to a large part, the Bosnians—saw the proper place for Bosnia as a part of Greater Serbia. But Austria had no intention of relinquishing control of the province, regardless of its Slavic population. In 1908, she formally annexed Bosnia into the Austro-Hungarian Empire, an act that infuriated the Serbs and nearly precipitated a crisis with Russia. By the end of 1913, a confrontation appeared immanent: in October of that year, the Austrian Foreign Minister, Count Berchtold, candidly discussed with Kaiser Wilhelm II the strong probability of a war with Serbia.

It is against this volatile background that the Archduke, Franz Ferdinand, chose to pay a visit to Sarajevo on June 28, 1914. This decision could not have been more ill-advised. The visit came on the anniversary of the Battle of Kosovo (1386), the occasion when Serbia was defeated and swallowed by Turkey. Albrecht-Carrié compares the insulting character of the Archduke's visit to the similar hatreds then found in Ireland:

> Had the heir to the British throne elected to visit Dublin on St. Patrick's day in 1916, the gesture would have been regarded as a manifestation of insensitive bad taste . . . It was no less rash of Archduke Franz Ferdinand [to visit Sarajevo that day] . . .

But visit he did, and in one of those terrible twists of fate, his motorcade took a wrong turn. Waiting there was Princip, one of a group of zealous nationalists bent on detaching Bosnia from Austria and uniting it with Serbia. Princip fired, killing both the Archduke and his wife Sophie, the Duchess of Hohenberg.

The month between the assassination and the opening of the war was marked by furious diplomatic activity in every Foreign Office in Europe. Central to all of the ferment were two great unknowns. First, would Austria regard the assassination as an act sponsored by the Serbian government?[14] And second, would any recrimination be confined as a local quarrel between Austria and Serbia?

On July 23, Austria delivered an ultimatum to Serbia. It was a particularly rude and brusque document, and to add to the insult, Serbia was given only forty-eight hours to respond, with no possibility of extension. As Robert Massie notes:

> The demands were those that a defeated state might expect from a victor. At least one Austrian was candid about the nature and implications of the note . . . "There will be a big war," said the Emperor, Franz Joseph.

On the advice of both Russia and Britain, Serbia made a strong effort at conciliation. Her response was to concede to almost all of the Austrian demands; she also included a proposal to submit the entire affair to an international tribunal. The response was perceived as a masterpiece of diplomacy; even Kaiser Wilhelm II remarked:

> A brilliant performance for a time limit of only forty-eight hours . . . This is more than one could have expected. A great moral victory for Vienna; with it, every reason for war drops away.

But Austria was not to be denied her vengeance, and on July 28, she declared war on Serbia. On the 29th, Russia, long a patron of the Slavic Serbs, mobilized her armies. Germany and France followed suit on August 1. Germany sent an ultimatum to France on the 2nd, and war between them erupted on the 3rd. Germany entered Belgium on the 4th, and Britain declared war on Germany on the 5th.

And thus World War I came to pass. The visceral hatreds that were unleashed ruled Europe for half a century. The fighting, and even more, the cancerous growth in technology that made the fighting ever more violent, were the first bout of an ever-expanding siege of military madness in whose shadow we live even now.

Some notes on the text. The monarchal references in the Ultimatum are not obvious: the phrase "the Royal Government" refers to the Serbians and "the Imperial and Royal Government" (also abbreviated below as "I. and R.") refers to Austria-Hungary

The citation in the opening of the Ultimatum refers to Serbia's unwilling agreement to the annexation of Bosnia in 1908.

---

[14] It is fascinating even now to observe the divergence of opinion from different historians about the Serbian Government's complicity. That there was some sort of cooperation between Serbian police and the assassins is sure. But beyond that, the record grows more Byzantine, as is, of course, Balkan history itself.

The Ultimatum also contained an appendix that described the results of Austria's investigation of the assassination, and which were the basis of Austria's accusation of Serbian complicity. I have included this appendix as another Page after the Ultimatum.

Finally, the Ultimatum was sent to the German Minister at Belgrade, von Gieslingen, to present to Serbia. It also contained the following message to von Gieslingen himself:

> On the occasion of handing over this note, would Your Excellency please also add orally that—in the event that no unconditionally positive answer of the Royal government might be received in the meantime—after the course of the 48-hour deadline referred to in this note, as measured from the day and hour of your announcing it, you are commissioned to leave the I. and R. Embassy with your personnel.

Archduke Franz Ferdinand with his family

Serbia recognizes that her rights were not affected by the state of affairs created in Bosnia, and states that she will accordingly accommodate herself to the decisions to be reached by the Powers in connection with Article 25 of the Treaty of Berlin. Serbia, in accepting the advice of the Great Powers, binds herself to desist from the attitude of protest and opposition which she has assumed with regard to the annexation since October last, and she furthermore binds herself to alter the tendency of her present policy toward Austria-Hungary, and to live on the footing of friendly and neighborly relations with the latter in the future.

Now the history of the past few years, and particularly the painful events of the 28th of June, have proved the existence of a subversive movement in Serbia, whose object it is to separate certain portions of territory from the Austro-Hungarian Monarchy. This movement, which came into being under the very eyes of the Serbian Government, subsequently found expression outside of the territory of the Kingdom in acts of terrorism, in a number of attempts at assassination, and in murders.

Far from fulfilling the formal obligations contained in its declaration of the 31st of March, 1909, the Royal Serbian Government has done nothing to suppress this movement. It has tolerated the criminal activities of the various unions and associations directed against the Monarchy, the unchecked utterances of the press, the glorification of the authors of assassinations, the participation of officers and officials in subversive intrigues; it has tolerated an unhealthy propaganda in its public instruction; and it has tolerated, finally, every manifestation which could betray the people of Serbia into hatred of the Monarchy and contempt for its institutions. This toleration of which the Royal Serbian Government was guilty, was still in evidence at that moment when the events of the twenty-eighth of June exhibited to the whole world the dreadful consequences of such toleration.

It is clear from the statements and confessions of the criminal authors of the assassination of the twenty-eighth of June, that the murder at Sarajevo was conceived at Belgrade, that the murderers received the weapons and the bombs with which they were equipped from Serbian officers and officials who belonged to the Narodna Odbrana, and, finally, that the dispatch of the criminals and of their weapons to Bosnia was arranged and effected under the conduct of Serbian frontier authorities. The results brought out by the inquiry no longer permit the Imperial and Royal Government to maintain the attitude of patient tolerance which it has observed for years toward those agitations which center at Belgrade and are spread thence into the territories of the Monarchy. Instead, these results impose upon the Imperial and Royal Government the obligation to put an end to those intrigues, which constitute a standing menace to the peace of the Monarchy.

In order to attain this end, the Imperial and Royal Government finds itself compelled to demand that the Serbian Government give official assurance that it will condemn the propaganda directed against Austria-Hungary, that is to say, the whole body of the efforts whose ultimate object it is to separate from the Monarchy territories that belong to it; and that it will obligate itself to suppress with all the means at its command this criminal and terroristic propaganda. In order to give these assurances a character of solemnity, the Royal Serbian Government will publish on the first page of its official organ of July 26/13, the following declaration:

> The Royal Serbian Government condemns the propaganda directed against Austria-Hungary, that is to say, the whole body of the efforts whose ultimate object it is to separate from the Austro-Hungarian Monarchy territories that belong to it, and it most sincerely regrets the dreadful consequences of these criminal transactions.

The Royal Serbian Government regrets that Serbian officers and officials should have taken part in the above-mentioned propaganda and thus have endangered the friendly and neighborly relations, to the cultivation of which the Royal Government had most solemnly pledged itself by its declarations of March 31, 1909.

The Royal Government, which disapproves and repels every idea and every attempt to interfere in the destinies of the population of whatever portion of Austria-Hungary, regards it as its duty most expressly to call attention of the officers, officials, and the whole population of the kingdom to the fact that for the future it will proceed with the utmost rigor against any persons who shall become guilty of any such activities, activities to prevent and to suppress which, the Government will bend every effort.

This declaration shall be brought to the attention of the Royal army simultaneously by an order of the day from His Majesty the King, and by publication in the official organ of the army.

Gavrillo Pronzep

The Royal Serbian Government will furthermore pledge itself:

1. to suppress every publication which shall incite to hatred and contempt of the Monarchy, and the general tendency of which shall be directed against the territorial integrity of the latter;

2. to proceed at once to the dissolution of the Narodna Odbrana to confiscate all of its means of propaganda, and in the same manner to proceed against the other unions and associations in Serbia which occupy themselves with propaganda against Austria-Hungary; the Royal Government will take such measures as are necessary to make sure that the dissolved associations may not continue their activities under other names or in other forms;

3. to eliminate without delay from public instruction in Serbia, everything, whether connected with the teaching corps or with the methods of teaching, that serves or may serve to nourish the propaganda against Austria-Hungary;

4. to remove from the military and administrative service in general all officers and officials who have been guilty of carrying on the propaganda against Austria-Hungary, whose names the Imperial and Royal Government reserves the right to make known to the Royal Government when communicating the material evidence now in its possession;

5. to agree to the cooperation in Serbia of the organs of the Imperial and Royal Government in the suppression of the subversive movement directed against the integrity of the Monarchy;

6. to institute a judicial inquiry against every participant in the conspiracy of the twenty-eighth of June who may be found in Serbian territory; the organs of the Imperial and Royal Government delegated for this purpose will take part in the proceedings held for this purpose;

7. to undertake with all haste the arrest of Major Voislav Tankosic and of one Milan Ciganovitch, a Serbian official, who have been compromised by the results of the inquiry;

8. by efficient measures to prevent the participation of Serbian authorities in the smuggling of weapons and explosives across the frontier; to dismiss from the service and to punish severely those members of the Frontier Service at Schabats and Losnitza who assisted the authors of the crime of Sarajevo to cross the frontier;

9. to make explanations to the Imperial and Royal Government concerning the unjustifiable utterances of high Serbian functionaries in Serbia and abroad, who, without regard for their official position, have not hesitated to express themselves in a manner hostile toward Austria-Hungary since the assassination of the twenty-eighth of June;

10. to inform the Imperial and Royal Government without delay of the execution of the measures comprised in the foregoing points.

The Imperial and Royal Government awaits the reply of the Royal Government by Saturday, the twenty-fifth instant, at 6 p.m., at the latest. A reminder of the results of the investigation about Sarajevo, to the extent they relate to the functionaries named in points 7 and 8 [above], is appended to this note.

Appendix to the Ultimatum

The crime investigation undertaken at court in Sarajevo against Gavrilo Princip and his comrades on account of the assassination committed on the 28th of June this year, along with the guilt of accomplices, has up until now led to the following conclusions:

1. The plan of murdering Archduke Franz Ferdinand during his stay in Sarajevo was concocted in Belgrade by Gavrilo Princip, Nedeljko Cabrinovic, a certain Milan Ciganovic, and Trifko Grabesch with the assistance of Major Voika Takosic.

2. The six bombs and four Browning pistols along with ammunition—used as tools by the criminals—were procured and given to Princip, Cabrinovic and Grabesch in Belgrade by a certain Milan Ciganovic and Major Voija Takosic.

3. The bombs are hand grenades originating from the weapons depot of the Serbian army in Kragujevatz.

4. To guarantee the success of the assassination, Ciganovic instructed Princip, Cabrinovic and Grabesch in the use of the grenades and gave lessons on shooting Browning pistols to Princip and Grabesch in a forest next to the shooting range at Topschider.

5. To make possible Princip, Cabrinovic and Grabesch's passage across the Bosnia-Herzegovina border and the smuggling of their weapons, an entire secretive transportation system was organized by Ciganovic. The entry of the criminals and their weapons into Bosnia and Herzegovina was carried out by the main border officials of Shabatz (Rade Popovic) and Losnitza as well as by the customs agent Budivoj Grbic of Losnitza, with the complicity of several others.«

Kaiser Wilhelm: Address to the Reichstag

The personality of Kaiser Wilhelm II is the kind that historical commentaries thrive on. Erratic, impulsive, whimsical, unpredictable, bellicose, yet often likable in spite of it all, the Kaiser struts through the story of those years with swagger and gusto. He personifies within himself many of the sharp political contrasts that flourished in Europe in the years before the Great War. And like his uncle, King Edward VII of England, he played a significant part in the events leading up to the war's outbreak.

Wilhelm II came to the throne in 1888, after the long reign of his grandfather, Wilhelm I (1861-1888).[15] During those three decades, Germany had actually been governed by the unshakable hand of Otto von Bismarck, perhaps the greatest master of international politics since Richelieu. As Chancellor of the Reich from 1862 to 1890, Bismarck was largely responsible for the creation of modern Germany. He had guided it from the federation of competing Prussian states that existed in 1850 into the Empire that dominated the Continent in 1880.

Bismarck is too often portrayed as a war-hungry militarist. To be sure, his most quoted remark was that "Not by speeches and majority resolutions are the great questions of the time decided . . . but by blood and iron." And it is also true that Bismarck regarded war as a useful mechanism to achieve his political objectives. He waged brief wars in 1864, 1866, and 1870, against Denmark, Austria, and France, which had the net effect of shifting the dominance in central Europe away from the Austro-Hungarian Empire and toward Germany. But Bismarck was in reality an utterly pragmatic politician. He did not seek war for its own sake, nor was he possessed by any bloodlust. If wars were necessary, they should be fought and won quickly. His simple goal was to make the German Empire supreme on the Continent, which he largely managed to do.

The new Kaiser was not as pliable as his grandfather. Though Wilhelm II admired Bismarck, he would not suffer him as the shadow ruler of the Empire. Within two years, relations between them soured, and by 1890, the Chancellor resigned, leaving Wilhelm as the ruler of Germany in fact as well as in name. Germany was, in truth, a constitutional monarchy, and the power of the Kaiser was far from

---

[15] Wilhelm I's son Frederick died after ruling for only three months in 1888. At his death, he was succeeded by his son Wilhelm II. Frederick's wife Victoria was the eldest daughter of Queen Victoria.

absolute. But this did not prevent Wilhelm from viewing his own position as central. "The King's will is the highest law" he wrote, soon after his coronation.

Three aspects of Wilhelm's personality are tightly intertwined, and are especially significant during the period that preceded the war. First, he loved the sea, and dreamed of making Germany a major naval power. He watched his British cousins with undisguised jealousy as they sailed the globe in their majestic ships; he was utterly delighted when Queen Victoria made him an honorary Admiral of the Fleet in 1889. His envy found expression two years later, when in a famous speech in 1891, Wilhelm remarked that "our future is on the water." Soon thereafter, he placed Alfred Tirpitz in charge of Germany's naval strategy. Tirpitz, like Wilhelm, believed in the importance of a navy for German military power; Tirpitz was the force behind the German naval buildup of great battleships around the turn of the century. This buildup was a direct challenge to Britain's very existence, and she matched Germany ship for ship. The naval arms race between them endured until the war.

Second, Wilhelm's envy of the British navy was a reflection of the fact that he both loved and hated England with deep intensity. "I adore England," he was wont to say, and this adoration was certainly true with respect to his grandmother Queen Victoria. The correspondence between them transforms the diplomatic relations between England and Germany into a fascinating record of maternal concern, stern admonition, and genuine affection between the elderly "Grandmama," and the errant and impetuous "Willy." But if Willy adored Victoria, he detested her eldest son, the Prince of Wales. Bertie[16] was everything Willy was not: charming, well-liked, stylish, and the heir to the throne of a world-wide empire. "He is a Satan," was the Kaiser's candid opinion of Bertie, and the dislike was returned in equal intensity. As Robert Massie notes:

> Bertie looked down on Wilhelm and Wilhelm's country as pushy and parvenu, and Wilhelm knew it.

Which leads to the third side of Wilhelm's personality: he was desperately anxious that Germany's greatness should be acknowledged by other nations. That England (and others) might look down on Germany or think Germans rude drove him to fury. He sought to affirm the nation's stature on every public occasion: "We have conquered for ourselves a place in the sun" he declared in a famous speech in 1901. And this notion of Germany's rightful place reappears like a leitmotiv; we see it reiterated in the present Page spoken thirteen years later: "We are inspired to protect the place in which God has set us."

---

[16] Though he reigned as Edward VII, the Prince's given name was Albert, and he was generally known as "Bertie" throughout his life.

Yet in his forceful advocacy of Germany's stature and German might, Wilhelm could be his own worst enemy, and often was the very cause for the Prince of Wales' disdain. When a German expedition was leaving to help quell the Boxer Rebellion, he addressed the troops thus:

> You are about to meet a crafty, well-armed, cruel foe! Meet him and beat him! Give him no quarter! Take no prisoners! Kill him when he falls into your hands!

The world-wide publicity that followed that speech did little to raise Germany in the esteem of Wilhelm's uncle or, for that matter, of anyone else.

The following Page is the address the Kaiser made to the Reichstag at the moment when Germany entered the war. It captures many of the contradictory characteristics of this fascinating man. It is interesting to remember, when reading this text, that Wilhelm actually opposed the war when it started. He had expected that Austria would be satisfied with Serbia's response to her ultimatum, and was surprised when Austria opened hostilities. But Wilhelm had promised to support his Austrian ally; he had conveyed his unqualified support in his disastrous "blank check" message, which promised Austria that, come what may, ". . . Rest assured that [Germany] will faithfully stand by Austria-Hungary . . ." As a loyal Teuton, therefore, fight he must. And fight he did, but the cost was bitter and grave.

Honored Gentlemen:

At a time great with consequences I have assembled the elected representatives of the German people around me. For nearly a half century we have been allowed to follow the ways of peace. The attempts to attribute to Germany warlike intentions and to hedge in her position in the world have often sorely tried the patience of my people. Undeterred, my government has pursued the development of our moral, spiritual, and economic strength as its highest aim, with all frankness, even under provocative circumstances!

The world has been witness that during the last years, under all pressure and confusion, we have stood in the first rank in saving the nations of Europe from a war between the great powers. The most serious dangers to which the events in the Balkans had given rise seemed to have been overcome—then suddenly an abyss was opened through the murder of my friend the Archduke Franz Ferdinand. My lofty ally, the Emperor and King Franz Joseph, was forced to take up arms to defend the security of his empire against dangerous machinations from a neighboring state. The Russian empire stepped in the way of the Dual Monarchy following out the just interests of Austria-Hungary.

Not only our duty as ally calls us to the side of Austria-Hungary, but it is our great task to protect our own position and the old community of culture between us against the attack of hostile forces. With a heavy heart I have had to mobilize the army against Russia, a neighbor with whom we have fought side by side on many a battlefield. With unfeigned sorrow I saw broken a friendship which had been faithfully preserved by Germany. The Imperial Russian Government, yielding to the pressure of an insatiable nationalism, has taken sides for a state which through its sanctioning of criminal attacks has brought about the evils of this war.

That France too should have taken sides with our enemy could not surprise us; too often have our attempts to come to friendlier relationships with the French Republic failed because of her old hopes and old resentments.

Honored Gentlemen, what human insight and power could do to equip a people for these uttermost decisions has been done with your patriotic assistance. The hostility which has been making itself felt in the east and in the west for a long time past has now broken out in bright flame. The present situation is not the result of passing conflicts of interests or of diplomatic conjunctions; it is the result of an ill will which has been active for many years against the power and the prosperity of the German Empire.

No lust of conquest drives us on; we are inspired by the unalterable will to protect the place in which God has set us for ourselves and all coming generations. From the documents which have been submitted to you, you will see how my government and especially my Chancellor have endeavored even to the last moment to stave off the inevitable. In a defensive war that has been forced upon us, with a clear conscience, and a clean hand, we take up the sword.

I issue my call to the peoples and stocks of the German Empire, that with their united strength they may stand like brothers with our allies in order to defend what we have created through the works of peace. Following the example of our fathers, staunch and true, earnest and knightly, humble before God, but with the joy of battle in the face of the enemy, we trust in the Almighty to strengthen our defense and guide us to good issue.

Honored Gentlemen, the German people gathered about their princes and leaders are today looking to you. Come to your decisions quickly and unanimously. Such is my most earnest wish.

Kaiser Wilhelm II

Woodrow Wilson: The Fourteen Points

The peace negotiations that took place in 1918 and 1919 to end the war were long and difficult. This fact is reflected in the breadth of effort that historians have invested in analysis and commentary about those events, for there is a very great amount of historical research, documented in a large literature, about the forging of the Treaty of Versailles. Most of these studies acknowledge that the Treaty was mortally flawed and that its defects contributed, in large part, to the resurgence of Germany in the 1930s and the resumption of war in 1939. The causes of the flaws are ascribed to many different sources. Depending on viewpoint, either the French, the English, the Americans, or the Italians were simplistic, selfish, or wise. France was too vindictive, America too naive. Clemenceau, Lloyd George, or Wilson were, singly or jointly, ideologues, patriots, or fools. Regardless of any specific historical bias, however, almost all observers agree that the Fourteen Points of President Woodrow Wilson, enunciated in a speech to Congress in January 1918, provided a central, perhaps the pivotal focus around which those negotiations revolved.

Wilson was a most unlikely candidate for filling so major a role in ending the war. At the onset of the conflict he was an ardent isolationist, pleading for neutrality on the part of all Americans. He fully expected to maintain the posture of avoiding European entanglements that stretched back to 1796, with the Farewell Address of Washington. But technology had brought him to a crisis: German submarine attacks against Allied shipping soon became attacks on U.S. citizens. The sinking of the Lusitania in 1915 provoked a huge outcry in America; the sinking of the Sussex in 1916 brought an ultimatum from Wilson to Germany demanding a halt to the U-boat attacks. When, in early 1917, Germany announced a new policy of unrestricted attacks on all shipping, belligerent or neutral, this was effectively a declaration of war against America. Four American merchantmen were sunk in mid-March, and Wilson had no other options. In the first week of April 1917, he asked for, and received, a declaration of war against Germany. Thus, against his will, he had been compelled to bring America into a European war, waged between European states, and fought for European causes.

On January 8, 1918, Wilson delivered an address to Congress that contained his idealistic vision of the future, a set of fourteen principles that could govern the postwar world.[17] He essentially called for a restoration of pre-war boundaries,

---

[17] David Lloyd George, the British Prime Minister, had made a very similar speech three days earlier. But the principles embedded in his speech were lost in the commotion and celebrity that surrounded Wilson's.

creation of a League of Nations, and the right of all peoples everywhere to self determination.

Among the European Allies, the general reaction to Wilson's Fourteen Points was cautious approval of their spirit, though with considerable concern about many of their particulars. Germany, however, saw a golden opportunity in Wilson's speech. By 1918, the long and terrible stalemate in the trenches between France and Germany had taken an enormous toll on both sides. But while both sides were exhausted, the Central Powers were especially eager to find a path toward peace. Even though the war on the Eastern front was over (because of the Russian Revolution in 1917), America's entry into the war meant that the probable conclusion would be a victory for the Allies. So Germany viewed the Fourteen Points with considerable optimism: Wilson's ringing and idealistic declarations seemed a very hopeful basis on which to negotiate a peace. In October, Germany sent a note to Wilson accepting the Fourteen Points as a basis for declaring an armistice. Wilson responded directly to the German government, and on November 11, the fighting ceased. But behind this simple recitation of facts lurks a cauldron of international rivalries and bitter diplomatic infighting.

First, most of the European Allies regarded Wilson with decidedly mixed feelings. They were extremely annoyed that he had, for all practical purposes, independently opened negotiations with Germany when he unilaterally responded to the October note. Their perception of America—not quite an Ally, somewhat of an outsider—was maintained throughout the entire negotiation process.[18]

Second, neither France nor Britain had ever accepted the Fourteen Points as in any way complete, correct, or binding. So Germany's acceptance of them as the basis for the armistice was totally immaterial to them. From their vantage point, some of the Points were simply in need of clarification; but others were completely unacceptable. (As an example, Britain rejected without qualification the notion of absolute freedom of the seas.) But most of all, everyone, except Wilson, perhaps, realized that the Fourteen Points were thoroughly unsuitable as a basis for resolving the complex European situation in 1918. They were filled with inconsistencies, too hazy in some places, far too precise in others. In historian Thomas Bailey's words:

> The Points were idealistic and vague enough to make a splendid platform for waging the war; but they were too illusory and contradictory to make an adequate platform upon which to construct the peace.

---

[18] In fact, America never declared itself as one of the Allied powers: it remained an "Associated" power for the duration of the war and the peace negotiations.

So the fighting stopped and the peace talks began. They went on until June 1919, first as a Council of Ten Allies, then of Five, finally of Four: Wilson, and the prime ministers of Great Britain, France, and Italy (Lloyd George, Clemenceau, and Orlando). In a brilliant display of short-sightedness, Germany was excluded from any participation. Issues such as reparations, national boundaries, and culpability were discussed, bitterly contested, and finally agreed to. At the end, the Austro-Hungarian Empire was dismembered, with a large number of small, independent, and weak states created in its place. France regained Alsace-Lorraine from Germany, which she had lost in the 1871 war; Germany also lost Danzig and the Polish Corridor. The German territory west of the Rhine was demilitarized and the Saar put under the protection of the League of Nations. Germany was commanded to pay a huge reparation, eventually set at $33 billion, and also, through the famous "war guilt clause," made to accept the responsibility for all of the loss and damage of the war, "caused by the aggression of Germany and her allies."

Wilson and Mrs. Wilson at his second inauguration

When presented with the Treaty, the Germans felt utterly betrayed. When the fighting had stopped, they were in a military position that was roughly equivalent to the Allies; they had not (not yet, at least) been conquered. They had agreed to the armistice based on the idealism of the Fourteen Points; the document they now must sign was more like the abject humiliation of one who was totally vanquished. The territorial settlements were probably inevitable. But the amount of reparations was staggering, given that Germany was exhausted and bled dry from the war. The war guilt clause was even more onerous; they never accepted it, and branded it a lie even as they signed the Treaty. (And, in fact, Wilson himself had loudly maintained before 1917 that no single nation had brought the catastrophe into existence.)

We often read that many people in Europe and America, after the conclusion of the Treaty in 1919, believed that war itself had finally been defeated; "the war to end all wars," and all that. Some, perhaps, may naïvely have thought this, but no one who knew much about history. In fact, rather than widespread naïvete, there are abundant indications that the terrible fragility of the Versailles settlement was obvious to a wide variety of observers who witnessed its creation. For instance, in a far-seeing analysis of the Treaty, Karl Radek reported to the Communist International that:

> No date can be fixed as to whether, or at which time [the existing European tensions] will become acute and result in a new world war.

The New York Call, a Socialist newspaper, made a more definitive and caustic forecast:

> Accept it [the Versailles Treaty], children with faith and resignation—and prepare for the next Armageddon.

And even Lloyd George, high among the great and mighty who fashioned the peace, made the following, astonishing prediction soon after the signing:

> [the Versailles Treaty] was all a great pity. We shall have to do the same thing all over again in twenty-five years, at three times the cost.

Would that the wisdom that lay behind his shrewd prediction had been more widespread among the Allies before the terms of the Treaty were forged, not after. As it was, the Treaty almost guaranteed that a Hitler would emerge, that Germany would throw off the impossible yoke, and that the war would resume. But in 1919, everyone was utterly weary, and eager for nothing but closure; so the Treaty was concluded in spite of its flaws. The horrors of the blitzkrieg, the Holocaust, and the Bomb were all still to come as the Great War went not into peace, but only into its long and fruitless armistice.

I   Open covenants of peace, openly arrived at, after which there shall be no private international understanding of any kind but diplomacy shall proceed always frankly and in the public view.

II   Absolute freedom of navigation upon the seas, outside territorial waters, alike in peace and in war, except as the seas may be closed in whole or in part by international action for the enforcement of international covenants.

III   The removal, so far as possible, of all economic barriers and the establishment of an equality of trade conditions among all the nations consenting to the peace and associating themselves for its maintenance.

IV   Adequate guarantees given and taken that national armaments will be reduced to the lowest point consistent with domestic safety.

V   A free, open-minded, and absolutely impartial adjustment of all colonial claims, based upon a strict observance of the principle that in determining all such questions of sovereignty the interests of the populations concerned must have equal weight with the equitable claims of the government whose title is to be determined.

VI   The evacuation of all Russian territory and such a settlement of all questions affecting Russia as will secure the best and freest cooperation of the other nations of the world in obtaining for her an unhampered and unembarrassed opportunity for the independent determination of her own political development and national policy and assure her of a sincere welcome into the society of free nations under institutions of her own choosing: and, more than a welcome, assistance also of every kind that she may need and may herself desire. The treatment accorded Russia by her sister nations in the months to come will be the acid test of their good will, of their comprehension of her needs as distinguished from their own, and of their intelligent and unselfish sympathy.

VII   Belgium, the whole world will agree, must be evacuated and restored, without any attempt to limit the sovereignty which she enjoys in common with all other free nations. No other single act will serve as this will serve to restore confidence among the nations in the laws which they have themselves set and determined for the government of their relations with one another. Without this healing act the whole structure and validity of international law is forever impaired.

VIII   All French territory should be freed and the invaded portions restored, and the wrong done to France by Prussia in 1871 in the matter of Alsace-Lorraine, which has unsettled the peace of the world for nearly fifty years, should be righted, in order that peace may once more be made secure in the interest of all.

IX   A readjustment of the frontiers of Italy should be effected along clearly recognizable lines of nationality.

X The peoples of Austria-Hungary, whose place among the nations we wish to see safeguarded and assured, should be accorded the freest opportunity of autonomous development.

XI Rumania, Serbia, and Montenegro should be evacuated; occupied territories restored; Serbia accorded free and secure access to the sea; and the relations of the several Balkan states to one another determined by friendly counsel along historically established lines of allegiance and nationality; and international guarantees of the political and economic independence and territorial integrity of the several Balkan states should be entered into.

XII The Turkish portions of the present Ottoman Empire should be assured a secure sovereignty, but the other nationalities which are now under Turkish rule should be assured an undoubted security of like and an absolutely unmolested opportunity of autonomous development, and the Dardanelles should be permanently opened as a free passage to the ships and commerce of all nations under international guarantees.

XIII An independent Polish state should be erected which should include the territories inhabited by indisputably Polish populations, which should be assured a free and secure access to the sea, and whose political and economic independence and territorial integrity should be guaranteed by international covenant.

XIV A general association of nations must be formed under specific covenants for the purpose of affording mutual guarantees of political independence and territorial integrity to great and small states alike.

Lloyd George, Orlando, Clemenceau, and Wilson at Versailles

The Munich Pact

The signing of the Munich Pact in September 1938 is often viewed as the singular event by which the West chose appeasement over confrontation with Hitler, the moment when Britain and France sold out the Czechs in a cowardly and hopeless attempt to avoid resuming war with Germany.

Important, yes, but not singular: the Munich Pact was only one in a series of such events, and was quite a logical step, given Hitler's previous successes. A moment at least equal in importance to Munich had occurred two years earlier, when Hitler, with no Allied opposition, remilitarized the Rhineland.[19] This step unilaterally voided the basic political balance that had existed since the signing of the Versailles Treaty. In the view of René Albrecht-Carrié:

> The 7th of March, 1936, is as significant a date as any ... during the entire period of the long armistice: the consequence of the success of the Hitlerian gamble [to move into the Rhineland] was the collapse of the structure of Europe that had existed since the restoration of peace.

And then in March 1938, six months before the Munich Pact, Hitler successfully incorporated Austria into the German Reich with barely a murmur from Britain or France, another moment that ranks high as an example of Allied appeasement. From Hitler's point of view, therefore, his strategy towards Czechoslovakia was essentially the same as in the Rhineland and Austria. It was based on his perception that Britain and France would avoid a general outbreak of war if given any other alternative. In Hitler's own words:

> I shall, however, only decide to take action against Czechoslovakia if, as in the case of the occupation of the demilitarized zone [the Rhineland] and the entry into Austria, I am convinced that France will not march and therefore Britain will not intervene either.

In fact, Hitler had set his sights on Czechoslovakia long before the signing of the Munich Pact. One reason was that Czechoslovakia sat on Germany's eastern flank as France did its western one, and France and Czechoslovakia were bound by a treaty of mutual assistance that dated from 1924. Another reason for Hitler to eye Czechoslovakia was the existence of a substantial industrial capacity that could be put to benefit in the service of Germany. But the crisis that brought about the Munich Pact itself was based on a much simpler cause: Hitler's revenge.

In the mid-1930's, Czechoslovakia was a significant presence in central Europe. It was a large, Democratic state, with a well-developed economic base. It had a

---

[19] By remilitarizing the Rhineland, Hitler specifically repudiated the Locarno Agreement of 1925.

sizable army, ample fortifications and supplies, and while perhaps not the military equal of Germany or France, nonetheless made a respectable contribution to the European balance of power. The country had been pieced together in 1919 after the breakup of the Austro-Hungarian Empire. It encompassed the old Kingdom of Bohemia, part of Ruthenia, and a part of the district of Teschen. The population of the country reflected the vast diversity of the old Empire, including Czechs, Slovaks, Ruthenians, Poles, Hungarians—and a large number of Germans in the region called Sudetenland, on Germany's eastern border.

As the Nazi zeal spread throughout the German-speaking portion of Central Europe, it was inevitable that the Sudeten Germans would be no less susceptible to its siren song than had been the Germans and Austrians. By 1935 a "Sudeten Deutsche Partei" had emerged and was agitating for redress of grievances (in large part imaginary ones); its real aim was for separation of the Sudetenland and union with the German Reich. The agitation grew throughout 1936 and 1937, and by the winter of 1937, much of European diplomacy was focused on "the Czechoslovakian problem."

In November 1937, Hitler drafted the plans for Operation Green, which called for a military operation against Czechoslovakia; liberation of the Sudeten Germans was to be the convenient excuse. However, the real goal of this move was to secure his eastern front, so that later he could safely concentrate on France, the greater enemy in the west. But there was no timetable given for Operation Green; it was only to occur when "Germany has attained full preparedness for war." During the Spring of 1938 the crisis within Czechoslovakia grew to a head, fueled by Hitler's own public pronouncements and the internal pressures that the Sudeten Germans were placing on the Czech government.

In May 1938, the Czech President, Eduard Benes, unexpectedly called Hitler's bluff. On the occasion of a spurious report of German troop movements near the border, he ordered the mobilization of a Czech division. This in turn triggered a French declaration to "provide the utmost help if Czechoslovakia were attacked." Britain, unwillingly, to be sure, also announced that she would support the Czechs by military force. Hitler was not at all prepared for actual fighting and backed down, with Germany making loud protestations of innocence. Almost unwittingly, the Czechs had demonstrated that standing up to Hitler did not automatically bring about war, but could keep him at bay. The press throughout the world proclaimed how Hitler had been bested.

The humiliation enraged Hitler, who immediately declared: "It is my unalterable intention to smash Czechoslovakia by military action in the near future." His words may appear curious, in light of his recent retreat. But he rightly perceived that, despite any declarations to the contrary, Britain and France were not anxious to go to war to save the Czechs. Throughout the Summer the Sudeten Germans continued to press for autonomy. On September 12, Hitler delivered a violent speech charging the Czech government with rampant persecution of the Sudeten Germans, and threatened military intervention. The lesson of May had indeed been lost: Hitler's threat provoked Neville Chamberlain, the British Prime Minister (and possibly the chief proponent of appeasing Germany) to offer to come to Germany to discuss a peaceful settlement with Hitler.[20]

Meeting in Berchtesgaden, Chamberlain and Hitler agreed that it would be a "just and reasonable" solution to the Czech problem if Germany were to annex the Sudetenland. (It is worth noting that neither the Czechs nor their French allies were party to this agreement.) Chamberlain returned to London where, after three days of Anglo-French talks, both Britain and France recommended to Czechoslovakia that she accept the proposal and cede the Sudetenland to Germany. In effect, France was renouncing her treaty of mutual defense.

Hitler now sensed his victory and made additional demands. In a wild speech on September 26, he insisted on a further dismemberment of Czechoslovakia, with large pieces going to Hungary and Poland (both of whom were quite willing to side with Germany and help themselves to parts of a vulnerable Czechoslovakia). These demands were totally unexpected, and partial mobilization orders were prepared in Britain, France, and Germany.

On September 28, through the urgings of Mussolini, Hitler agreed to a four-party meeting between Britain, France, Germany, and Italy (but not Czechoslovakia). The result of that meeting was the Munich Pact, truly one of the saddest Pages of History. By it, the Czechs were made to realize that if they opposed Hitler, they would do so alone. By it, Germany seized most of Czechoslovakia's fortifications and a huge area of land on its western border. Some thirty military divisions, a potential threat to Hitler's eastern flank, were neutralized. Hungary seized portions of Slovakia and all of Ruthenia. Poland took Teschen, 800 square kilometers containing iron and steel works and chemical plants. In all, Czechoslovakia lost 11,000 square miles of territory, 70% of her iron and steel capacity, 86% of her chemical industry, and 70% of her electrical capability.

After signing the Pact, Chamberlain returned to London with the cheers of a large crowd welcoming him. At his landing, he made his famous "Peace with honour ... Peace in our time" proclamation. The peace lasted less than a year. His proclamation is probably among the bitterest legacies that any leader has ever left to posterity.

Note that, as with many documents of that time, there is also an Annex with a Declaration and Supplementary Declaration; these are appended as a separate Page.

---

[20] On hearing that Chamberlain would travel to meet with Hitler, the Italian leader Mussolini remarked: "There will not be war. But this is the liquidation of English prestige." For a year, at least, he was absolutely correct.

Germany, the United Kingdom, France and Italy, taking into consideration the agreement, which has been already reached in principle for the cession to Germany of the Sudeten German territory, have agreed on the following terms and conditions governing the said cession and the measures consequent thereon, and by this agreement they each hold themselves responsible for the steps necessary to secure its fulfillment:

(1) The evacuation will begin on 1st October.

(2) The United Kingdom, France and Italy agree that the evacuation of the territory shall be completed by the 10th October, without any existing installations having been destroyed, and that the Czechoslovak Government will be held responsible for carrying out the evacuation without damage to the said installations.

(3) The conditions governing the evacuation will be laid down in detail by an international commission composed of representatives of Germany, the United Kingdom, France, Italy and Czechoslovakia.

(4) The occupation by stages of the predominantly German territory by German troops will begin on 1st October. The four territories marked on the attached map will be occupied by German troops in the following order:

The territory marked No. I on the 1st and 2nd of October; the territory marked No. II on the 2nd and 3rd of October; the territory marked No. III on the 3rd, 4th and 5th of October; the territory marked No. IV on the 6th and 7th of October. The remaining territory of preponderantly German character will be ascertained by the aforesaid international commission forthwith and be occupied by German troops by the 10th of October.

(5) The international commission referred to in paragraph 3 will determine the territories in which a plebiscite is to be held. These territories will be occupied by international bodies until the plebiscite has been completed. The same commission will fix the conditions in which the plebiscite is to be held, taking as a basis the conditions of the Saar plebiscite. The commission will also fix a date, not later than the end of November, on which the plebiscite will be held.

(6) The final determination of the frontiers will be carried out by the international commission. The commission will also be entitled to recommend to the four Powers, Germany, the United Kingdom, France and Italy, in certain exceptional cases, minor modifications in the strictly ethnographical determination of the zones which are to be transferred without plebiscite.

(7) There will be a right of option into and out of the transferred territories, the option to be exercised within six months from the date of this agreement. A German-Czechoslovak commission shall determine the details of the option, consider ways of facilitating the transfer of population and settle questions of principle arising out of the said transfer.

(8) The Czechoslovak Government will within a period of four weeks from the date of this agreement release from their military and police forces any Sudeten Germans who may wish to be released, and the Czechoslovak Government will within the same period release Sudeten German prisoners who are serving terms of imprisonment for political offences.

Munich, September 29, 1938.

Chamberlain, Daladier, Hitler, and Mussolini

Annex: His Majesty's Government in the United Kingdom and the French Government have entered into the above agreement on the basis that they stand by the offer, contained in paragraph 6 of the Anglo-French proposals of the 19th September, relating to an international guarantee of the new boundaries of the Czechoslovak State against unprovoked aggression. When the question of the Polish and Hungarian minorities in Czechoslovakia has been settled, Germany and Italy for their part will give a guarantee to Czechoslovakia.

Declaration: The heads of the Governments of the four Powers declare that the problems of the Polish and Hungarian minorities in Czechoslovakia, if not settled within three months by agreement between the respective Governments, shall form the subject of another meeting of the Heads of the Governments of the four Powers here present.

Supplementary Declaration: All questions which may arise out of the transfer of the territory shall be considered as coming within the terms of reference to the International Commission.

Composition of the International Commission: The four Heads of Governments here present agree that the international commission provided for in the agreement signed by them today shall consist of the Secretary of State in the German Foreign Office, the British, French and Italian Ambassadors accredited in Berlin, and a representative to be nominated by the Government of Czechoslovakia.

Adolf Hitler

Neville Chamberlain

Edouard Daladier

Benito Mussolini

Winston Churchill: Initial Broadcast as Prime Minister

It is usually simplistic to regard great or catastrophic events of history as caused by a single individual. Hitler, for instance, did not bring the 1939 war into existence all by himself. The punitive nature of the peace settlement in 1919, the economic disasters of the 1920s, the generally dismal performance by the British and French governments of the 1930s, the leftover ethnic rivalries stretching from the Rhine to the Volga: these factors and more were all contributors to its coming. Hitler, vicious though he was, was as much a consummate opportunist as devil incarnate, and he certainly capitalized on these convenient realities as he erected the horror of his Nazi Reich.

But it is probably not too simplistic to acknowledge that a single individual looms large in opposition. Because indeed, one man truly was the Enemy of Hitler: Winston Churchill, Prime Minister of Great Britain from 1940 to 1945, and quite possibly the greatest personification of indomitable and charismatic leadership of the twentieth century, and many other centuries as well.

Churchill's presence in Western history spans the whole of the century's first half, from long before the First war to well after the Second. He had fought as an infantryman during the Boer War, was made First Lord of the Admiralty in 1911, and was a major voice urging Britain to maintain her naval superiority over Germany before the outbreak of war in 1914. He served as a Member of Parliament for several terms; throughout the 1930s, he made increasingly strong arguments against the growing menace of a rearming Germany and Hitler's ambitions.

He bitterly opposed the appeasement policies of Chamberlain, though he had few allies that supported him. Until the late 30s, not many British politicians were willing to admit that the foundation of Chamberlain's policies—that lasting peace could be maintained by reasonable agreements between reasonable leaders of reasonable nations—was utterly invalid in the wake of the Treaty of Versailles and against the rabid appetite of Hitler. Yet even after Munich, when the folly of appeasement should have been obvious, Churchill was regarded by most of his peers as a scold and a nuisance rather than a prescient statesman.

Churchill never doubted the rightness of his views. He perceived Hitler's goals with unerring accuracy, and he saw, correctly, that only by a determination such as his own could Hitler be stopped. Nor was he beset by any concerns about his own fitness to lead; when he became Prime Minister, he said of himself:

> I was conscious of a profound sense of relief. At last I had the authority to give directions over the whole scene ... My warnings over the last six years had been so numerous, so detailed, and were now so terribly vindicated, that no one could gainsay me ... I was sure I should not fail.

As was also true of Hitler, one of Churchill's greatest weapons was his voice. His words alone probably counted as much as a dozen divisions of soldiers. And his greatest speeches have enriched the English language with unforgettable phrases. Through him, England vowed to fight with her blood, her sweat, and her tears. The world learned of the superhuman valour of the Royal Air Force when Churchill told the world of their finest hour. And he warned Hitler that every English man, every English woman, and every English child would fight on the beaches, in the fields, and in the streets, a promise that very probably would have been kept if need be.

Most of Churchill's immortal speeches are well known, and in fact are too lengthy for the purposes of this volume. However, on the occasion of his becoming Prime Minister, he delivered a truly wonderful address over the BBC that is not often reprinted, but that is, to my mind, one of surpassing quality. In it he describes the military situation just before Dunkirk and the fall of Paris. In it he shows his hatred of Hitler and the Reich, and reveals his profound and lasting will to triumph.

Any description of Churchill's role in the war, even in brief, must also include what happened at the war's end. In the Summer of 1945, just as the war was being won, the British public voted to replace Churchill as Prime Minister by Clement Attlee. Coming on the heels of so great an Allied victory, in which Churchill stands out as a prime architect, his ejection from office is striking. Though he wrote of it almost casually— in his account of the evening five years earlier, when he took office—the simple yet caustic words are heavy with a bitterness that sears the soul:

> Thus, on the night of the tenth of May [1940], at the outset of this mighty battle, I acquired the chief power in the state, which henceforth I wielded in ever-growing measure for five years and three months of world war, at the end of which time, all our enemies having surrendered unconditionally or being about to do so, I was immediately dismissed by the British electorate from all further conduct of their affairs.

The tale of why and how that happened is beyond our purview here. For now, we turn to the Page at hand, in which Churchill for the first time spoke to the nation as its leader. Some of the text is jarring now; Churchill's hopes that the French could resist Hitler have a painful, almost naive quality when we recall how quickly France was to fall. But Churchill's unbending will, his refusal to despair, and his abiding belief in his own ability to stand against the menace of Hitler shine through every sentence of this address. The conclusion contains lines that are the equal of any of his more famous speeches, and the final paragraph still echoes with profound righteousness, even after nearly a century has dimmed the peril that England and the world then faced.

Winston Churchill

I speak to you for the first time as Prime Minister in a solemn hour for the life of our country, of our Empire, of our allies, and, above all, of the cause of freedom. A tremendous battle is raging in France and Flanders. The Germans, by a remarkable combination of air bombing and heavily armoured tanks, have broken through the French defences north of the Maginot Line, and strong columns of their armoured vehicles are ravaging the open country, which for the first day or two was without defenders. They have penetrated deeply and spread alarm and confusion in their track. Behind them there are now appearing infantry in lorries, and behind them, again, the large masses are moving forward. The regroupment of the French armies to make head against, and also to strike at, this intruding wedge has been proceeding for several days, largely assisted by the magnificent efforts of the Royal Air Force.

We must not allow ourselves to be intimidated by the presence of these armoured vehicles in unexpected places behind our lines. If they are behind our front, the French are also at many points fighting actively behind theirs. Both sides are therefore in an extremely dangerous position. And if the French Army, and our own Army, are well handled, as I believe they will be; if the French retain that genius for recovery and counter-attack for which they have so long been famous; and if the British Army shows the dogged endurance and solid fighting power of which there have been so many examples in the past, then a sudden transformation of the scene might spring into being.

It would be foolish, however, to disguise the gravity of the hour. It would be still more foolish to lose heart and courage or to suppose that well-trained, well-equipped armies numbering three or four millions of men can be overcome in the space of a few weeks, or even months, by a scoop, or raid of mechanized vehicles, however formidable. We may look with confidence to the stabilization of the front in France, and to the general engagement of the masses, which will enable the qualities of the French and British soldiers to be matched squarely against those of their adversaries. For myself, I have invincible confidence in the French Army and its leaders. Only a very small part of that splendid army has yet been heavily engaged; and only a very small part of France has yet been invaded. There is good evidence to show that practically the whole of the specialized and mechanized forces of the enemy have been already thrown into the battle; and we know that very heavy losses have been inflicted upon them. No officer or man, no brigade or division, which grapples at close quarters with the enemy, wherever encountered, can fail to make a worthy contribution to the general result. The armies must cast away the idea of resisting behind concrete lines or natural obstacles, and must realize that mastery can only be regained by furious and unrelenting assault. And this spirit must not only animate the High Command, but must inspire every fighting man.

In the air—often at serious odds—often at odds hitherto thought overwhelming—we have been clawing down three or four to one of our enemies; and the relative balance of the British and German Air Forces is now considerably more favourable to us than at the beginning of the battle. In cutting down the German bombers, we are fighting our own battle as well as that of France. My confidence in our ability to fight it out to the finish with the German Air Force has been strengthened by the fierce encounters which have taken place and are taking place. At the same time, our heavy bombers are striking nightly at the tap-root of German mechanized power, and have already inflicted serious damage upon the oil refineries on which the Nazi effort to dominate the world directly depends.

We must expect that as soon as stability is reached on the Western Front, the bulk of that hideous apparatus of aggression which gashed Holland into ruin and slavery in a few days, will be turned upon us. I am sure I speak for all when I say we are ready to face it; to endure it; and to retaliate against it to any extent that the unwritten laws of war permit. There will be many men, and many women, in this island who when the ordeal comes upon them, as come it will, will feel comfort, and even a pride that they are sharing the perils of our lads at the front—soldiers, sailors and airmen, God bless them—and are drawing away from them a part at least of the onslaught they have to bear. Is not this the appointed time for all to make the utmost exertions in their power? If the battle is to be won, we must provide our men with ever-increasing quantities of the weapons and ammunition they need. We must have, and have quickly, more aeroplanes, more tanks, more shells, more guns. There is imperious need for these vital munitions. They increase our strength against the powerfully armed enemy. They replace the wastage of the obstinate struggle; and the knowledge that wastage will speedily be replaced enables us to draw more readily upon our reserves and throw them in now that everything counts so much.

Our task is not only to win the battle but to win the war. After this battle in France abates its force, there will come the battle for our island for all that Britain is, and all that Britain means. That will be the struggle. In that supreme emergency we shall not hesitate to take every step, even the most drastic, to call forth from our people the last ounce and the last inch of effort of which they are capable. The interests of property, the hours of labour, are nothing compared with the struggle for life and honour, for right and freedom, to which we have vowed ourselves.

I have received from the Chiefs of the French Republic, and in particular from its indomitable Prime Minister, M. Reynaud, the most sacred pledges that whatever happens they will fight to the end, be it bitter or be it glorious. Nay, if we fight to the end, it can only be glorious.

Having received His Majesty's commission, I have formed an administration of men and women of every party and of almost every point of view. We have differed and quarrelled in the past; but now one bond unites us all to wage war until victory is won, and never to surrender ourselves to servitude and shame, whatever the cost and the agony may be. This is one of the most awe-striking periods in the long history of France and Britain. It is also beyond doubt the most sublime. Side by side, unaided except by their kith and kin in the great Dominions and by the wide Empires which rest beneath their shield side by side, the British and French peoples have advanced to rescue not only Europe but mankind from the foulest and most soul-destroying tyranny which has ever darkened and stained the pages of history. Behind them—behind us—behind the armies and fleets of Britain and France gather a group of shattered and bludgeoned races: the Czechs, the Poles, the Norwegians, the Danes, the Dutch, the Belgians—upon all of whom the long night of barbarism will descend, unbroken even by a star of hope, unless we conquer, as conquer we must; as conquer we shall.

Today is Trinity Sunday. Centuries ago words were written to be a call and a spur to the faithful servants of truth and justice: 'Arm yourselves, and be ye men of valour, and be in readiness for the conflict; for it is better for us to perish in battle than to look upon the outrage of our nation and our altar. As the Will of God is in Heaven, even so let it be.'

The Atlantic Charter

The Atlantic Charter was the result of a secret conference held between Franklin Roosevelt and Winston Churchill in 1941. The conference took place aboard the British battleship HMS *Prince of Wales* and the American cruiser USS *Augusta*, anchored off the coast of Newfoundland; it lasted from August 9th through the 12th.

This meeting came at a perilous time for Britain. She had held off the Luftwaffe in the Battle of Britain, but still stood alone in the West against the victorious German armies that swarmed over most of Europe. Churchill's hopes, therefore, were immediate and pragmatic: he wanted a stronger U.S. participation in the war effort:

> I had the keenest desire to meet Mr. Roosevelt, with whom I had now corresponded with increasing intimacy for nearly two years. Moreover, a conference between us would proclaim the ever closer association of Britain and the United States, would cause our enemies concern, make Japan ponder, and cheer our friends.

Roosevelt was far more circumspect. Biographer James MacGregor Burns notes that:

> Roosevelt wanted merely to meet Churchill,[21] feel him out, exchange ideas and information, and achieve a moral and symbolic unity.

The two leaders discussed many things. High on the agenda was the current state of the Nazi invasion of Russia. Leningrad was surrounded, and Germany was apparently on the brink of overrunning the Ukraine. But they also discussed England's plan to occupy the Canary Islands, Churchill's increasing worries about the Japanese threat, and—presuming an Allied victory—the need for agreements on how to shape the postwar years.

On the 10th, Churchill gave Roosevelt a draft of a "Joint Anglo-American Declaration of Principles," which became the basic text of the Atlantic Charter. The discussions and negotiations that transformed this draft into the final document were essentially continuations of the different goals—Churchill's desire for U.S. commitment, and Roosevelt's determination to remain clearly neutral—that each man had for the meeting.

---

[21] The issue of whether this really was the first meeting for the two is somewhat unclear. According to Burns, Roosevelt at one point recalled meeting Churchill many years earlier, but Churchill did not remember the occasion.

Roosevelt and Churchill aboard the HMS *Prince of Wales*

The projection concerning the postwar years was an especially sharp point of difference. Churchill wanted an explicit mention of some international organization, much like the League of Nations. But Roosevelt could not agree. He was painfully aware of the residue of opinion in America about the failed League of Nations, and insisted that the wording be as diffuse as possible. (The text in question is in the eighth article, which is indeed quite vague.)

Churchill's desire for U.S. commitments were, for the most part, unfulfilled. As Burns describes it:

> Churchill was still upset ... by Roosevelt's proposal that their joint statement make clear that there had been no commitments ... Commitments were precisely what Churchill wanted to bring back.

Ultimately, however, Churchill was content with the outcome. His expressed desire for greater U.S. participation notwithstanding, he was satisfied for the moment with lofty sentiments; specifics could follow later. He expresses this realistic (and perhaps somewhat cynical) assessment in a note to Clement Attlee:

> We must regard this as an interim and partial statement of war aims.

And, in fact, the Charter does spell out America's intention, at the highest moral level, that Britain emerge victorious: the Sixth Article, containing the words "after the final destruction of the Nazi tyranny..." could mean nothing else.

Some obvious parallels exist between the principles of the Atlantic Charter and the principles found in Wilson's Fourteen Points. Both, for instance, mention the need for reduction of armaments, the inherent right of nations to govern themselves, and the need for free trade. The differences are pronounced, however: Wilson's principles are far more detailed about rectifying the wrongs done to certain nations and about restoring prewar boundaries, while the Charter remains at a generally high level of lofty international sentiment.

There were varying reactions to the Atlantic Charter. Felix Frankfurter congratulated Roosevelt on his far-seeing and courageous action. The New York Times predicted that it marked the end of American isolationism. And the Chicago Tribune, clearly unhappy with the document, branded the Charter as a sellout to the British, with Roosevelt playing the role of traitorous Tory:

> Roosevelt is a true descendant of that James Roosevelt . . . who . . . took the oath of allegiance to the British King.

HMS *Prince of Wales*

The President of the United States of America and the Prime Minister, Mr. Churchill, representing His Majesty's Government in the United Kingdom, being met together, deem it right to make known certain common principles in the national policies of their respective countries on which they base their hopes for a better future for the world.

FIRST, their countries seek no aggrandizement, territorial or other;

SECOND, they desire to see no territorial changes that do not accord with the freely expressed wishes of the peoples concerned;

THIRD, they respect the right of all peoples to choose the form of government under which they will live; and they wish to see sovereign rights and self-government restored to those who have been forcibly deprived of them;

FOURTH, they will endeavor, with due respect for their existing obligations, to further the enjoyment by all States, great or small, victor or vanquished, of access, on equal terms, to the trade and to the raw materials of the world which are needed for their economic prosperity;

FIFTH, they desire to bring about the fullest collaboration between all nations in the economic field with the object of securing, for all, improved labor standards, economic adjustment and social security;

SIXTH, after the final destruction of the Nazi tyranny, they hope to see established a peace which will afford to all nations the means of dwelling in safety within their own boundaries, and which will afford assurance that all the men in all the lands may live out their lives in freedom from fear and want;

SEVENTH, such a peace should enable all men to traverse the high seas and oceans without hindrance;

EIGHTH, they believe that all of the nations of the world, for realistic as well as spiritual reasons, must come to the abandonment of the use of force. Since no future peace can be maintained if land, sea or air armaments continue to be employed by nations which threaten, or may threaten, aggression outside of their frontiers, they believe, pending the establishment of a wider and permanent system of general security, that the disarmament of such nations is essential. They will likewise aid and encourage all other practicable measures which will lighten for peace-loving peoples the crushing burden of armaments.

Franklin D. Roosevelt

Winston S. Churchill

Franklin Roosevelt: Address to the Nation after Pearl Harbor

Less than five months after the Atlantic Charter was signed, America was drawn into the war, not by any German action, as many had feared, but by Japan's surprise attack on Pearl Harbor. From our comfortable vantage point of almost a century later, Japan's march toward war with America seems inexorable; it may seem to us that the attack on Pearl Harbor should have been no surprise at all. Yet as those days unfolded, the key players in the drama apparently saw many different possible paths, and the Pacific war did not have the inevitability we consider it to have today.

It is true that there were some observers in America who expected the Pearl Harbor bombing. General Billy Mitchell many years earlier had shown a near-clairvoyant awareness of Japanese war aims when he predicted, in remarkably correct detail, a Japanese air attack. By the onset of the 1940s. there were a few other voices that repeated his prediction. The American ambassador to Japan, Joseph Grew, noted in his diary in January 1941, that

> There is a lot of talk around town to the effect that the Japanese, in case of a break with the United States, are planning to go all out in a surprise attack on Pearl Harbor.

But Mitchell's and Grew's perceptions were shared by few others. On the contrary, there was considerable hope that, while war with Germany was a strong possibility, a war with Japan could be avoided.[22]

It is "surprise" that seems to typify not only the attack on Pearl Harbor but the whole rise of Japanese military might in the first half of the twentieth century. If we go back to the turn of the century, for instance, the general European (and American) view of Japan was of a minor power only recently arrived at the international table. That she should claim or be accorded Great Power status was, to many people, unexpected—and surprising. This was partly a geographical phenomenon. Europe has historically considered itself as the central player in world history. The southern border of Europe is, after all, the sea 'at the middle of the world,' and three centuries of imperial legacy had taught Europeans that the role of the outlying continents was primarily colonial, furnishing goods and markets, but certainly having no central political or historical importance. A

---

[22] One fascinating, and very early, prediction of Japanese–American friction in the Pacific was voiced by Karl Radek, in his report to the Communist International in 1922.

global perspective (which we claim to have today), where a nation like Japan is as weighty a player as Britain or Germany, did not occur to the European of 1900.

Yet Japan had, surprisingly, defeated China—an ancient Great Power, whose Mongols had once terrified Europe—in a war in 1894-95. And when Japan suddenly attacked Port Arthur in 1904, that move certainly surprised the Russians, a reaction that was painfully heightened when the Japanese humbled the Russian fleet in the Tsushima Strait.

Although Japan did not figure heavily during the 1914-1918 fighting, Japanese troops did invade Siberia in 1918, when Russia was in chaos (and when American, British, and French troops were marching in Russia as well); Japan was also a significant presence at the negotiations in Versailles. Certainly by the 1930s, it became obvious, or should have become obvious, that Japan was building a powerful military capability, and would use it boldly as an instrument of national policy. The focus of Japan's immediate interest was Asia. China was the target of Japanese aggression in 1931, when Manchuria was invaded, and again in 1936–37, when Shanghai was captured and Nanking raped. In 1937, a new Japanese government under Premier-Prince Fumimaro Konoe began extending Japanese interests into Indochina, at which point the United States took very serious notice.

With Konoe in power, the progression toward a Pacific war really was, in all probability, inevitable. The Tripartite Pact in 1940 between Japan, Germany, and Italy was a tacit permission from Germany for Japan to expand its sphere of influence to Thailand, Burma, and even Australia. Roosevelt now realized that Japan represented a threat equal to that of Germany. But from Roosevelt's point of view, while a war with Germany was likely, one with Japan would be, in James MacGregor Burns' words, "the wrong war, in the wrong ocean, at the wrong time."

In July 1941, Japan invaded Indochina, a move that provoked an American embargo of steel and iron shipments to Japan. It was now Japan's turn to register surprise, and a short period of apparent conciliation set in. In August, Ambassador Nomura met with Roosevelt in the White House. He indicated that Premier Konoe wished a meeting with Roosevelt in the mid-Pacific, much like Roosevelt's meeting with Churchill in the Atlantic. Roosevelt thought the meeting a good idea; he perceived a change in mood in the Japanese government, and hoped to put it to advantage. Although that meeting never took place, negotiations between Japan and America continued over the next four months. The talks could not have been more fruitless: the two sides were seeking entirely different goals. For Roosevelt, the major goal was a Japanese commitment to ignore the Tripartite Pact should America enter the war in Europe. For Japan, the overriding goal was securing an American admission that Japan had military and political sway over Southeast Asia.

By the Autumn, Japan fully expected war with the United States. At a meeting on November 1, attended by Premier Tojo and the military high command, a decision was reached to attack America unless a diplomatic rapprochement was reached by November 30. Roosevelt, even at that point, did not see war as inevitable. As late as December 6, a day before the attack, he was working on a message to Emperor Hirohito urging Japanese withdrawal from Indochina. And if Japan refused to withdraw, Roosevelt assumed that any overt Japanese military move would be in the Philippines or in the Dutch East Indies.

On December 7, the Japanese attacked Pearl Harbor. Given the litany of events described above, we might think that no one should have been surprised. Yet the overwhelming reaction throughout the entire American population was one of shock. Whether Roosevelt should have expected the attack, or could have taken steps to prevent it will never now be known. But it was a stunned and somber President that addressed the Congress and the nation. His speech resounded with anger, and made a righteous call for vengeance. His opening sentence has entered the ranks of immortal phrases; in that moment, he united the nation in dreadful purpose.

Destruction of the USS *Arizona* at Pearl Harbor

Roosevelt addressing Congress and the Nation

Yesterday, December 7, 1941—a date which will live in infamy—the United States of America was suddenly and deliberately attacked by naval and air forces of the Empire of Japan. The United States was at peace with that Nation and, at the solicitation of Japan, was still in conversation with its Government and its Emperor looking toward the maintenance of peace in the Pacific. Indeed, one hour after Japanese air squadrons had commenced bombing in the American Island of Oahu, the Japanese Ambassador to the United States and his colleague delivered to our Secretary of State a formal reply to a recent American message. And while this reply stated that it seemed useless to continue the existing diplomatic negotiations, it contained no threat or hint of war or of armed attack.

It will be recorded that the distance of Hawaii from Japan makes it obvious that the attack was deliberately planned many days or even weeks ago. During the intervening time the Japanese Government has deliberately sought to deceive the United States by false statements and expressions of hope for continued peace. The attack yesterday on the Hawaiian Islands has caused severe damage to American naval and military forces. I regret to tell you that very many American lives have been lost. In addition American ships have been reported torpedoed on the high seas between San Francisco and Honolulu. Yesterday the Japanese Government also launched an attack against Malaya. Last night Japanese forces attacked Hong Kong. Last night Japanese forces attacked Guam. Last night Japanese forces attacked the Philippine Islands. Last night the Japanese attacked Wake Island. And this morning the Japanese attacked Midway Island

Japan has, therefore, undertaken a surprise offensive extending throughout the Pacific area. The facts of yesterday and today speak for themselves. The people of the United States have already formed their opinions and will understand the implications to the very life and safety of our Nation. As Commander in Chief of the Army and Navy, I have directed that all measures be taken for our defense. But always will our whole Nation remember the character of the onslaught against us.

No matter how long it may take us to overcome this premeditated invasion, the American people in their righteous might will win through to absolute victory. I believe that I interpret the will of the Congress and of the people when I assert that we will not only defend ourselves to the uttermost but we will make it very certain that this form of treachery shall never again endanger us. Hostilities exist. There is no blinking at the fact that our people, our territory, and our interests are in grave danger. With confidence in our armed forces; with the unbounding determination of our people, we will gain the inevitable triumph, so help us God. l ask that the Congress declare that since the unprovoked and dastardly attack by Japan on Sunday, December 7, 1941, a state of war has existed between the United States and the Japanese Empire.

The Japanese Instrument of Surrender

The Great War started in the first days of August 1914. Thirty-one years later, in August 1945, the fighting finally ended. But it was an ending that no other war in history had ever witnessed: the long and bitter World War of the twentieth century ended with a baptism, a terrible baptism by fire that came as the new world of the Atom was born in the flames of Hiroshima and Nagasaki. This Page, the document by which Japan surrendered to the Allies, was signed in the aftermath of those flames.

After Germany capitulated in May 1945, it was inevitable that Japan would soon do likewise. She had exhausted nearly all of her resources and had suffered a series of military reverses so decisive that no other outcome was possible. Yet the war dragged on for three painful and fateful months, until hostilities ceased on August 15.[23] What provoked this extension of the Japanese fighting? If defeat truly was inevitable, why prolong the agony?

Toshikazu Kase, a member of the Japanese wartime Foreign Office, and one of the Japanese officials present at the signing of the surrender, explains it as follows:

> Why did not Japan lay down her arms at the time of the German surrender? The answer is that we could not. The domineering militarists were still directing our national destiny ... the military position was indeed desperate. The leaders of the armed forces, however, could not now withdraw the repeated assurances of ultimate victory with which they had for years fed the gullible nation.

This was at least partially true. Even on the afternoon of August 9, 1945, after the second Atomic Bomb had destroyed Nagasaki, the Japanese Army Minister, Korechika Anami argued for continuing the war. Historian Dennis Wainstock quotes Anami as saying:

> If it comes to a final battle on Japanese soil, we could at least for a time repulse the enemy, and might thereafter find life out of death.

Yet this explanation of laying the blame for continuing the war solely at the feet of an unyielding military is somewhat unsatisfying. It is, at least, incomplete.

---

[23] The fighting went on until the very end. On August 14, the U.S. submarine Torsk sank two Japanese frigates; these were the last enemy sinkings of the war. The Torsk is still afloat, on exhibit at the Maritime Museum in the Baltimore Inner Harbor.

For one thing, the impasse concerning unconditional surrender looms large in all of the accounts of those three months. The Allies demanded it; the Japanese refused it. Neither side really understood the other's position. From the Japanese side, it was imperative that they not be forced to accept the dishonor that unconditional surrender implied. In April 1945, the newly appointed Prime Minister, Suzuki, stated that:

> The enemy is now urging an unconditional surrender on us such as would only aim at [the destruction of Japan.] There is but one way for our nation to follow, and that is to fight to the very end.

Two things give this statement a grim irony. First, Suzuki actually desired a quick end to the war; the Emperor had appointed him for precisely that reason. Second, Suzuki's concern for "the destruction of Japan" was probably unrelated to territory or treasure. Japan must have expected to lose everything it had gained by conquest; she certainly expected no better treatment than Germany had received. The basis of Suzuki's refusal, and the essence of the horror of dishonor, was rooted in concern about the Emperor. The Emperor's role was much more than that of a monarch in the European tradition. As Kase points out, he embodied:

> a fusion of political and theocratic ideas . . . Emperors of flesh and blood were worshipped as immortal gods.

In an unconditional surrender, this immortal god's fate would be unknown. Citing Wainstock:

> The United States might try him as a war criminal, imprison, or execute him.

From the Allied side, however, it was unthinkable that Japan should dictate the terms of her own surrender. It was Japan that had been the aggressor at Pearl Harbor, it was Japan that had subsequently been crushed, and it was Japan that now must pay whatever price the Allies demanded. And those victorious Allies, America in particular, were in no mood to ponder the nuances of different cultures, or be concerned about what constituted dishonor. The Pacific war had been bloody, fought without pity on either side, and was now nearly won. The final step was for Japan to give up.

So the weeks of May and June passed with no visible movement toward a settlement. It was becoming apparent that, barring the surrender that the Allies demanded, it would be necessary to force Japanese capitulation by invasion, the strategy that had produced a similar result in Europe. And here, the Japanese rhetoric was fateful. The Allies took Suzuki's words at face value, and conjectured what the cost of an invasion would be. There was a vivid and bloody example immediately at hand. The fighting for Okinawa raged on until June 21, the Japanese defending every inch with suicidal fury. Any speculation about the cost of an assault on the Japanese homeland, surely a battle more bitter than Okinawa, produced a staggering estimate of lives to be lost.

Nor were these estimates pure conjecture. Even in her weakened state, Japan could mount a strong defense against an Allied invasion. Of particular concern was the existence of 9,000 airplanes, more than half of which had been converted to kamikaze status. A sizable army existed as well; in an attack on Kyushu, the southernmost island of Japan, the Allies expected to meet an opposing force of 350,000 Japanese troops.

Into these deliberations, like an ancient Greek "deus ex machina"—but a deity of unmatched fury—came the Atomic Bomb. The first test of the bomb was made on July 16, as the Potsdam Conference was underway. The existence of this weapon provided an alternative to invasion, and could hasten the end of the war. There has been lengthy debate over the wisdom or folly of using the Bomb. Aside from whether the decision was the proper one, which can never be objectively decided, the words of President Truman are very precise about his own perspective:

> Let there be no mistake . . . I regarded the bomb as a military weapon and never had any doubt that it should be used.

On July 26, the Potsdam Declaration, signed by America, Britain, and China, called once again for unconditional surrender. On July 28, the Japanese Foreign Minister formally rejected it.[24] One week later, on August 6, the *Enola Gay* dropped an Atomic Bomb on Hiroshima. Japan made no response. On August 9, another bomb fell on Nagasaki. At this point—and against considerable opposition—the Emperor commanded that the surrender be agreed to. Yet even at this point, the Japanese insisted on conditions. As Wainstock notes, Prime Minister Suzuki's declaration was that

> His Majesty expressed the opinion that this Government should accept the terms of the Potsdam Declaration with one stipulation—that our national polity and our imperial system be maintained.

The jockeying back and forth between Japan and the Allies about this stipulation went on for nearly a week (while the fighting still continued). The Allies were keenly aware of the authority of the Emperor, and the valuable role he could play in an occupied Japan; they agreed that some accommodation was needed. The

---

[24] Another nuance, this time of language: The Japanese response was actually to "ignore it through silence." In the views of at least some authors on the war, this was not quite the same thing as rejection.

final solution came in the American response to Suzuki's declaration, suggesting the following wording:

> From the moment of surrender, the authority of the Emperor . . . shall be subject to the Supreme Commander of the Allied Powers who will take such steps as he deems proper to effectuate the surrender terms.

In Truman's more gutsy phrasing:

> They wanted to keep the Emperor . . . We told 'em we'd tell 'em how to keep him.

On September 2, at 9:04, on board the USS *Missouri*, anchored in Tokyo Bay, Mamoru Shigemitsu, the Japanese Foreign Minister, and Gen. Yoshijiro Umezu signed the peace accord, formally called the "Instrument of Surrender." General Douglas MacArthur, the Supreme Commander of the Allies, accepted the surrender in the name of United States, China, the United Kingdom, and the Union of Soviet Socialist Republics, and also "in the interests of the other United Nations at war with Japan."

There is an interesting postscript to this story. In 2002, the author Studs Terkel had an interview with Paul Tibbets, pilot of the *Enola Gay*. During their discussion, Tibbets mentioned two facts that are generally not known.[25] First, he described the initial orders he received from General Uzal Ent, in September 1944. In his description, he quotes the General as follows:

> Then he laid out what was going on and it was up to me now to put together an organization and train them to drop atomic weapons on both Europe and the Pacific–Tokyo.

It is not clear whether this assertion means that Truman had that intention, but it seems clear that some in the Air Force certainly did, the truce with Germany still being several months away.

Second, he described his experience during the days after the second bomb fell:

> Unknown to anybody else—I knew it, but nobody else knew—there was a third one. See, the first bomb went off and they didn't hear anything out of the Japanese for two or three days. The second bomb was dropped and again they were silent for another couple of days. Then I got a phone call from General Curtis LeMay [chief of staff of the Strategic Air Forces in the Pacific]. He said, "You got another one of those damn things?" I said, "Yes sir." He said, "Where is it?" I said,

---

[25] The story is repeated but in a slightly different manner by Yoichi Funabashi in "The Third Atomic Bomb," The Asia-Pacific Journal, August 9, 2003.

"Over in Utah." He said, "Get it out here. You and your crew are going to fly it." I said, "Yes sir." I sent word back and the crew loaded it on an airplane and we headed back to bring it right on out to Tinian and when they got it to California debarkation point, the war was over. [Studs Terkel:] What did General LeMay have in mind with the third one? [Paul Tibbets:] Nobody knows.

We truly have great reason, therefore, to be glad that both the Germans and the Japanese surrendered when they did. So now, to the "Instrument of Surrender."

Signing of the Instrument of Surrender on board the USS *Missouri*

We, acting by command of and in behalf of the Emperor of Japan, the Japanese Government and the Japanese Imperial General Headquarters, hereby accept the provisions set forth in the declaration issued by the heads of the Government of the United States, China, and Great Britain on 26 July 1945 at Potsdam, and subsequently adhered to by the Union of Soviet Socialist Republics, which four powers are hereafter referred to the Allied Powers

We hereby proclaim the unconditional surrender to the Allied Powers of the Japanese Imperial General Headquarters and of all Japanese armed forces and all armed forces under Japanese control wherever situated.

We hereby command all Japanese forces wherever situated and the Japanese people to cease hostilities forthwith, to preserve and save from damage all ships. aircraft, and military and civil property and to comply with all requirements which may be imposed by the Supreme Commander for the Allied Powers or by agencies of the Japanese Government at his direction.

We hereby command the Japanese Imperial General Headquarters to issue at once orders to the Commanders of all Japanese forces and all forces under Japanese control wherever situated to surrender unconditionally themselves and all forces under their control.

We hereby command all civil, military, and naval officials to obey and enforce all proclamations, orders, and directives deemed by the Supreme Commander for the Allied Powers to be proper to effectuate this surrender and issued by him or under his authority and we direct all such officials to remain in their posts and to continue to perform their non-combatant duties unless specifically relieved by him or under his authority.

We hereby undertake for the Emperor, the Japanese Government and their successors to carry out the provisions of the Potsdam Declaration in good faith, and to issue whatever orders and take whatever action may be required by the Supreme Commander for the Allied Powers or by any other designated representative of the Allied Powers for the purpose of giving effect to that Declaration.

We hereby command the Japanese Imperial Government and the Japanese Imperial General Headquarters at once to liberate all allied prisoners of war and civilian internees now under Japanese control and to provide for their protection, care, maintenance and immediate transportation to places as directed.

The authority of the Emperor and the Japanese Government to rule the state shall be subject to the Supreme Commander for the Allied Powers who will take such steps as he deems proper to effectuate these terms of surrender.

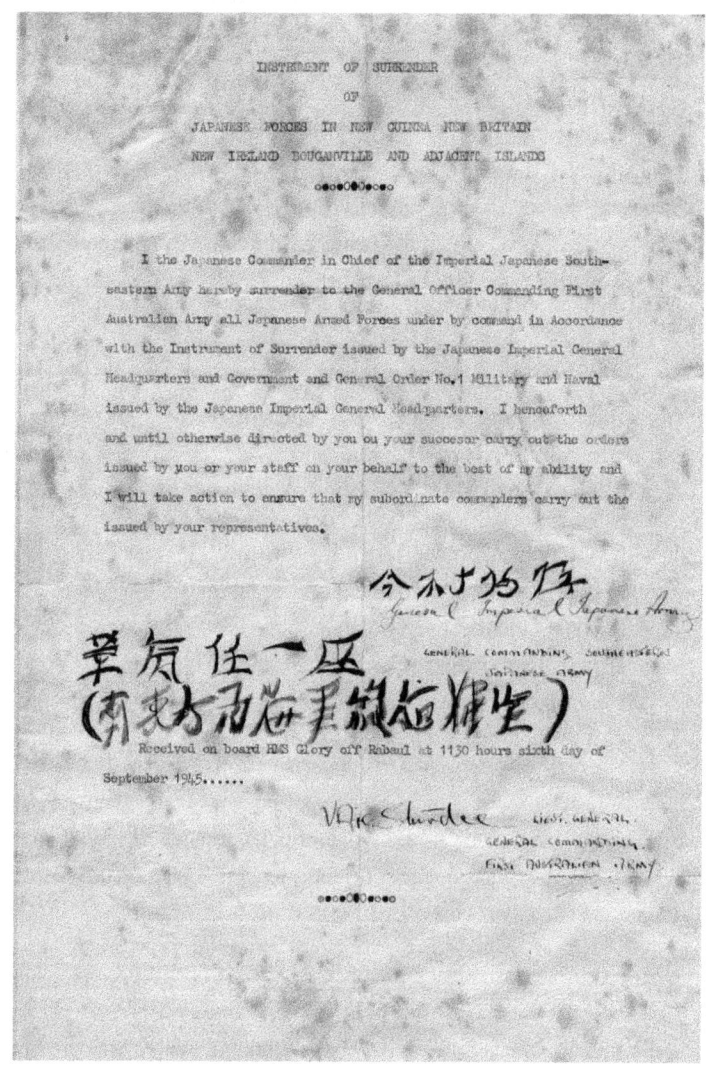

The Instrument of Surrender

FAITH AND RELIGION

If God did not exist, it would be necessary to invent him. (Voltaire, Épîtres, no. 96)
There is only one religion, though there are a hundred versions of it. (Shaw, Plays Pleasant and Unpleasant)

This section brought with it some very interesting questions and a good deal of fascinating reading. The result, however, is somewhat less fulsome than the other sections in the volume. This is partly because, although there are many religious works that have had signal impact on History, very few of them are single Pages. Powerful, pivotal, or critical religious works tend to be lengthy works, ponderous even, and would collide with my First Principle by simply occupying too much space. Thus, for instance, an item that I truly hoped could be included here, Luther's Ninety-Five Theses, was too long no matter how I fudged margins, reduced font size, and searched out the leanest translations.

It is true that many significant religious works—the Bible, for instance—are really collections of shorter documents. However, it is equally true that of those portions of the Bible that are of major importance, few can stand alone as a single Page. Conversely, those that are single Pages are seldom of signal interest. Hence, though one of the shorter Epistles might have been included, that would have been unfair both to it as a text and to the integrity of the volume. As a result, there is only one item from the Bible here, the Decalogue of Moses. The rationale? Remember that this text, we are told, was originally written on two stone tablets. This was close enough to claim a kinship with a single Page (written on two sides, of course).

The Page from the Roman Martyrology was chosen partly because it is very beautiful, it concerns the foundation of Christianity, and provided a selection from the early years of the church, before its sundering into the Roman, Orthodox, and Protestant camps. True, its identity as a separate Page is tenuous; this is an occasion where I was willing to bend my self-imposed rules about excerpts.

The remaining three Pages are perhaps more interesting to the church historian than to the cleric. First, the great sermon of Urban II that began the Crusades had a profound importance for all of the European peoples. It is an oft-stated truth that through the Crusades, the resulting cross-fertilization of men, culture, and science across the Mediterranean had a direct impact on the subsequent Renaissance and Enlightenment that brought Europe into the Modern era. Next, the decision of Henry VIII to break with Rome and establish a state religion in England set in motion any number of deep historical currents: the whole course of the English monarchy for several centuries, the Puritan flight to America, even the ongoing struggle whose echoes still persist today in Ireland: what might not have happened if Henry had chosen to accept the Pope's will? And finally, the King James Bible, represented here by its Preface, is as critical to the art of translation as it is to faith or religion, and the decisions that were made as ancient languages gave way to English were as much influenced by rhetorical considerations as by theology.

So I have been cautious, as is perhaps wise with such potentially volatile subjects as faith and religion. But not, I hope, too stingy. The following five Pages are indisputably significant to several great religions. And I believe—an apt word for this section—that these selections are equally proper choices for this volume.

Michaelangelo, *The Last Judgement*

The Decalogue of Moses
(The Ten Commandments)

In his masterful book "The Religions of Man," Huston Smith estimates that one-third of Western civilization shows the impact of our common ancestry in Judaism. He goes on to ascribe much of this impact to the Ten Commandments:

> . . . it is through the Ten Commandments that Hebraic morality has made its greatest impact in the world. Taken over by Christianity and Islam, the Ten Commandments constitute the moral foundation of half the world's population.

Smith is by no means alone in his estimate. The great Reformer John Calvin said of the Commandments:

> Our God, to remove all possibility of excuse, willed to set forth more fully and clearly by the Ten Commandments everything connected with the honor, fear, and love of him, and everything pertaining to the love of man.

And St. Augustine, somewhat more poetically, referred to them thus:

> . . . the Three and the Seven, that harp of ten strings, thy Decalogue, O God, most high and sweet.

When the Ten Commandments appeared in the world, there were many similar legal codes used by peoples in the Near East to govern their lives. The Babylonian Code of Hammurabi is the best known (and the source of the notion of "an eye for an eye"), but the Sumerians, the Assyrians, and the Hittites all had complex sets of legal strictures as well. The signal difference between the Ten Commandments and these other codes of law (and thus between the ancient Hebrews and their neighbors) lies in the difference between what is called casuistic and apodictic law. The Jesuit scholar John Huesman distinguishes these as follows:

> The basis of [these other codes] is casuistic law: If so-and-so does this, then the following penalty is operative. In [the Ten commandments], we meet the characteristic apodictic law: Thou shalt, or shalt not, do such-and-such, but with no introductory conditional element.

It is sometimes surprising to many people that there are several places in the Bible where the Decalogue (literally, "ten words") appears. Exodus 20, where Moses goes to the top of Mt. Sinai, is generally considered the "real" source of the text. But in Deuteronomy 5, a slightly different version can be found; the text about keeping the Sabbath has some notable differences, and the order of "thy neighbor's house . . . thy neighbor's wife" are reversed. And even within Exodus itself, in a later chapter (34), after Moses has destroyed the original stone tablets in his anger, we find the Covenant (sometimes called the "Ritual Decalogue"), a text that repeats some of the Exodus Commandments (i.e., those about having no other gods, and keeping the sabbath), but which are otherwise quite different, focusing mostly on appropriate forms of ritual.

Gustave Doré, *Moses Coming Down From Mt. Sinai*

I have taken the simplest approach and used the version from Exodus 20. But then came another quandary: which Bible to quote? Making this decision was illuminating, because even apart from differences in text that result from different translations, the division of the Commandments varies between the religious traditions. At least three numbering schemes exist. For Jews, the commandment to "have no other gods" is the Second Commandment, but for Greeks, it is part of the First. For Lutherans, the commandments about "thy neighbor's wife" and "thy neighbor's house" are divided into the Ninth and Tenth Commandments; for Reformed churches, these are both part of the Tenth.

There was no solution that appeared as optimal. So from a very, very wide number of possibilities, I chose the Jerusalem Bible as the source for the text to use here. I make no claim that this version is in any way more correct, more right, or more authoritative. It is simply the one that I liked best.

This distinction about the division of the Commandements even hit home as I was preparing this Page, since the earlier citation from Augustine, where he speaks of "the Three and the Seven," refers to a division that separates the Commandments that pertain to worship and those that pertain to human activity. This implies that the division Augustine followed was not the one on the following Page, since the command to keep the Sabbath holy would be part of "the Three," and here, it is the Fourth.

I   I am Yahweh your God who brought you out of the land of Egypt, out of the house of slavery. You shall have no gods except me.

II   You shall not make yourself a carved image or any likeness of anything in heaven or on earth beneath or in the waters under the earth; you shall not bow down to them or serve them. For I, Yahweh your God, am a jealous God and I punish the father's fault in the sons, the grandsons, and the great-grandsons of those who hate me; but I show kindness to thousands of those who love me and keep my commandments.

III   You shall not utter the name of Yahweh your God to misuse it, for Yahweh will not leave unpunished the man who utters his name to misuse it.

IV   Remember the sabbath day and keep it holy. For six days you shall labour and do all your work, but the seventh day is a sabbath for Yahweh your God. You shall do no work that day, neither you nor your son nor your daughter nor your servants, men or women, nor your animals nor the stranger who lives with you. For in six days Yahweh made the heavens and the earth and the seas and all that these hold, but on the seventh day he rested; that is why Yahweh has blessed the sabbath day and made it sacred.

V   Honour your father and your mother so that you may have a long life in the land that Yahweh your God has given to you.

VI   You shall not kill.

VII   You shall not commit adultery.

VIII   You shall not steal.

IX   You shall not bear false witness against your neighbour.

X   You shall not covet your neighbour's house. You shall not covet your neighbour's wife, or his servant, man or woman, or his ox, or his donkey, or anything that is his.

Preface to The Martyrology for Christmas Day

The beautiful text on the following Page comes from a rather unusual source, a document called the "Roman Martyrology" that traces its roots back to the most ancient works of the Christian church. This document is not well known, so at the risk of losing the Reader by wandering too far down the dusty road of ecclesiastical scholarship, a brief lesson in hagiography—the study of the lives of saints—is in order.

A martyrology is essentially a catalogue of the honored dead, a collection of names of martyrs, saints, and bishops, listed in order of the calendar days on which they are venerated. Such lists began to be kept very early in the life of the Christian church; the practice possibly goes back to the time of the catacombs. The earliest extant example dates from the fourth century, and several other examples from the fifth and sixth centuries exist as well. Originally, individual churches and towns kept their own lists, preserving for Christians living in small communities the names of their forefathers who had died in the early persecutions. As the church became more and more unified, the lists of martyrs correspondingly became more universal, and began to favor those martyrs and saints venerated by the church as a whole.

In the eighth century, a new type of martyrology appeared. Up until then, these lists had been simple commemorations. But Bede the Venerable, the great English cleric, introduced a new type of martyrology that added information about the life of each saint. This changed, in a subtle but significant manner, the function of the document, making it a small-scale ecclesiastical history. The most important example of this type was written in 875, by one Usuard of St. Germain. Usuard's Martyrology, though amended with new names often, remained in general use until the Reformation.

By then, several centuries later, with Christianity fractured, the Catholic church was engaged in a massive "Counter-Reformation" that aimed to win back the ground lost to the Protestant reformers. Among other things, this entailed revising and updating many of the ancient practices that had become encrusted with centuries of accretion and abuse. Pope Gregory XIII (1572-1585) was an avid participant in this great ecclesiastical shake-up. The year 1582 found him in an active temperament indeed, bubbling over with plans for modernizing the church. He had just promulgated his reform of the astronomical calendar, correcting the ancient Julian calendar which by then was behind the actual solar year by ten days. The issue of the calendar settled, his next step was to consider the martyrology, a document that depended entirely on the calendar. Gregory appointed a commission to fully revise the document. Published in 1584, the new version was called the Roman Martyrology. It consists of a series of pages ordered like a diary, in which each day of the year commemorates a number of saints by first briefly describing their lives and then, usually in vivid and gory detail, the way they went to their deaths. Though updated on many occasions, this is the document still officially in use in the Catholic church, and used in some Anglican churches as well.

Like the rest of the days of the year, December 25, Christmas Day, has an entry in the Roman Martyrology. Like the others, that entry has its allotted selection of martyrs who are memorialized on that date. But given the special significance of Christmas, the Martyrology for December 25th has a special added preface; this is the text on the following Page. The Christmas preface does not recount the sufferings of any martyrs. Instead, it is a graceful and moving litany of the many different ways to describe the year of Christ's birth. It takes dates from various Jewish, Greek, and Roman modes of reckoning time, arranging them as a sequence of progressively smaller counts of years.[26] The result has a masterful subtlety; it actually seems to gather urgency as each line is read. (After this touching preface, the proper reading for December 25th reverts to the suffering of martyrs, starting with an appropriately gruesome description of how St. Anastasia was dismembered during the persecution of the Emperor Diocletian.)

The Martyrology is generally used only in monastic communities. But the tiny Christmas preface is often read in Catholic churches as part of the Midnight Mass. To those familiar with it, the reading is a favorite moment, enumerating the tale of years from Creation to Nativity. This text has a unique character; somehow quiet and joyous at the same time, and a wonderful summation of history as a writer of the Middle Ages would have known it. There could not be a nicer Christmas gift.

---

[26] When reading this text, note that one item is counted in "olympiads," which are really four-year periods. Thus, though it may appear out of sequence, it really does fit where it is placed.

December
The five and twentieth Day

In the 5199th year from the Creation of the world, when in the beginning God created Heaven and Earth;

In the 2957th year from the flood of Noah;

In the 2015th year from the Nativity of Abraham;

In the 1510th year from Moses and the coming forth of the people of Israel out of Egypt;

In the 1032nd year from the anointing of David as King;

In the 65th week according to the Prophecy of Daniel;

In the 194th Olympiad;

In the 752nd year from the building of the City of Rome;

In the 42nd year of the Empire of Octavian Augustus, in the sixth Age of the World, when the whole world was at peace;

Jesus Christ, Eternal God, and Son of the Eternal Father,
    intending to sanctify the world with His most blessed Presence,
    having been conceived of the Holy Ghost,
    and nine months being past after his conception,
    was made man,
    born in Bethlehem in Judah of the Virgin Mary.

Botticelli, *Madonna of the Eucharist*

Pope Urban II: The Call for a Crusade

The end of the eleventh century was a rollicking time in Western Europe. By comparison, we today live in a decorous age indeed. The politics of the eleventh-century world were wildly fluid, in large part because sacred and secular questions were not really distinguishable. The great and mighty European rulers—the Roman Pope, the German Emperor, the French King—quarreled and squabbled with vigor and abandon over life, religion, and civil laws, all of which were tightly intertwined. In the events that lie behind this Page, after a bitter dispute over papal authority, the Pope excommunicated the Emperor, who promptly invaded Rome and set a rival pope on the throne of St. Peter. The King of France, charged with adultery (even then, the French were very French), was also excommunicated, though almost without losing a beat, the Pope asked the French nobles to go to war in a holy Crusade against the heathen Turks. Those French nobles responded with unexpected gusto, catapulting Europe into two centuries of headstrong idealism, useless conquest, and inglorious defeat. The long misadventure cost too many lives and too much treasure, and was all in the furtherance of a quest that could never succeed.

Yet those same two centuries were the foundation for the flowering of Western literature, science, and humanism that was the Renaissance; the Crusades paved the way for what we know as Modern History. And it all started with a sermon by Pope Urban II at the Council of Clermont in 1095, where he called on the faithful to do good deeds, atone for their sins, love their neighbor, and beat the hell out of the pagan Moslems. It was, as I say, a rollicking time.

In truth, the specific cause for Urban making his summons to the Crusade was quite serious. He had received an urgent request from Alexius, Emperor of Byzantium, the "second Rome," the heart of the Eastern Empire that still preserved intact its lineage from the ancient Roman Caesars. In 1071, the Seljuk Turks had inflicted a decisive defeat on the Byzantine army and were now threatening Byzantium itself. These highly aggressive people, migrating west from Turkestan, had conquered most of Asia Minor and had adopted Islam. Now strong enough to challenge the Byzantine Empire, they could, if left unchecked, easily reinvigorate the militant spirit of the whole Moslem world. And although the attempted Moslem conquest of Europe in the west, through Spain, had been halted, a resurgent Moslem zeal in the east could jeopardize all of Christendom, and even menace Rome.

Pope Urban had other concerns as well. For one thing, the Turks were much less tolerant than the Palestinians had been toward Christian pilgrims in the Holy Land. Travelers, rich and poor alike, were at risk, and incidents of mistreatment, even outright attacks on pilgrims, were growing. Closer to home, it was also apparent that Urban viewed the Crusade as a convenient social mechanism. The internal disorders of Europe had become acute, evidenced by sundry occasions of robbery and mayhem. By channeling the widespread urge toward violence against a common external foe, a social ill could perhaps be put to good use and possibly even cured at the same time.

But probably the most interesting aspect of Urban's call to arms appears when we consider the larger European backdrop of papal and imperial politics in 1095. And to understand the burning question that dominated Urban's attention, we must go back two decades to the reign of his great predecessor, Pope Gregory VII.[27]

Gregory VII was a man of great personal sanctity, and a zealous reformer. By the eleventh century, there were many abuses that had crept into the Church—probably a normal occurrence for any institution that reaches a thousand years of age—and Gregory undertook the task of uprooting these ills and revitalizing the Church. One issue, known as "lay investiture," was particularly contentious. This was the common practice by the ruling monarchs in each country of naming that country's bishops. The monarchs considered it their right; Gregory considered it a major cause of the current laxity in faith and morals. And on this issue, Gregory locked horns with the German Emperor Henry IV, who had no intention of relinquishing his privilege. When Gregory issued a Papal Decree in 1075 prohibiting lay investiture, Henry loudly and publicly refused; his letter to the Pope almost sizzles:

> Let another ascend the throne of St. Peter, who shall not practice violence under the cloak of religion, but shall teach the sound doctrine of St. Peter. I, Henry, King by the grace of God, do say unto thee: descend, descend, to be damned through the ages.

Pope Gregory, no less capable of sizzle, responded with a writ of excommunication:

> In the name of the Almighty God, Father, Son, and Holy Ghost, I withdraw, through Thy power and authority, from Henry the King, son of

---

[27] Urban II was actually once removed from Gregory VII. After Gregory died, his immediate and unwilling successor was the monk Desiderius, who was elected in 1086, but resisted consecration for a year. Desiderius finally took office as Victor III, but he died a few months later, and was succeeded by Urban II, who reigned from 1088 to 1099.

Henry the Emperor, who has risen against thy Church with unheard of insolence, the rule over the whole Kingdom of the Germans and over Italy. And I absolve all Christians from the bonds of the oath which they have made or shall make to him; and I forbid any one to serve him as King.

In retribution, Henry prevailed on the German Bishops to elect a rival Pope, Clement III, and then invaded Rome in 1081, setting Clement on the Papal throne as "antipope." Gregory was rescued by a French army, but died in 1085 with the dispute still unsettled (and the antipope still claiming legitimacy).

This was the situation that Urban inherited in 1088, and it dominated his reign. He spent his first few papal years as an exile, while the antipope sat in Rome, propped up by Henry's troops. By 1094, however, internal revolt had weakened Henry's rule over Germany and Italy; with Henry's support failing, Urban finally was able to unseat the antipope and claim his proper place on St. Peter's throne.[28]

Given such an unstable foundation for his reign, it is not hard to imagine the attraction that a great and noble cause like a Crusade might hold for Urban. By unifying the bickering forces of Christendom against a common enemy, the terrible internecine fighting could cease, and wounds could heal. (That healing would take some time; very few German knights took part in the first Crusade.) So whether his summons to the Crusade, made at the Council of Clermont in 1095, was motivated by a pure desire to save the Faith, or was more a golden opportunity to solidify his hard-won victory over Henry, it is easy to believe that Urban put a great effort into his sermon that summoned the French to battle.

It must have been stirring and compelling. The chronicles report that on hearing Urban's command to go forth and smite the infidel, a great cry of *"Deus lo volt!* (God wills it!)" went up from the crowd. And the movement spread like fire through dry tinder. Within two years, thousands of French knights had embarked on their holy quest. By July 1099, Jerusalem was conquered, and the city passed—for oh, so short a time— into the hands of the Crusaders. For the next two centuries, French, English, and German armies, sometimes led by great leaders, sometimes a motley rabble, departed for the East. There, they fought the Infidel in a vain attempt to conquer the Holy Land for Christendom; they had few successes and many failures. Finally, in 1291, a Moslem army retook Acre, the last Christian stronghold, and the era of the Crusades came to an end.

---

[28] Having depended on French support for several years, it was only at this point that Urban felt secure enough to excommunicate the King of France for abandoning his wife and carrying on a very public affair with the wife of one of his vassals. Even a Pope must bow to pragmatism.

To end this long commentary, we must also point out that two decades before Urban's address, Pope Gregory VII had issued a very similar call for a Crusade, but it produced no response comparable to Urban's. Why Gregory's words fell on deaf ears and Urban's struck such a mighty spark is impossible to know. But whatever the reason, it is to Urban that historians give the honor (or blame) of igniting the flames of the Crusading era. *Deus lo volt.*

Some notes on the text. There is no extant copy of Urban's actual speech to the Council, but there are several reconstructions set down by eyewitnesses. The one most often cited is the following Page, written by one Fulcher of Chartres. Fulcher's account divides the text into two distinct halves. In the first part, Urban is addressing the Bishops as shepherds of the faithful, responsible for guiding their flocks of wayward sinners. In the second part, Urban speaks more generally, and is obviously appealing to a larger, non-clerical audience.

Jean Colombe, ***Pope Urban II preaching at the Council of Clermont***

Most beloved brethren: Urged by necessity, I, Urban, by the permission of God chief bishop and prelate over the whole world, have come into these parts as an ambassador with a divine admonition to you, the servants of God. I hoped to find you as faithful and as zealous in the service of God as I had supposed you to be. But if there is in you any deformity or crookedness contrary to God's law, with divine help I will do my best to remove it. For God has put you as stewards over his family to minister to it. Happy indeed will you be if he finds you faithful in your stewardship. You are called shepherds; see that you do not act as hirelings. But be true shepherds, with your crooks always in your hands. Do not go to sleep, but guard on all sides the flock committed to you. For if through your carelessness or negligence a wolf carries away one of your sheep, you will surely lose the reward laid up for you with God. And after you have been bitterly scourged with remorse for your faults, you will be fiercely overwhelmed in hell, the abode of death. For according to the gospel you are the salt of the earth. But if you fall short in your duty, how, it may be asked, can it be salted? O how great the need of salting! It is indeed necessary for you to correct with the salt of wisdom this foolish people which is so devoted to the pleasures of this world, lest the Lord, when He may wish to speak to them, find them putrefied by their sins unsalted and stinking. For if He shall find worms, that is, sins, in them, because you have been negligent in your duty, He will command them as worthless to be thrown into the abyss of unclean things. And because you cannot restore to Him His great loss, He will surely condemn you and drive you from His loving presence. But the man who applies this salt should be prudent, provident, modest, learned, peaceable, watchful, pious, just, equitable, and pure. For how can the ignorant teach others? How can the licentious make others modest? And how can the impure make others pure? If anyone hates peace, how can he make others peaceable? Or if anyone has soiled his hands with baseness, how can he cleanse the impurities of another?

We read also that if the blind lead the blind, both will fall into the ditch. But first correct yourselves, in order that, free from blame, you may be able to correct those who are subject to you. If you wish to be the friends of God, gladly do the things which you know will please Him. You must especially let all matters that pertain to the church be controlled by the law of the church. And be careful that simony does not take root among you, lest both those who buy and those who sell church offices be beaten with the scourges of the Lord through narrow streets and driven into the place of destruction and confusion. Keep the church and the clergy in all its grades entirely free from the secular power. See that the tithes that belong to God are faithfully paid from all the produce of the land; let them not be sold or withheld. If anyone seizes a bishop let him be treated as an outlaw. If anyone seizes or robs monks, or clergymen, or nuns, or their servants, or pilgrims, or merchants, let him be anathema.[29] Let robbers and incendiaries and all their accomplices be expelled from the church and anathematized. If a man who does not give a part of his goods as alms is punished with the damnation of hell, how should he be punished who robs another of his goods? For thus it happened to the rich man in the gospel; for he was not punished because he had stolen the goods of another, but because he had not used well the things which were his.

You have seen for a long time the great disorder in the world caused by these crimes. It is so bad in some of your provinces, I am told, and you are so weak in the administration of justice, that one can hardly go along the road by day or night without being attacked by robbers; and whether at home or abroad, one is in danger of being despoiled either by force or fraud. Therefore it is necessary to reenact the truce, as it is commonly called, which was proclaimed a long time ago by our holy fathers. I exhort and demand that you, each, try hard to have the truce kept in your diocese. And if anyone shall be led by his

---

[29] The liturgical manner of saying: "Let him be cursed."

cupidity or arrogance to break this truce, by the authority of God and with the sanction of this council he shall be anathematized.

At this point in his account, Fulcher adds the following:
After those and various other matters had been attended to, all who were present, clergy and people, gave thanks to God and agreed to the Pope's proposition. They all faithfully promised to keep the decrees. Then the Pope said that in another part of the world Christianity was suffering from a state of affairs that was worse than the one just mentioned. He continued:

Although, O sons of God, you have promised more firmly than ever to keep the peace among yourselves and to preserve the rights of the church, there remains still an important work for you to do. Freshly quickened by the divine correction, you must apply the strength of your righteousness to another matter which concerns you as well as God. For your brethren who live in the east are in urgent need of your help, and you must hasten to give them the aid which has often been promised them. For, as the most of you have heard, the Turks and Arabs have attacked them and have conquered the territory of Romania[30] as far west as the shore of the Mediterranean and the Hellespont, which is called the Arm of St. George. They have occupied more and more of the lands of those Christians, and have overcome them in seven battles. They have killed and captured many, and have destroyed the churches and devastated the empire. If you permit them to continue thus for awhile with impunity, the faithful of God will be much more widely attacked by them. On this account I, or rather the Lord, beseech you as Christ's heralds to publish this everywhere and to persuade all people of whatever rank, foot-soldiers and knights, poor and rich, to carry aid promptly to those Christians and to destroy that vile race from the lands of our friends. I say this to those who are present, it meant also for those who are absent. Moreover, Christ commands it.

All who die by the way, whether by land or by sea, or in battle against the pagans, shall have immediate remission of sins. This I grant them through the power of God with which I am invested. O what a disgrace if such a despised and base race, which worships demons, should conquer a people which has the faith of omnipotent God and is made glorious with the name of Christ! With what reproaches will the Lord overwhelm us if you do not aid those who, with us, profess the Christian religion! Let those who have been accustomed unjustly to wage private warfare against the faithful now go against the infidels and end with victory this war which should have been begun long ago. Let those who for a long time, have been robbers, now become knights. Let those who have been fighting against their brothers and relatives now fight in a proper way against the barbarians. Let those who have been serving as mercenaries for small pay now obtain the eternal reward. Let those who have been wearing themselves out in both body and soul now work for a double honor. Behold! on this side will be the sorrowful and poor, on that, the rich; on this side, the enemies of the Lord, on that, his friends. Let those who go not put off the journey, but rent their lands and collect money for their expenses; and as soon as winter is over and spring comes, let them eagerly set out on the way with God as their guide.

---

[30] The Byzantine Empire.

The Act of Supremacy
(The Establishment of the Anglican Church)

The second quarter of the sixteenth century witnessed the start of the English Reformation. It was a time of great religious confusion, with dramatic events following each other with rapidity. The turmoil continued throughout the following century, as England oscillated between Protestant and Catholic, with Edward VI, Mary, Elizabeth, the Stuarts, and Cromwell each bringing a particular bias to the throne. Whatever the importance of these later monarchs, however, the spotlight of History seems centered on the man who started it all; the starring role in the English Reformation was played by Henry VIII, the brilliant, talented, and egotistical man who is, quite possibly, the most famous character in English history.

In the popular mind, Henry is unshakeably linked with lustful desire: he broke with Rome because the Pope refused to let him divorce Catherine of Aragon to marry Anne Boleyn. And he then went on to have several other wives, a model of marital variety unmatched until the film stars of the twentieth century. But as with most simple notions of history, it is not quite correct, and the real story is more subtle. Henry may indeed have been the manly gent he is imagined to be, but there is more to the tale than his libido.

Long before Luther's break with Rome in 1517, the spirit of religious reform was abroad in several places in Europe, and was certainly so in England. John Wycliffe (1320–1384) was an early voice for reform, proclaiming many of the issues that later marked the major Protestant movements. He denounced Papal supremacy, rejected the ornate Roman church practices, and insisted on the primacy of the Bible in Christian life. His followers were known as "Lollards," and they established a tradition of English religious dissent that persisted throughout the fifteenth century. The Lutheran revolt in 1517 was centered in Germany, but it found considerable support in England from those who had kept alive the Lollard ideals.

But when the English Reformation actually began, toward the end of the 1520s, the immediate causes were as much political as religious. One issue was Papal authority. Aside from any implied theological supremacy he might have, the Pope's civil authority extended into many areas, and this was the source of considerable friction. The anger was especially directed at Cardinal Wolsey, the Papal Legate. A. G. Dickens, eminent historian of the English Reformation, describes Wolsey as a man:

> ... for whom the mass of Englishmen, clerical as well as lay, had developed an intense dislike. His tactlessness and financial demands in Parliament, his repression of the nobility ... his voracious appetite for other clergymen's privileges, the Roman basis for his authority as Legate, each of these features attracted powerful enemies.

A more pressing issue for Henry was the lack of a male heir to the throne. His father, Henry VII, had two sons, Arthur and Henry; Arthur died in 1502. Soon after Henry VIII was crowned, in 1509, he took the unusual step of marrying Arthur's widow, Catherine of Aragon. To do this, he requested, and received, from Pope Julius II, a Papal dispensation.[31]

Catherine dutifully bore many children; but all died soon after birth except one daughter, Mary, born in 1516. By the mid-1520s, it had become clear that there would be no male heir to the throne. For any monarch of that period this might have caused some concern; but Henry was keenly aware of the special danger for England. The bitter civil strife over dynastic succession (called the Wars of the Roses) between the houses of York and Lancaster had finally ceased in 1485, when Henry's father defeated Richard III at Bosworth Field. Now, if Henry VIII died without a son, there was as yet no precedent for a Queen to reign; the spectre of renewed civil war filled Henry (and many others) with dread.

These two issues—disaffection with Papal authority and the lack of a Royal Prince—were central in Henry's mind by 1525. When, in the hope of begetting a son from another wife, Henry appealed to the Pope (by then, Clement VII) for a divorce from Catherine, his appeal was denied; the two issues then became inextricably fused into one.

In truth, Henry's stated justification for the divorce was somewhat curious. He maintained that the original dispensation should never have been granted—even though it was he himself that had requested it—and hence his marriage to Catherine was never valid. He was not alone in this reasoning. As A. G. Dickens points out:

> There had existed genuine doubts among the canon lawyers of Europe concerning the validity of the unusual dispensation by which Julius II had permitted the child-marriage of Henry and Catherine.

---

[31] The dispensation was needed because of a prohibition in Leviticus against a man marrying his brother's wife; those who do so are cursed, and "shall die childless."

But it cannot be denied that Henry's amorous interest was at least partially a factor in his request; there are love letters from Henry to Anne Boleyn that date from 1527, at just the time when he was pressing his appeal to the Pope.

His justification, warranted or otherwise, made little difference; His Holiness refused to grant the divorce. The Pope had his own political, and very practical reason, one that was far removed from any theological question. The wife Henry wished to get rid of, Catherine of Aragon, was also the Aunt of the German Emperor, Charles V. Not only was Charles very powerful, his Imperial armies were just next door to the Pope; the amorous Henry was far away in England. In 1527, Charles' troops sacked the city of Rome; with the Emperor's soldiers virtually outside his bedroom, the Pope was hardly prepared to insult the Emperor's Aunt Catherine by letting Henry cast her aside.

Henry's hopes for a legal divorce thus quashed, he began a slow but inexorable march toward an Anglican Church. The shift took place over several years, and was accomplished entirely as a steadily increasing appropriation of ecclesiastical authority. Unlike Luther or Calvin, Henry never contested the essential doctrinal beliefs of the Roman Church. Citing Sir Maurice Powicke:

> The Reformation in England was a parliamentary transaction. All the important changes were made under statutes ... Henry had no immediate intention of breaking with Rome [i.e., in the sense of a theological separation]. He was declared to be head of the Church in England, not of a separate Church.

Henry first dismissed Wolsey, in 1529, and summoned a Parliament, now known as the "Reformation Parliament." Over the next five years, an array of Laws and Statutes were enacted that, bit by bit, broke the ties between England and the Papacy, and established the authority of the English Monarch as head of the Church. The following Page, the Act of Supremacy, was passed in 1534, and essentially concluded this shift in power.

From then on, England became irreversibly bound with the growing Protestant movements on the Continent. Henry himself resisted an alliance with Protestantism; even after his break with Rome, he tried to keep the English Church away from the influence of the German Reformers. But he was trying to stem an unstoppable tide: immediately after Henry's death, the English Church, under the steady guidance of men like Thomas Cranmer, moved to embrace a great many of the reformist principles of Luther, Calvin, and Zwingli.

There has been considerable disagreement about whether the Anglican Church would ever have come into existence had the divorce issue not been present. Dickens sums it up thus:

> The place of the royal divorce in the history of the Reformation will always remain a subject for argument. Protestant writers have tended to dismiss it as a mere "occasion" ... Catholics have sometimes regarded the divorce as the chief cause of the cataclysm. To the present writer neither of these views seems wholly acceptable ... Had Henry obtained his divorce he would most likely have tried, and with some success, to hold his realm in some sort of spiritual allegiance to Rome ... On the other hand, the divorce suit did not create either Protestantism or those anti-papal and anti-sacerdotal forces which smoothed its path.

Clearly ambiguous, the way most real history usually is. And, like that turbulent time, just confusing enough to give writers of history books an excuse to carry on their work.

Hans Holbein the Younger, *Portrait of Henry VIII*

The King's Grace to be authorized Supreme Head

Albeit the king's majesty justly and rightfully is and ought to be the supreme head of the Church of England, and so is recognized by the clergy of this realm in their convocations, yet nevertheless for corroboration and confirmation thereof, and for increase of virtue in Christ's religion within this realm of England, and to repress and extirp all errors, heresies, and other enormities and abuses heretofore used in the same;

Be it enacted by authority of this present Parliament, that the King our sovereign lord, his heirs and successors, kings of this realm, shall be taken, accepted, and reputed the only supreme head in earth of the Church of England, called Anglicana Ecclesia;

And shall have and enjoy, annexed and united to the imperial crown of this realm, as well the title and style thereof, as all honours, dignities, pre-eminences, jurisdictions, privileges, authorities, immunities, profits, and commodities to the said dignity of supreme head of the same Church belonging and appertaining;

And that our said sovereign lord, his heirs and successors, kings of this realm, shall have full power and authority from time to time to visit, repress, redress, reform, order, correct, restrain, and amend all such errors, heresies, abuses, offences, contempts, and enormities, whatsoever they be, which by any manner spiritual authority or jurisdiction ought or may lawfully be reformed, repressed, ordered, redressed, corrected, restrained, or amended, most to the pleasure of Almighty God, the increase of virtue in Christ's religion, and for the conservation of the peace, unity, and tranquillity of this realm;

Any usage, custom, foreign law, foreign authority, prescription, or any other thing or things to the contrary hereof notwithstanding.

Dedication of the King James Bible

The Bible—Biblos—"The Book"—is the centerpiece of Western religious tradition. Its first five books (the Pentateuch) preserve the heritage of Moses and are the foundation of Judaism. Its four Gospels, accounts written soon after the death of Jesus, were the formative documents of Christianity. And translating the Bible into the contemporary European languages of the sixteenth century was one of the key battlegrounds over which the Protestant Reformation was fought.

To be sure, there were matters other than scriptural translation that stood between Luther and the Pope, and even the dispute of the vernacular Bible itself was based on authority as much as on language. But Biblical translation was at least as significant as any of the other issues for the Reformers, and was especially thorny in England.

The root of the problem lay in ancient history. The early Christian church had grown from a band of Jewish zealots in the first century to become a major cultural and social institution in the fourth and fifth centuries, eventually replacing the Roman Empire as the dominant factor in European civilization. By then, the role of sacred scripture had become less one of missionary persuasion and more one of providing a consistent text that unified the diverse populations that had adopted Christianity. Thus, though the Latin language itself was losing common usage in Europe, the Latin Bible was still a very visible symbol of the universality—and authority—of the Church, and also of the Pope, the Bishop of Rome. Much later, as the Renaissance blossomed, and with it the growth of learning and humanism, the preservation of the Latin Scriptures had become a bulwark against heresy: if Everyman could read scripture, what perversions of official doctrine might emerge?

Yet the notion of rendering the sacred Scriptures into a contemporary tongue was a hallowed tradition within the ancient Church. Hebrew texts had been brought into Aramaic, then into Greek, and at the end of the fourth century, into the Latin of St. Jerome's "Vulgate," the language of the common man. And while the Vulgate maintained its status as the official version for over a millennium, ongoing translations into other languages did not cease, but continued as the European languages themselves changed and mutated. In 735, the Venerable Bede translated the Gospel of John into Anglo-Saxon; many of the Psalms appeared throughout the ninth century; and in the tenth century the monk Aelfric brought large portions of the Old Testament into the Saxon language that he spoke and preached in.

The language known as Middle English, the language of Chaucer, coalesced toward the end of the twelfth century, at the very time that the question of Biblical translation was becoming inexorably bound up with reformation. John

Wycliffe, an early champion of church reform in England, translated the whole of the Vulgate into Middle English; his translation appeared in 1384, the year of his death. By the middle of the fifteenth century, Wycliffe's translation was widely known throughout England, in spite of ecclesiastical prohibition.

In Germany, Luther's break with the Pope occurred in 1517, and one of his first actions was to translate the Bible into German: by now, scriptural translation had become an act of political defiance. The spirit of reform was gaining strength in England as well. In 1525, William Tyndale translated the New Testament into English, and in 1530, the first part of the Old Testament. Miles Coverdale, building on Tyndale's work, issued a complete Bible in 1535; this was later revised as the "Great" Bible of 1539.[32] One thing that characterized these early sixteenth century English translations, and affected all of their successors, was their recourse to sources other than Latin. Tyndale's translation did not begin with the Latin Vulgate, but had returned to the Greek and Hebrew texts. This practice continues up to the present day: a considerable proportion of scriptural scholarship is intimately bound up with understanding the nuances of language, and the subtle changes that occur when a portion of Scripture goes from one language into another.[33]

The work of Tyndale and Coverdale came at just the time when Henry VIII was engaged in his confrontation, and eventual break, with Rome (1534). So although Tyndale began his work as an outlaw, within a decade—the time that Coverdale was revising his complete Bible—the need for an English Bible had become officially sanctioned. Several English Bibles soon appeared, each of which had some debt to Tyndale and Coverdale: the Geneva Bible, the "Bishops' Bible," and eventually, Catholic translations, first of the New Testament (called the "Rheims" version) and then the Old Testament (the Douai version).

The appearance of the Catholic translations was significant. They were, first of all, tacit acceptance by Rome that a vernacular Bible was necessary. But they also provided a golden opportunity for Rome to attack the Protestant translations, Tyndale and all his successors, as flawed in scholarship and dubious in doctrine. As Gerald Hammond, an authority on the King James Bible, notes:

> The Rheims version not only stood as a stylistic contrast to the Protestant versions, but its powerful presentation of the text was designed to persuade readers that it offered the last word in scholarship ... Not only the church fathers but modern commentators too are given copious citation ... This extends as far as printing Greek words in the

---

[32] Coverdale read neither Greek nor Hebrew. His Bible actually depends on the work of other translators, especially Tyndale, who truly was a Greek and Hebrew scholar.

[33] The issue still exists. The Latin text of the Lord's Prayer states "Pater noster, qui es **in coelis** ... sicut **in coelo** ..." The first underlined word is properly translated as "in heaven" and the second as "in the heavens." This distinction has been lost in the English version, but is preserved in the contemporary French version.

commentary, as well as the occasional Hebrew word—something without precedent in any earlier English Bible.

By the start of the seventeenth century in England, none of the existing texts had both universality and official sanction: the need for an official Protestant text, and one superior to any challenge from Rome, was obvious. In 1604, therefore, a great effort, authorized by the new Stuart King, James I, was begun to make such a Bible. The project enlisted fifty-four scholars from Oxford, Cambridge, Westminster, and London. They examined and built on all of the earlier versions, even including the Catholic Rheims version. They did not set out to make an entirely new translation, but consciously based their effort on all of the previous work:

> We never thought . . . that we should need to make a new translation . . . but to make a good one better, or out of many good ones one principal good one.

They labored for seven years, and finally published the new version in 1611. It was dedicated to King James (the dedication is the following Page) and thereafter became, for the Anglican Protestant Church, the "Authorized Version," a name by which it is still known.

The Authorized Version is not a translation in the sense that Tyndale's was. But it represents a unique marriage of two things: the fruit of nearly a century of scrupulous scholarship over ancient texts, and the gracious and powerful language of the early seventeenth century (the fifty-four did their work as the greatest lines of Shakespeare were first echoing in London). The subtle power of the Authorized Version can be seen in the following comparison of three translations of a text from Proverbs:

> Coverdale's Bible: Her wayes are pleasant wayes, and all her paths are peaceable.

> Geneva Bible: Her wayes are wayes of pleasure and all her paths prosperitie.

> Authorized Version: Her wayes are wayes of pleasantness, and all her paths are peace.

In his account of the English Bible, F. C. Grant cites this example from the Authorized Version as:

> . . . a perfect rendering of the Masoretic Hebrew texts . . . its final note is that sublime conception which runs throughout the ancient Scripture: Shalōm, peace . . .

In later years, revisions of the Authorized Version have been made, and many other new translations have appeared. But to this day, the Authorized Version, that keeps alive the name of King James, endures and thrives. It is still in use in some Christian churches, and its beauty is admitted by most others, Protestant and Catholic alike. Countless idioms, expressions, and familiar phrases of our language can be traced to its pages. It can rightfully be said, in fact, that among its pages are some of the most beautiful Pages of History. In some future book, perhaps, constrained by some different rules, it will be a joy to include some of them. For now, the florid dedication to King James will have to suffice.

One postscript: Scripture scholars will have had ample occasion in the preceding discussion to note where I have simplified, perhaps to a perilous degree, the details of the how the Bible came into Jacobean English. As I noted in the book's Preface, these introductory commentaries are only meant to set the stage, not to provide scholarly discourse. However, the story of the Bible's translation is an especially diverse one, and I am painfully aware of how much is omitted here. So to those readers who can cite Origen, or have read the Greek of Theodotion, I ask that you might grant to me, in the spirit of the fifty-four inspired men of 1611, your forgiveness, that I too may rest secure "having walked in the ways of simplicity."

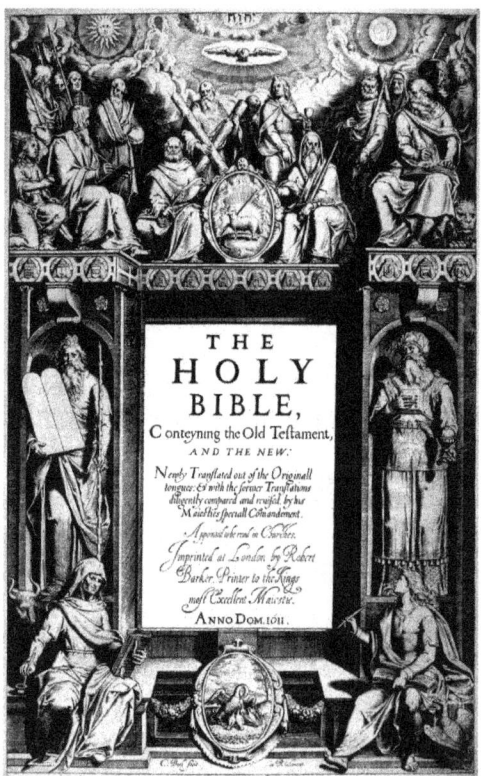

Frontispiece to the King James Bible, 1611

To the Most High and Mighty Prince
JAMES
by the Grace of God
King of Great Britain, France, and Ireland
Defender of the Faith, etc.
The Translators of the Bible wish
Grace, Mercy, and Peace
Through Jesus Christ Our Lord

Great and manifold were the blessings, most dread Sovereign, which Almighty God, the Father of all mercies, bestowed upon us the people of England, when first he sent Your Majesty's Royal Person to rule and reign over us. For whereas it was the expectation of many, who wished not well unto our Sion, that upon the setting of that bright Occidental Star, Queen Elizabeth of most happy memory, some thick and palpable clouds of darkness would so have overshadowed this Land, that men should have been in doubt which way they were to walk; and that it should hardly be known, who was to direct the unsettled State; the appearance of Your Majesty, as of the Sun in his strength, instantly dispelled those supposed and surmised mists, and gave unto all that were well affected exceeding causes of comfort; especially when we beheld the Government established in Your Highness, and Your hopeful Seed, by an undoubted Title, and this also accompanied with peace and tranquility at home and abroad.

But among all our joys, there was no one that more filled our hearts, than the blessed continuance of the preaching of God's sacred Word among us; which is the inestimable treasure, which excelleth all of the riches of the earth; because the fruit thereof extendeth itself, not only to the time spent in this transitory world, but directeth and disposeth men unto that eternal happiness which is above in heaven.

Then not to suffer this to fall to the ground, but rather to take it up, and to continue it in that state, wherein the famous Predecessor of Your Highness did leave it; nay, to go forward with the confidence and resolution of a Man in maintaining the truth of Christ, and propagating it far and near, is that which hath so bound and firmly knit the hearts of all Your Majesty's loyal and religious people unto You, that Your very name is precious among them; their eye doth behold You with comfort, and they bless You in their hearts, as that sanctified Person, who, under God, is the immediate Author of their true happiness. And this their contentment doth not diminish or decay, but every day increaseth and taketh strength, when they observe, that the zeal of Your Majesty toward the house of God doth not clack or go backward, but is more and more kindled, manifesting itself in the farthest parts of Christendom, by writing in defense of Truth, (which hath given such a blow unto that man of sin, as will not be healed,) and every day at home, by religious and leaned discourse, by frequenting the house of God, by hearing the Word preached, by cherishing the Teachers thereof, by caring for the Church as a most tender and loving nursing Father.

There are infinite arguments of this right Christian and religious affection in Your Majesty; but none is more forcible to declare it to others than the vehement and perpetuated desire of accomplishing and publishing of this work, which now with all humility we present unto Your Majesty. For when Your Highness had once out of deep judgement apprehended how convenient it was, that out of the Original Sacred Tongues, together with comparing of the labours, both in our own, and other foreign Languages, of many worthy men who went before us, there should be one more exact Translation of the holy Scriptures into the English Tongue; Your Majesty did never desist to urge and to excite those to whom it was commended, that the work might be hastened, and that the business might be expedited in so decent a manner, as a matter of such importance might justly require.

And now at last, by the mercy of God, and the continuance of our labours, it being brought unto such a conclusion as that we have great hopes that the Church of England shall reap good fruit thereby; we hold it our duty to offer it to Your Majesty, not only as to our King and Sovereign, but as to the principal Mover and Author of the work: humbly craving of Your most Sacred Majesty, that since things of this quality have ever been subject to the censures of illmeaning and demented persons, it may receive approbation and patronage from so learned and judicious a Prince as Your Highness is, whose allowance and acceptance of our labours shall more honour and encourage us, than all the calumniations and hard interpretations of other men shall dismay us. So that it, on the one side, we shall be traduced by Popish Persons at home or abroad, who therefore will malign us, because we are poor instruments to make God's holy Truth to be yet more and more known unto the people, whom they desire still to keep in ignorance and darkness; or if, on the other side, we shall be maligned by self-conceited Brethren, who run their own ways, and give liking unto nothing, but what is framed by themselves and hammered on their anvil; we may rest secure, supported within by the truth and innocency of a good conscience, having walked the ways of simplicity and integrity, as before the Lord; and sustained without by the powerful protection of Your Majesty's grace and favour, which will ever give countenance to honest and Christian endeavours against bitter censures and uncharitable imputations.

The Lord of heaven and earth bless Your Majesty with many and happy days, that, as his heavenly head hath enriched Your Highness with many singular and extraordinary graces, so You may be the wonder of the world in this latter age for happiness and true felicity, the honour and glory of that great God, and the good of his church, through Jesus Christ our Lord and only Saviour.

ART & SCIENCE, WISDOM & UNDERSTANDING

Practical wisdom is a virtue and not an art (Aristotle. Nicomachean Ethics, VI.5)
Wisdom is to be desired above all things (Cicero, De Officiis, II,5)

The Pages in this section are the most varied and unconnected documents of this book. To some extent, this is a reflection of the bundling together of these apparently diverse topics into one chapter. But that diversity was not always apparent. For instance, in our present understanding of the words "art" and "science," we normally hold that the former refers to free and imaginative invention, and the latter to empirically-based factual knowledge. But this is hardly true for other ages: to Aristotle, as well as to other thinkers of ancient days, "art" and "science" had a significant overlap. Similarly, making a clear distinction between such words as "wisdom" and "understanding" (as well as their brethren "knowledge" and "truth") is perilous: a simple web search will overpower the reader with definitions that offer slightly varying distinctions that most often define one in terms of the others.

All of this notwithstanding, there is in fact a common thread that relates all of these Pages: they reflect the individual: his deeply held beliefs, his unusual insight, or his mysterious ability to create things that change the world. And these traits represent a deep and personal urge toward expression that originates in the self.

The oldest of these Pages, the Hippocratic Oath, dates from the Golden Age of Pericles, roughly the fifth century BCE. It concerns the contributions of Hippocrates, the leading physician of antiquity, and a man widely considered the "Father of Medicine." The issues he discusses were significant in his own time, and are no less significant today, perhaps even moreso, as the ethical questions faced by the physisicnas of today are vastly more complex than those of Hippocrates' time (e.g.,the medical crisis facing the world in 2020 is a telling example).

Galileo's capitulation to the Pope concerning whether the sun revolves around the earth or the reverse is widely regarded as an intellectual contest between science and religion. Yet the whole tale is considerably more entangled, and shows the powerful role that politics plays in both domains.

In publishing the First Folio of Shakespeare's plays, Heminge and Condell, who were two actors who had been in Shakespeare's company, made a profound contribution to the ages. Former Harvard president Charles Eliot regards the book that they published as "the most important book in the imaginative literature of the world."

The Pages that concern music focus on two of the greatest musical minds in all history, Johann Sebastian Bach, and Ludwig von Beethoven. Through the words with which Bach dedicated his pieces, we can see that the place of the musician of the 1700s was to be a servant of the noble classes. With the oration at the funeral of Beethoven, we see this role transformed, and the great composer has become the voice of immortality. And that same composer's "Heiligenstadt Testament" is a painful personal letter to his brothers in which he shakes his fist at the heavens as laments his growing deafness.

Aristotle contemplating a Bust of Homer: Rembrant van Rijn

The Futurist Manifesto, by F.T. Marinetti, is a curiosity of sorts, but it offers remarkable insight into the cauldron of contradictory artistic currents that were bubbling in Europe in the first two decades of the twentieth century. Much of the savagery of the First World War, as well as the growing dissonance of the painting, music and literature of those years is reflected in this violent statement of modernism.

The importance of the letter from Einstein to President Roosevelt, that ultimately resulted in the creation of the atomic bomb, cannot be overestimated in importance. Like a pebble before an avalanche, that single Page changed the world more profoundly than most other documents of our history. We now live the Age of the Atom, and the political conduct of men and of nations is now wholly bound up with the threats and dangers of nuclear war. A difficult commentary on our age, perhaps. But the importance of this letter cannot be doubted, and it provides a fitting conclusion to this journey through the Pages of History.

Explosion of the Atomic Bomb at Hiroshima

The Hippocratic Oath

Hippocrates (c. 460 BCE–c. 374 BCE) was a Greek physician during the Age of Pericles, a time during which Athens saw an enormous flowering of culture, learning, and power. Hippocrates was then, and is still, known as the leading physician of ancient times, and is sometimes called "the Father of Medicine." Unlike previous practitioners of medicine, he disapproved of curing illness through rituals or prayers intoned by priests. Instead, he believed in curing disease through rigorous scientific principles and rational observations of cause and effect. The result of his teachings essentially established medicine as a profession.

He was highly regarded throughout the intellectual community of Greece. Plato spoke highly of him during his own time, and his fame survived the long transition from the Graeco-Roman centuries into the Christian era, According to Professor Gottfried Roth at the University of Vienna:

> During the patristic age [starting at the end of the first century CE] there was an abundance of quotations from the authentic works of Hippocrates ... and these have survived to us. Indeed, Cyprian of Carthage, Gregory Nazianzen, Gregory of Nyssa, and Eusebius of Cesarea [churchmen of the third and fourth centuries] all held to a theory of the natural sciences about the origins and causes of illness which went back to Hippocrates.

Dante (c.1265-1321) includes him in his depiction of Limbo in the "The Divine Comedy" (Inferno, The Virtuous Heathen: Canto IV.):

> When I raised my eyes a little higher ... I saw Socrates and Plato ... and I saw Orpheus, Cicero, Linus, and Seneca the moralist, Euclid the geometer, and Ptolemy, Hippocrates, Avicenna, Galen, and Averroes ...

While we know very little about Hippocrates himself, there is still extant a collection of some 60 medical documents, most of which date from the time in which he lived, and which reflect his teachings; it is called the Hippocratic Corpus. It contains treatises on various medical issues, e.g., "On the Heart," "Epidemics," "On the Diseases of Women." The majority of these documents date from between the end of the fifth century BCE and the middle of the fourth century BCE; some are earlier, and a few appear to be from the first century CE. Regardless of their dates, these texts reflect the influence of Hippocrates and the scientific basis of his medical practice. As an example from the Corpus, here is a telling condemnation of the healer-priest from a document that focuses on epilepsy, then regarded as "the sacred disease":

> These are the people who pretend to be very pious and be particularly wise. By invoking a divine element they are able to screen their own failure to give suitable treatment and so called this a "sacred" malady to conceal their ignorance of its nature. I believe that this disease is not in the least more divine than any other but has the same nature as other diseases and a similar cause.

The Page we will now encounter is the most famous member of the Corpus, the Hippocratic Oath. This document contains both abstract principles and practical advice, and has provided the basis for all succeeding studies of medical ethics. While it bears Hippocrates's name, most contemporary scholars believe that he was not the author, although no other author has been proposed. Regardless of its author, the Oath has endured, in highly various forms, until the present day.

Paulus Pontius, after Peter Paul Rubens, *Portrait of Hippocrates*

The Oath is traditionally taken by physicians as they complete their medical training. It is a text that primarily focuses on ethical issues, and enumerates several practices and behaviors that should guide beginning doctors as they start their medical practice. Although the Oath in its original form dates from 400 BCE, we have little knowledge of its subsequent role in medical practice until relatively recent times. Steven Miles, author of an authoritative analysis of the Oath, notes that the earliest copy we possess dates from about 300 CE, 700 years after it was written:

> There are two citations of the Oath in the fourth century CE, two more from the fifth to the eleventh centuries ... Medieval scholars rediscovered it and began altering it or interpreting it to conform to Christian doctrines ... From the eighteenth century onward, various versions of the Oath have been widely, though never universally, used in medical school graduation ceremonies in Europe and the United States.

After the text of the Oath was rediscovered by German scholars during the sixteenth century, knowledge of it gradually became universal; by two centuries later, it had taken its place as an expected culminating element of a medical education. But during all of this time, and lurking behind Miles' mention of "... altering it or interpreting it..." is a fascinating history of documental evolution and re-creation.

One issue that faced Europeans when they read the Oath was that a significant amount of its content was rooted in Greek culture of the fourth century BCE. The very opening of the Oath shows this resoundingly:

> I swear by Apollo ... and all the gods and goddesses ...

During a period when Christian Europe was witnessing its long battle between the Papacy and its reformers, this was an unacceptable statement, no matter what the rest of the document might say.

The Greek text also showed a calm acceptance of slavery:

> ... Whatever houses I may visit, I will come for the benefit of the sick ... be they free or slaves ...

And then as now, the question of abortion was of significance:

> ... I will not give a woman a destructive pessary ... [34]

Inevitably, and on numerous occasions, the text of the Oath has been revised, and sometimes actually rewritten, toward more contemporary sensibilities. One well-known revision is that of Louis Lasagna of Tufts University Medical School, made

---

[34] This clause has various translations: one uses the words "a destructive pessary" while another translates it as "a pessary to cause an abortion." Probably the most straightforward definition of "pessary" is found in Wikipedia: A pessary is a prosthetic device inserted into the vagina for structural and pharmaceutical purposes.

in 1964. This revision omits all reference to Greek culture: the original opening phrase from Hippocrates:

> I swear by Apollo Healer, by Asclepius, by Hygieia, by Panacea, and by all the gods and goddesses, making them my witnesses, that I will carry out, according to my ability and judgment, this oath and this indenture.

is replaced by:

> I swear to fulfill, to the best of my ability and judgment, this covenant:

Another issue dealt with euthanasia: where Hippocrates writes:

> Neither will I administer a poison to anybody when asked to do so, nor will I suggest such a course.

Lasagna is more nuanced:

> But it may also be within my power to take a life; this awesome responsibility must be faced with great humbleness and awareness of my own frailty.

A somewhat different approach was taken by students at the School of Medicine at Bristol University, where the medical students wished to create a statement of the values that would guide their careers. The result was the Bristol Promise, whose values include conscience, integrity, confidentiality, and care for the public's wellbeing.

And there are numerous other translations, revisions, and substitutions, all intended to bring the document in line with modern sensibilities. But all of these changes inevitably bring into question the degree to which the oath that young doctors swear as they start their careers is in truth an oath at all. Dr. David Graham, writing in the Journal of the American Medical Association, posed the question:

> The original oath is redolent of a covenant, a solemn and binding treaty ... By contrast, many modern oaths have a bland, generalized air of 'best wishes' about them, being near-meaningless formalities devoid of any influence on how medicine is truly practiced.

As evidence for that assertion, a survey of 150 U.S. and Canadian medical schools showed that:

> ... only 14 percent of modern oaths prohibit euthanasia, 11 percent hold covenant with a deity, 8 percent foreswear abortion, and a mere 3 percent forbid sexual contact with patients—all maxims held sacred in the classical version.

And perhaps more significant:

> ... while the classical oath calls for "the opposite" of pleasure and fame for those who transgress the oath, fewer than half of oaths taken today insist the taker be held accountable for keeping the pledge.

So the record is decidedly mixed in terms of whether or not the statement that is said as young doctors enter their profession is, in fact, an oath. For some it is merely a promise, for others it is a serious statement of intentions, and for others it truly has the binding nature of a sworn oath; a complex mix, just as is the practice that these young doctors are entering.

Yet, when all is said and done, the use of an oath, considered as a genuine oath or as no more than a statement of intention, seems to remain a desirable rite of passage. Whether using the words of Hippocrates or some modern replacement, an oath seems to persist as a culminating moment of a medical education. Steven Miles sums it up nicely:

> The percentages of American medical schools reciting an oath increased from twenty-four percent in 1928 ... to ninety-eight percent in 1993. Half of these schools use a variant of the Hippocratic Oath; the rest use other texts ... I think that oaths endure because they require the physicians to speak of their values. At some level, physicians recognize that a personal revelation of moral commitments is necessary to the practice of medicine.

Well said; now let us look at the Oath itself.

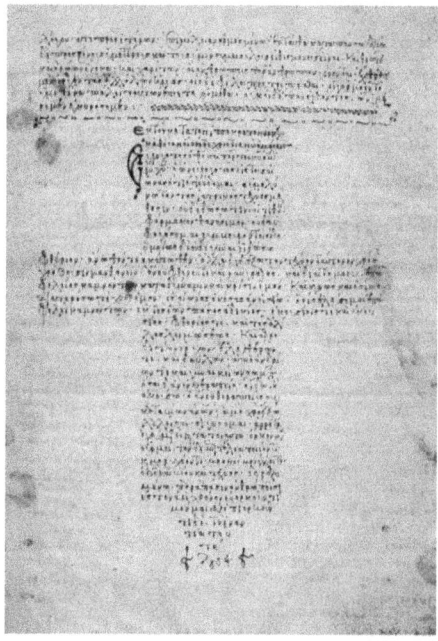

Manuscript of the Oath from the twelfth century in the form of a cross

I swear by Apollo Healer, by Asclepius, by Hygieia, by Panacea, and by all the gods and goddesses, making them my witnesses, that I will carry out, according to my ability and judgment, this oath and this indenture.

To hold my teacher in this art equal to my own parents; to make him partner in my livelihood; when he is in need of money to share mine with him; to consider his family as my own brothers, and to teach them this art, if they want to learn it, without fee or indenture; to impart precept, oral instruction, and all other instruction to my own sons, the sons of my teacher, and to indentured pupils who have taken the Healer's oath, but to nobody else.

I will use those dietary regimens which will benefit my patients according to my greatest ability and judgment, and I will do no harm or injustice to them.[7] Neither will I administer a poison to anybody when asked to do so, nor will I suggest such a course. Similarly I will not give to a woman a pessary to cause abortion. But I will keep pure and holy both my life and my art. I will not use the knife, not even, verily, on sufferers from stone, but I will give place to such as are craftsmen therein.

Into whatsoever houses I enter, I will enter to help the sick, and I will abstain from all intentional wrong-doing and harm, especially from abusing the bodies of man or woman, bond or free. And whatsoever I shall see or hear in the course of my profession, as well as outside my profession in my intercourse with men, if it be what should not be published abroad, I will never divulge, holding such things to be holy secrets.

Now if I carry out this oath, and break it not, may I gain for ever reputation among all men for my life and for my art; but if I break it and forswear myself, may the opposite befall me.

Galileo Galilei: Abjuration to the Inquisition

Great indeed are the things which in this brief treatise I propose for observation and consideration by all students of nature . . . It is a very beautiful thing, and most gratifying to the sight, to behold the body of the moon . . . so that its diameter appears almost thirty times larger . . . as when viewed with the naked eye

Thus, in 1610, did Galileo Galilei begin his treatise, "The Starry Messenger," in which he told an astonished world of the astronomical wonders he had seen through his telescope. And thus was set in motion, almost with the inexorable quality of a Greek tragedy, the chain of events that would culminate some two decades later, in his famous trial before an ecclesiastical court in Rome, where he abjured himself of his heretical belief that the earth revolves around the sun.

Galileo's battle with the Roman authorities, and his eventual submission, are often viewed as the archetype of the bitter tension between learning and ignorance, science and faith, wisdom and superstition. Yet it was not really quite that simple, as numerous scholars have attested. And, as is true of any good Greek tragedy, there is a healthy amount of myth involved. Michael Segre's study of Galileo notes that:

> Galileo became a myth even in his own day and . . . much energy has been spent over the past three centuries in either strengthening or denouncing this myth . . . the Galileo myth has given him the peculiar status of official martyr-saint of science.

Some of this mythic character comes about because the boundaries of the affair were hazy. It was not simply a dispute between scientific and theological perspectives; it was in large part a political battle, with the leaven of temperamental personalities thrown in for good measure. And those events must be viewed from the perspective of the seventeenth century, a time of bitter religious strife, when anywhere in Europe, whether Catholic or Protestant locale, the distinction between civil and ecclesiastical authority was very slim indeed.

The scientific issue was called "heliocentrism" (from the Greek word for the sun, "helios"), and certainly was not original with Galileo. Its most famous proponent had been Nicholas Copernicus, a Polish astronomer—and Catholic priest—who had published a lengthy treatise on heliocentrism entitled "On the Revolutions of Celestial Bodies" nearly seventy years earlier, in 1543. And Copernicus was himself reviving the far more ancient proposal, made by Aristarchus of Samos in the third century BCE, that all of the planets, including the earth, revolve around the sun. But the heliocentric view won few adherents either in antiquity or in later days. The geocentric system, with the earth at the center of the universe, was the belief that most people, wise and simple alike, shared. It was the foundation of Aristotle's Physics, and the system was later brought to a high degree of sophistication by the great astronomer Ptolemy. This cosmology was then adopted by Christian philosophers and theologians, since it had much to recommend it. It agreed with common sense (with one's own eyes, one can see the sun move around the earth). It reconciled most of the observable phenomena of astronomy. And it best of all, it seemed to conform to the words of Scripture.

So a contrary view (that the earth moved around the sun), which seemed to make the Scriptures false, was bound to cause controversy. And, in fact, when Copernicus published his work in 1543, he got his share of censure. Luther, for instance, was strongly opposed to Copernicus's theories:

> People give ear to an upstart astrologer who strove to show that the earth revolves ... this fool wishes to reverse the entire science of astronomy; but Sacred Scripture tells us that Joshua commanded the sun to stand still, not the earth.

Francesco Villamena, *Galileo Galilei*

The controversy lay dormant until 1613, when Galileo, now quite famous, publicly embraced the heliocentric theory, based on his observations of the skies. He won support from many sides, including many churchmen. He also won bitter condemnation as well. Historian Stillman Drake notes how one Dominican priest, Thomas Caccini, thoroughly denounced Galileo, Copernicus, and all mathematics; and in rebuttal, another Dominican priest apologized to Galileo for Caccini's words, regretting that "such stupidities should have been uttered by a member of his own religion." Finally, in 1616, the controversy came to a head, when the Holy Office, the guardian of Catholic orthodoxy, decided to condemn this belief:

> ... the doctrine of the mobility of the earth and the immobility of the sun ... is false and completely contrary to the divine Scriptures ...

The basis of this condemnation rested on a subtle distinction, namely, that Galileo's work had crossed the fine line between a scientific theory as a hypothesis, and the same theory as a true description of the world as it actually was. While we today might find this distinction a shadowy one, it was of paramount importance then. Segre notes how the same fine distinction had been equally important for Copernicus:

> Whether Copernicus intended his model to be a true description of the world, not simply a mathematical device that more accurately predicted celestial events, are topics of wide scholarly debate.

Also, for Galileo to propose turning the known universe upside down would require scientific proof, not simply assertion. Cardinal Robert Bellarmine, a leading theologian, observed that revising the traditional view, and rethinking the Bible, would require just that—proof:

> I say that if there were a true demonstration that the sun was in the center of the universe ... then it would be necessary to proceed with great caution in explaining the passages of Scripture which seemed contrary ... But I do not believe that there is any such demonstration; none has been shown to me.

And, in fact, though we now have voluminous scientific evidence about the solar system, and send satellites around the earth and robots to Mars, we easily forget how little of this evidence was then available to Galileo. As Jerome Langford notes:

> Though he tried, Galileo did not prove the earth moves. He did succeed in showing that it is not impossible ... Unfortunately, the kind of evidence with which he could have won the day simply was not available. Such proof presupposed a new physics, the gravitational laws of Newton, the experiments of Foucault, the parallax observed in 1838 by Bessel.

So there the matter rested for several years. In 1623, a new Pope, Urban VIII, was elected. Urban had been a supporter of Galileo, and now urged him to continue his research, though in an impartial and hypothetical sense: Urban pointedly did not revoke the decree of 1616. Eventually, in 1632, Galileo published his definitive work, "Dialogue on the Great World Systems." It takes the form of a conversation among three characters during four "days" of scientific debate. In this work,

Galileo presented as conclusively as he could his argument for the Copernican theory.

The "Dialogue" was anything but impartial and hypothetical. Galileo had gone much farther than the Pope had suggested, and was obviously intending to persuade the reader of the essential truth of the heliocentric view. He made two terrible miscalculations. First, he really had no better proof than before. But the greater error, which had nothing to do with science or theology, was that one of the book's characters, the one who speaks for the orthodox geocentric view, was named Simplicio; this character often appears foolish, and hopelessly outweighed by the scientific evidence. Many people believed that Simplicio was intended to be a caricature of the Pope (the Pope himself thought so), and, in fact, it was hard not to agree with this interpretation. With such a perceived betrayal of the Pope's support, and in light of such a public insult, some sort of reaction was virtually guaranteed. Galileo was summoned to Rome, where between April and June 1633, a series of hearings was held. When all was said and done, Galileo bowed to the inevitable; he had gambled and lost. As Giorgio de Santillana puts it:

> [Galileo] had realized at last that the authorities were not interested in truth, but only in authority. They did not expect him to change his mind
> . . .

During the Spring months, he made a series of formal statements, called "depositions." In the second one especially (the first of the following Pages) we can see Galileo vainly trying to submit to ecclesiastical authority without fully abandoning his position; until its last paragraph, he admits nothing except an error in rhetorical stress. But in its last paragraph, Galileo capitulates: he recants his belief in heliocentrism. And several weeks later, on June 22, Galileo was commanded to make a full and formal "abjuration" of his theories. This is by far the most forceful of his refutations of the heliocentric theory; it is the second of the following Pages.

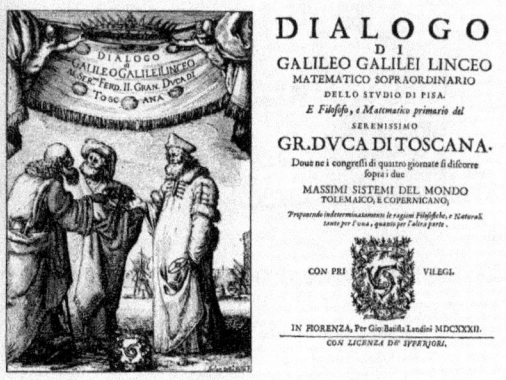

Frontispiece and title page of Galileo's "Dialogues"

The end of this tale, like any proper Greek drama, has its quota of irony. Galileo's abjuration took place in the convent of Santa Maria Sopra Minerva. This chapel, dating from the eighth century, still stands, and tourists still admire its famous artwork, Michelangelo's "Christ the Redeemer," that stands near the altar. The irony lies in the fact that the church had been erected near the site of the old Roman temple to the goddess Minerva. And on June 22, 1633, the date of his bitter abjuration, probably even Galileo failed to recall that Minerva was the goddess of wisdom, technology, and invention.

There is also an epilogue. On October 31, 1992, three hundred fifty-nine years after Galileo's abjuration, a Pontifical Commission created by Pope John Paul II produced a report that admitted that Galileo's judges had "believed, quite wrongly" that Copernicanism was a threat to Christianity, and that in condemning Galileo they had made a "subjective error of judgment."

Slow but sure moves the might of the Gods (Euripides)

Galileo offering his Telescope to Urania, goddess of astronomy

Galileo's Second Deposition (April 30, 1633)

For several days I have been thinking continuously and directly about the interrogations I underwent on the 16th of this month, and in particular about the question whether sixteen years ago I had been prohibited, by order of the Holy Office, from holding, defending, and teaching in any way whatever the opinion, then condemned, of the earth's motion and sun's stability. It dawned on me to reread my printed Dialogue, which over the last three years I had not even looked at. I wanted to check very carefully whether, against my purest intention, through my oversight, there might have fallen from my pen not only something enabling readers or superiors to infer a defect of disobedience on my part, but also other details through which one might think of me as a transgressor of the orders of Holy Church.

Being at liberty, through the generous approval of superiors, to send one of my servants for errands, I managed to get a copy of my book, and I started to read it with the greatest concentration and to examine it in the most detailed manner. Not having seen it for so long, I found it almost a new book by another author. Now, I freely confess that it appeared to me in several places to be written in such a way that a reader, not aware of my intention, would have had reason to form the opinion that the arguments for the false side, which I intended to confute, were so stated as to be capable of convincing because of their strength, rather than being easy to answer.

In particular, two arguments, one based on sunspots and the other on the tides, are presented favorably to the reader as being strong and powerful, more than would seem proper for someone who deemed them to be inconclusive and wanted to confute them, as indeed I inwardly and truly did, and do hold them to be inconclusive and refutable. As an excuse for myself, within myself, for having fallen into an error so foreign to my intention, I was not completely satisfied with saying that when one presents arguments for the opposite side with the intention of confuting them, they must be explained in the fairest way and not be made out of straw to the disadvantage of the opponent, especially when one is writing in dialogue form. Being dissatisfied with this excuse, as I said, I resorted to that of the natural gratification everyone feels for his own subtleties and for showing himself to be cleverer than the average man, by finding ingenious and apparent considerations of probability even in favor of false propositions. Nevertheless—even though to use Cicero's words, "I am more desirous of glory than is suitable"—if I had to write out the same arguments now, there is no doubt that I would weaken them in such a way that they could not appear to exhibit a force which they really and essentially lack. My error then was, and I confess it, one of vain ambition, pure ignorance, and inadvertence. This is as much as I need to say on this occasion, and it occurred to me as I reread my book.

And for greater confirmation that I neither did hold nor do hold as true the condemned opinion of the earth's motion and the sun's stability, is, as I desire, I am granted the possibility and the time to prove it more clearly, I am ready to do so. The occasion for it is readily available since in the book already published the speakers agree that after a certain time they should meet again to discuss various physical problems other than the subject already dealt with. Hence, with this pretext to add one of two other Days, I promise to reconsider the arguments already presented in favor of the said false and condemned opinion and to confute them in the most effective way that the blessed God will enable me. So I beg this Holy Tribunal to cooperate with me in this good resolution by granting me the permission to put it into practice. I Galileo Galilei, affirm the above.

Galileo's Abjuration (June 22, 1633)

I Galileo, son of the late Vincenzo Galilei of Florence, seventy years of age, arraigned personally for judgement, kneeling before you Most Eminent and Most Reverend Cardinals Inquisitors-General against heretical depravity in all of Christendom, having before my eyes and touching with my hands the Holy Gospels, swear that I have always believed, I believe now, and with God's help I will believe in the future all that the Holy Catholic and Apostolic Church holds, preaches, and teaches. However, whereas, after having been judicially instructed with injunction by the Holy Office to abandon completely the false opinion that the sun is the center of the world and does not move and the earth is not the center of the world and moves. and not to hold, defend, or teach this false doctrine in any way whatever, orally or in writing; and after having been notified that this doctrine is contrary to Holy Scripture; I wrote and published a book in which I treat of this already condemned doctrine and adduce very effective reasons in its favor without refuting them in any way; therefore, I have been judged vehemently suspected of heresy, namely of having held and believed that the sun is the center of the world and motionless and the earth is not the center and moves.

Therefore, desiring to remove from the minds of Your Eminences and every faithful Christian the vehement suspicion, rightly conceived against me with a sincere heart and unfeigned faith I abjure, curse, and detest the above-mentioned errors and heresies, and in general each and every other error, heresy, and sect contrary to the Holy Church; and I swear that in the future I will never again say or assert, orally or in writing, anything which might cause a similar suspicion about me; on the contrary, if I should come to know any heretic or anyone suspected of heresy, I will denounce him to this Holy Office, or to the Inquisitor or Ordinary of the place where I happen to be.

Furthermore, I swear and promise to comply with and observe completely all the penances which have been or will be imposed upon me by this Holy Office; and should I fail to keep any of these promises and oaths, which God forbid, I submit myself to all the penalties and punishments imposed and promulgated by the sacred canons and other particular and general laws against similar delinquents. So help me God and these Holy Gospels of His, which I touch with my hands.

I, the above-mentioned Galileo Galilei, have abjured, sworn, promised, and obligated myself, as above; and in witness of the truth I have signed with my own hand the present document of abjuration and have recited it word for word in Rome, at the convent of the Minerva, this twenty-second day of June, 1633.

I Galileo Galilei, have abjured as above, by my own hand.

The First Folio

As I noted in my opening words, I felt compelled to omit selections of great literature from this volume, a painful but pragmatic choice. It was a happy discovery, therefore, that one of the most significant Pages in the volume should be about great literature, namely the Preface to the first full edition of Shakespeare's plays, usually called the First Folio.

The importance of the First Folio can hardly be overstated. Shakespeare is one of the very few imaginative writers whose position at the apex of literary greatness is undisputed. Homer, probably, and Dante, perhaps, are in the same small circle. But for most other great talents, even such giants as Goethe, Pushkin, Cervantes, or Moliere, it is unlikely that singling any of them as Shakespeare's equal would pass without disagreement from one quarter or another. Harry Levin aptly describes Shakespeare's importance not only as a literary figure, but in wider terms:

> Shakespeare's works have ... been accorded a place in our culture above and beyond their topmost place in our literature. They have been virtually canonized as humanistic scriptures, the tested residue of pragmatic wisdom, a general collection of quotable texts, and usable examples. Reprinted, reedited, commented on, and translated into most languages, they have preempted more space on the library shelves than the books of—or about— any other author.

The First Folio is so named because the printed sheets were folded once, then sewn together. (Publications that used two folds per sheet were called "quartos," and those with three folds were "octavos.") When the First Folio was issued in 1623, numerous copies, versions, corruptions, and adaptations of Shakespeare's plays were in existence. Nineteen plays had been published individually (generally as quartos). Some of these were reasonably accurate (called by scholars the "good quartos") while others, based on various actors' reconstructions or recollections, were much less true (and called, surprisingly enough, the "bad quartos").

Bringing together the texts of the plays into the First Folio was the work of John Heminge and Henry Condell, the last survivors of Shakespeare's acting company. They had worked with Shakespeare for two decades, and undertook the task of restoring the authentic texts of the plays both to remove the corruptions as well as make the works known to a wider public. These two men were actors, and their edition was essentially an acting edition. They gathered together thirty-six of the thirty-eight plays generally ascribed to Shakespeare. ("Pericles" and "The Two Noble Kinsmen" do not appear.).

Title page of the First Folio

While subsequent scholarship has pointed out many errors, the First Folio is probably close to what Shakespeare actually wrote for the stage. Shakespearean scholar W.W. Greg states:

> On the whole they performed their task in a reasonably conscientious manner and at times went to considerable trouble to provide their readers with what they believed to be an authentic text.

Subsequent to the First Folio, a Second Folio was issued in 1632, a third in 1634, and a fourth in 1685.

From that point a torrent of editions, revisions, and restorations has flowed (and continues to flow) unabated. Indeed, buried in the earlier statement from Levin are the words "reprinted" and "reedited." Behind these innocent two words lies a vast army of scholars that has labored for nearly four centuries, engaged in the enormous enterprise aimed at establishing once and for all the final, true, and authentic version of these plays. (And as with any army, they bring with them the inevitable camp followers who revel in conspiracy theories about Shakespeare's works being written by almost anyone except William Shakespeare.)

Two last notes. The 1623 publication also contained a memorial poem by Ben Jonson, containing one of the loveliest expressions of admiration ever penned:

> He was not of an age, but for all time!
> And all the muses still were in their prime
> When, like Apollo, he came forth to warm
> Our ears, or like a Mercury to charm!

And finally, if any claims about the importance of the First Folio might still seem inflated, I add the following estimation from Charles Eliot:

> When one considers what would have been lost had it not been for the enterprise of [Heminge and Condell], it seems safe to say that the volume they introduced by the quaint and not too accurate preface, is the most important book in the imaginative literature of the world."

Well said. Now on to the Page itself. The Preface opens with a letter to the Earl of Pembroke and the Earl of Montgomery, followed by the body of the Preface, addressed to "the great variety of Readers." The variant spellings are maintained, and where impenetrable to modern readers, have explanatory notes in parentheses.

Shakespeare performing before Queen Elizabeth and her court

MR. William
SHAKESPEARES
Comedies, Histories & Tragedies,
Published according to the True Original Copies
London Printed by Ifaac Iaggard, and Ed, Bount. 1623

TO THE MOST NOBLE AND INCOMPARABLE PAIRE OF BRETHREN
WILLIAM Earle of Pembroke, &c;. Lord Chamberlaine to the Kings most Excellent Majesty.
AND
PHILIP Earle of Montgomery,&c;. Gentleman of his Majesties Bed-Chamber.
Both Knights of the most Noble Order of the Garter, and our singular good L O R D S.

Right Honourable,

Whilst we studie to be thankful in our particular for the many favors we have received from your L.L. [*Lordships*], we are fallen upon the ill fortune, to mingle two the most diverse things that can be: feare, and rashnesse—rashnesse in the enterprize, and feare of the successe. For, when we valew the places your H.H. sustaine, we cannot but know their dignity greater, then to descend to the reading of these trifles: and, while we name them trifles, we have depriv'd our selves of the defence of our Dedication. But since your L.L. have beene pleas'd to thinke these trifles some-thing, heeretofore; and have prosequuted both them, and their Authour living, with so much favour: we hope, that (they out-living him, and he not having the fate, common with some, to be exequutor to his owne writings) you will use the like indulgence toward them, you have done unto their parent. There is a great difference, whether any Booke choose his Patrones, or finde them: This hath done both. For, so much were your L.L. likings of the severall parts, when they were acted, as before they were published, the Volume ask'd to be yours. We have but collected them, and done an office to the dead, to procure his Orphanes, Guardians; without ambition either of selfe-profit, or fame: onely to keepe the memory of so worthy a Friend, & Fellow alive, as was our S H A K E S P E A R E , by humble offer of his playes, to your most noble patronage. Wherein, as we have justly observed, no man to come neere your L.L. but with a kind of religious addresse; it hath bin the height of our care, who are the Presenters, to make the present worthy of your H.H. by the perfection.

But, there we must also crave our abilities to be considerd, my Lords. We cannot go beyond our owne powers. Country hands reach foorth milke, creame, fruites, or what they have : and many Nations (we have heard) that had not gummes & incense, obtained their requests with a leavened Cake. It was no fault to approach their Gods, by what meanes they could: And the most, though meanest, of thins are made more precious, when they are dedicated to Temples. In that name therefore, we most humbly consecrate to your H.H. these remaines of your servant Shakespeare; that what delight is in them, may be ever your

L.L. the reputation his, & the faults ours, if any be committed, by a payre so carefull to shew their gratitude both to the living, and the dead, as is.

Your Lordshippes most bounden,

JOHN HEMINGE.
HENRY CONDELL.

To the great Variety of Readers.

From the most able, to him that can but spell: There you are number'd. We had rather you were weighed. Especially, when the fate of all Books depends upon your capacities: and not of your heads alone, but of your purses. Well! It is now public, and you will stand for your priviledges we know: to read, and censure. Do so, but buy it first. That doth best commend a Book, the Stationer says. Then, how odds soever your brains be, or your wisdoms, make your license the same, and spare not. Judge your sixe-pen'worth, your shillings worth, your five shillings worth at a time, or higher, so you rise to the just rates, and welcome. But, when ever you do, Buy. Censure will not drive a Trade, or make the Jacke go. And though you be a Magistrate of wit, and sit on the Stage at Black-Friares, or the Cock-pit, to arraigne Plays daily, know, these Plays have had their trial already, and stood out all Appeals; and do now come forth quitted rather by a Decree of Court, then any purchased Letters of commentation.

It had been a thing, we confess, worthy to have been wished, that the Author himselfe had lived to have set forth, and overseen his own writings; But since it hath been ordain'd otherwise, and he by death departed from that right, we pay you do not envy his Friends, the office of their care, and pain, to have collected and publish'd them; and so to have publish'd them, as where (before) you were abused with diverse stolen, and surreptitious copies, maimed and deformed by the frauds and stealths of iniurious imposters, that exposed them; even those, are now offer'd to your view cured, and perfect of their limbs; and all the rest, absolute in their numbers, as he conceived them. Who, as he was a happy imitator of Nature, was a most gentle expresser of it. His mind and hand went together: And what he thought, he uttered with that easiness, that we have scarce received from him a blot in his papers. But it is not our province, who only gather his works, and give them to you, to praise him. It is yours that read him. And there we hope, to your diverse capacities, you will find enough, both to draw, and hold you; for his wit can no more lie hid, then it could be lost. Read him, therefore; and again, and again; And if then you do not like him, surely you are in some manifest danger, not to understand him. And so we leave you to other of his Friends, whom if you need, can be your guides: if you need them not, you can lead your selves, and others. And such Readers we wish him.

Johann Sebastian Bach: Two Dedications

We sometimes hear the claim that music is the greatest of the arts. This is, of course, a hopelessly unprovable statement. Still, many people would at least agree that music contributes, in some undefinable way, something utterly necessary to one's humanity. When Shakespeare has Lorenzo say:

> The man that hath no music in himself,
> Nor is not moved with concord of sweet sounds,
> Is fit for treasons, stratagems, and spoils . . .
> Let no such man be trusted. (Merchant of Venice, V,i),

he echoes a sentiment that has been expressed often, from the most ancient times to the present.

Because music has such transcendent power, the creators of great music, men who have changed our lives profoundly, have a special mystique that attends them. While we might speak glowingly of Rembrandt or Da Vinci as men of genius, they remain human. But the names of Mozart or Beethoven are often intoned almost as though they were quasi-divine beings, channels to us mere mortals of a celestial language that no one but they can hear.

And so it is often disconcerting to find out the details about the lives of these great composers. Quasi-divine they may have been. But Mozart was inordinately fond of vulgar and scatological humor; Beethoven, especially in his last, unhearing years, was eccentric, irascible, and rude. And Bach, the great Johann Sebastian, about whom Albert Schweitzer could say "German art . . . comes to completion in him and is exhausted in him," turns out to be a most human person indeed. Reproved by the civil authorities for brawling on one occasion, tossed in jail for a month on another, old J.S. definitely had a headstrong side to him. And he must have had a tangy side as well; according to Bach scholar Hans David:

> [Bach, a church organist] could dryly point out that a healthy year had deprived him of many of the funeral fees he might normally have expected . . . [or complain to a cousin] that high import duties and transportation costs made his gift of a cask of wine hardly worth receiving.

It is equally disconcerting, particularly from today's perspective, to understand the social position that a man like Bach occupied. His career took place in the mid-eighteenth century, before the social upheavals that leveled the old aristocratic order. In Bach's day, a composer might well be famous, but he was a commoner and an artisan. He might be favored by princes and kings, but he was always at their service. It was not until the nineteenth century that we see the cult of the artist-genius, the lonely individual possessed by a divine madness, who lives outside the social norms. And only toward the end of the nineteenth century could anyone imagine such excesses as those enjoyed by Richard Wagner, who could virtually snap his fingers and the King of Bavaria would jump.

For Bach, in the early 1700s, such behavior was unthinkable. He was a craftsman who did his job; that job was making music, and it was his by family tradition. Whatever he truly thought of his own talents, he was not effusive. According to Charles Sanford Terry, when Bach was asked about the secret of his musical powers, his response was "I worked hard."

We can clearly see, in his letters and dedications, the social conventions that Bach followed in dealing with his royal patrons; the following Pages are the dedications by Bach of two of his greatest works, the Brandenburg Concerti and the Musical Offering. Bach addresses his aristocratic listeners as though they had a level of musical skill and artistic discernment far in excess of his own, the humble Bach who merely wrote the notes. The flowery, exorbitant language Bach uses is startling when one first encounters it. The apparent self-abasement ("... the small talent which Heaven has given me for music ...") from so great a genius is unexpected; we certainly do not believe that Bach thought it was true. But that is The Way It Was at the time, and Bach, at least as shown in these dedications, was quite willing to accept the existing conventions of class and rank.

In the first Page, Bach dedicates a set of six instrumental concertos to the Margrave of Brandenburg, a person about whom we know very little. The Margrave may have been a paragon of virtue, or a churl. But that he is remembered at all is entirely due to Bach's dedication of six concertos to him, a fact that music historians often chuckle over. As Archibald Davison put it:

> I have often thought that it would have been the neatest stroke of poetic justice if [the Margrave] could have known that for posterity, his sole distinction would lie in his having possessed the first autograph copy of the immortal Brandenburg Concertos.

And we do not even know whether the Margrave liked these pieces; it is possible that he never heard them. Audiences today, however, know the Brandenburg

Concertos well. Written in one of Bach's most fertile periods, they are wonderful works of genius. By turns jubilant, serene, and majestic, they remain among the most popular works from the eighteenth century.

The second dedication came twenty-six years later, and though similar in wording, it reflected a very different circumstance. Frederick the Great, King of Prussia and a major figure in the history of the eighteenth century, was a devoted lover of music. Frederick also had a deep and abiding respect for Bach. So, in 1747, when Bach (then near the end of his life) visited Frederick's court at Potsdam, it was an important event for both men. The King took Bach throughout the palace, proudly showing him his collection of instruments. Then Frederick himself played a theme (a short, rather sinuous melody) for Bach, and challenged him to improvise a three-part fugue on the theme; Bach did so to the King's delight. Frederick then gave Bach a greater challenge, to improvise a six-part fugue on the same melody. At this, Bach demurred, suggesting that he was not up to the occasion.[35] But Bach promised to compose such a piece, and to send it to the King.

In the next several weeks, Bach created a dazzling royal gift. He sent the King the six-part fugue that Frederick had requested, but surrounded it by a set of highly complex canons, a sonata, and one more fugue, each of them based on the "royal" theme; all in all, a staggering display of compositional skill. Called the "Musical Offering," this work occupies an exalted place in the musical cosmos, and has few peers in the literature of music (though another of Bach's last works, the "Art of the Fugue" is indeed one of those peers). Unlike the Margrave's silence about his concertos, King Frederick's reaction to Bach's tribute is known to us. More than a quarter century later, in a conversation with the Austrian ambassador, Frederick fondly recalled the occasion of Bach's visit to Potsdam, and spoke glowingly of Bach and his great musical mastery.

History echoes Frederick's sentiment. Bach's works stand at the pinnacle of musical genius, and more than two and one-half centuries after his death, he remains a presence in our daily lives. He was a commoner, an artisan, and a most human individual. Yet he changed the world in a way that few mortals have, and through his works the rest of us share in his genius. Not a "quasi-divine being," perhaps; but a man who touched the sky.

---

[35] It is extremely difficult to describe in non-technical terms the immense complexity of these two challenges. Suffice to say that improvising even a three-part fugue (on any theme at all) with any degree of quality is beyond the skill of most musicians today. And on that occasion, Bach actually did improvise a six-part fugue for the King, but on a theme of his own, not the "royal" theme.

Elias Gottlob Haussmann, *Johann Sebastian Bach*

Title Page of the Brandenburg Concerti

To His Royal Highness, My Lord Christian Louis Elector of Brandenburg, &c, &c, &c

Your Royal Highness,

As I had a couple of years ago the pleasure of appearing before Your Royal Highness, by virtue of Your Highness' commands, and as I noticed then that Your Highness took some pleasure in the small talents which Heaven has given me for Music, and as in taking leave of Your Royal Highness, Your Highness deigned to honor me with the command to send Your Highness some pieces of my Composition: I have then in accordance with Your Highness' most gracious orders taken the liberty of rendering my most humble duty to Your Royal Highness with the present Concertos, which I have adapted to several instruments; begging Your HIghness most humbly not to judge their imperfections with the rigor of the fine and delicate taste which the whole world knows Your Highness has for musical pieces; but rather to infer from them in benign Consideration the profound respect and the most humble obedience which I try to show Your Highness therewith. For the rest, Sire, I beg Your Royal Highness very humbly to have the goodness to continue Your Highness' gracious favor toward me, and to be assured that nothing is so close to my heart as the wish that I may be employed on occasions more worthy of Your Royal Highness and of Your Highness' service—I, who am without equal in zeal am,

Sire, Your Royal HIghness' most humble and obedient servant.

Jean Sebastien Bach

Cothen, March 24, 1721

Frederick the Great's Palace at the Sanssouci Park

Most gracious King,

In deepest humility I dedicate herewith to Your Majesty a musical offering, the noblest part of which derives from Your Majesty's own august hand. With awesome pleasure I still remember the very special Royal grace when, some time ago, during my visit to Potsdam, Your Majesty's Self deigned to play to me a theme for a fugue upon the clavier, and at the same time charged me most graciously to carry it out in Your Majesty's most august presence. To obey Your Majesty's command was my most humble duty. I noticed very soon, however, that for lack of necessary preparation, the execution of the task did not fare as well as such an excellent theme demanded. I resolved therefore and promptly pledged myself to work out this right Royal theme more fully, and then make it known to the world. This resolve has now been carried out as well as possible, and it has none other than this irreproachable intent, to glorify, if only in a small point, the fame of monarch whose greatness and power, as in all the sciences of war and peace, so especially in music, everyone must admire and revere. I make bold to add this most humble request: may Your Majesty deign to dignify the present modest labor with a gracious acceptance, and continue to grant Your Majesty's most Royal grace to

Your Majesty's

most humble and obedient servant,

the author.

Leipzig, July 7, 1747

Beethoven's Heiligenstadt Testament

Ludwig van Beethoven was born in December 1770. His musical career got off to an auspicious start, with his first work published at age 13. At 21, he moved to Vienna, then the capital of the musical world, and studied with Haydn, and soon became widely known as a virtuoso pianist. Unlike Haydn, who spent most of his career as an employee of wealthy noblemen, Beethoven was admired and even courted by them; for example, Prince Lichnowsky, a Prussian nobleman, sought to become his patron. In one sense, his future looked bright indeed.

Yet even before his 30th birthday, in 1800, he realized that he was losing his hearing; thus began several years of vainly searching for some sort of cure from his ailment. By 1801, he had begun complaining about a continual whistling sound in his ears that was constant. Finally, in 1802, on the advice of his doctor, he traveled to Heiligenstadt, a small village about eight miles from Vienna, to see if the peace and quiet of the countryside might facilitate some surcease from his malady.

Sadly, it brought no respite. But while there, he wrote the following Page, a painful outpouring of his agony and despair about losing the one sense on which his very existence depended. It takes the form of a letter to his two brothers, Carl and Johann, and gives us an unprecedented insight into the inner life of a great genius. The text describes his increasing sense of isolation, and a growing terror and fear of death.

In the following year, Beethoven premiered an oratorio entitled "*Christus Am Oelberge*" (Christ on the Mount of Olives) describing the period in Christ's life during his arrest. Beethoven scholar Barry Cooper, along with many Beethoven scholars, sees a clear parallel between Beethoven's depiction of the suffering of Christ, and his own personal agony as revealed in the painful words of the Heiligenstadt Testament. As Cooper describes it:

> The subject matter of Beethoven's oratorio *Christus Am Oelberge* . . . is unusual in that it does not cover the whole of Christ's Passion but concentrates entirely on the scene on the Mount of Olives, just before and during his arrest. The text, by Franz Xaver Huber, places much emphasis on Christ's agony and suffering, his struggle against adversity, and his ultimate triumph through his love of mankind. . . . Both texts [the oratorio and the Testament] contain ideas of extreme and undeserved suffering, expressions of terror, fear of imminent death, and a sense of isolation and loneliness . . . there is a certain stoicism and resignation to fate, and a willingness to fight the fierce battles that lie ahead, even if they end in death . . . And there is the

anticipation of ultimate triumph over adversity, with the struggle and agony being resolved in death and eternal joy.

Musicologists have analyzed the Testament closely, because in spite of the despair that it describes, this time in Beethoven's life is the period when his genius truly sprang forth. Even in the pain and suffering he endured at Heiligenstadt, he nonetheless began work on the Third Symphony, ("Eroica"), [36] which is arguably the first of his truly monumental compositions. It broke many of the boundaries of the classical symphony as practiced by Mozart and Haydn (the first movement alone is as long as many classical symphonies). Though it has some reflection of his tragic despair – the second movement is a funeral march – the work exhibits boundless energy, and novelty of form and orchestration.

And thereafter, for nearly the next quarter century, Beethoven poured out masterwork after masterwork. In spite of finally becoming totally deaf (in 1819, seven years after Heiligenstadt), he composed several more symphonies, including the majestic Ninth Symphony, which also shattered the boundary between symphony and oratorio. He composed amazing string quartets, of which the final four are among the highest pinnacles of chamber music. He produced piano concertos, many of which are still the mainstays of a pianist's concert life. And he wrote the glorious *Missa Solemnis*, about which musicologist Hugh Macdonald wrote*:*

> He regarded it as his greatest work. At the head of the score he wrote: "Von Herzen – möge es wieder zu Herzen gehen!" (From the heart: may it go to the heart). If any work from his last years reveals Beethoven's complicated view of existence, it is the *Missa solemnis*, more than the Ninth Symphony, which is a vigorous paean for human brotherhood and aspiration, and more than the late string quartets, which are too far removed from the certainties of language to be lightly interpreted with any human reference.

All in all, a mighty recovery indeed from the depths of despair he felt those long years before in Heiligenstadt; one further indication of the greatness of this titanic man.

Some interesting points about the text of the Testament. The document is written to both of his brothers, but only Carl's name appears, while Johann's name is omitted. There have been various conjectures that this may have derived from

---

[36] The symphony was originally intended to be dedicated to Napoleon, as the original manuscript shows. Beethoven considered Napoleon to be the embodiment of the anti-monarchial spirit of the French Revolution. As he was completing the manuscript, however, Beethoven learned that Napoleon had been crowned Emperor, and flying into a rage, changed the dedication to read "Heroic Symphony, Composed to celebrate the memory of a great man."

Beethoven's unhappy relationship with his father, an alcoholic abuser, and whose name was also Johann.

The Testament contains a reference that is unfamiliar to most readers: "... I hope my determination will remain firm to endure until it please the inexorable parcae to break the thread ..." The Parcae were the Roman deities that were descended from the Greek Moirai; these are usually called in English the Fates. One of these (Nona) was believed to have spun the original thread of one's life, the second (Decima) used her rod to measure the thread, and the third (Morta) chose the time and manner of one's death, at which point she would break the thread.

And finally, the text of the Testament is written as a single long paragraph, which I would have preferred to have broken into several smaller paragraphs. But a glance through the literature shows that no editor that I have encountered has dared to tamper with the original layout Beethoven gave us. I surmised that in dealing with any work of Beethoven, even his prose, tinkering with it would probably be a poor decision.

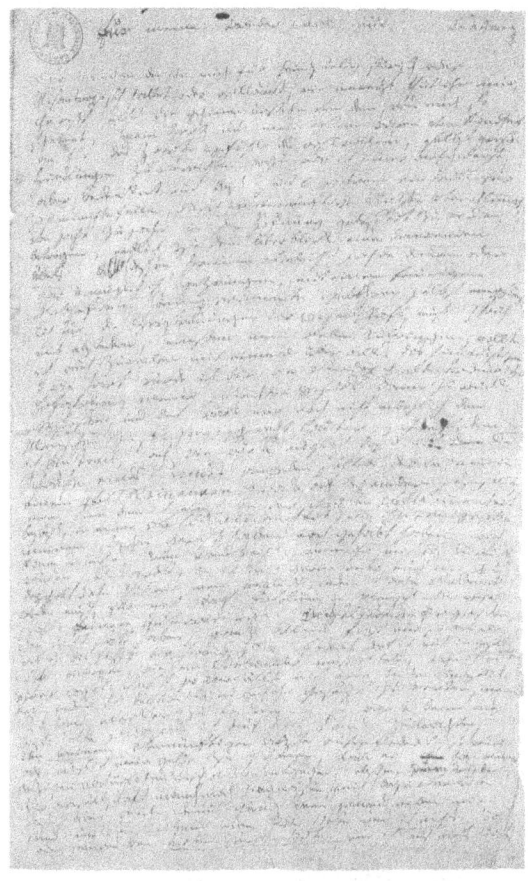

Handwritten text of the Heiligenstadt Testament

For my brothers Carl and [Johann] Beethoven

O ye men who think or say that I am malevolent, stubborn or misanthropic, how greatly do ye wrong me, you do not know the secret causes of my seeming, from childhood my heart and mind were disposed to the gentle feelings of good will, I was even ever eager to accomplish great deeds, but reflect now that for six years I have been a hopeless case, aggravated by senseless physicians, cheated year after year in the hope of improvement, finally compelled to face the prospect of a *lasting malady* (whose cure will take years or, perhaps, be impossible), born with an ardent and lively temperament, even susceptible to the diversions of society, I was compelled early to isolate myself, to live in loneliness, when I at times tried to forget all this, O how harshly was I repulsed by the doubly sad experience of my bad hearing, and yet it was impossible for me to say to men speak louder, shout, for I am deaf. Ah how could I possibly admit such an infirmity in the one sense which should have been more perfect in me than in others, a sense which I once possessed in highest perfection, a perfection such as few surely in my profession enjoy or have enjoyed—O I cannot do it, therefore forgive me when you see me draw back when I would gladly mingle with you, my misfortune is doubly painful because it must lead to my being misunderstood, for me there can be no recreations in society of my fellows, refined intercourse, mutual exchange of thought, only just as little as the greatest needs command may I mix with society. I must live like an exile, if I approach near to people a hot terror seizes upon me, a fear that I may be subjected to the danger of letting my condition be observed—thus it has been during the past year which I spent in the country, commanded by my intelligent physician to spare my hearing as much as possible, in this almost meeting my natural disposition, although I sometimes ran counter to it yielding to my inclination for society, but what a humiliation when one stood beside me and heard a flute in the distance and *I heard nothing,* or someone heard *the shepherd singing* and again I heard nothing, such incidents brought me to the verge of despair, but little more and I would have put an end to my life—only art it was that withheld me, ah it seemed impossible to leave the world until I had produced all that I felt called upon me to produce, and so I endured this wretched existence—truly wretched, an excitable body which a sudden change can throw from the best into the worst state—Patience—it is said that I must now choose for my guide, I have done so, I hope my determination will remain firm to endure until it please the inexorable parcae to break the thread, perhaps I shall get better, perhaps not, I am prepared. Forced already in my 28th year to become a philosopher, O it is not easy, less easy for the artist than for anyone else—Divine One thou lookest into my inmost soul, thou knowest it, thou knowest that love of man and desire to do good live therein. O men, when some day you read these words, reflect that ye did me wrong and let the unfortunate one comfort himself and find one of his kind who despite all obstacles of nature yet did all that was in his power to be accepted among worthy artists and men. You my brothers Carl and [Johann] as soon as I am dead if Dr. Schmid is still alive ask him in my name to describe my malady and attach this document to the history of my illness so that so far as possible at least the world may become reconciled with me after my death. At the same time I declare you two to be the heirs to my small fortune (if so it can be called), divide it fairly, bear with and help each other, what injury you have done me you know was long ago forgiven. To you brother Carl I give special thanks for the attachment you have displayed towards me of late. It is my wish that your lives be better and freer from care than I have had, recommend virtue to your children, it alone can give happiness, not money, I speak from experience, it was virtue that upheld me in misery, to it next to my art I owe the fact that I did not end my life with suicide.—Farewell and love each other—I thank all my friends, particularly *Prince Lichnowsky* and *Professor Schmid*—I desire that the instruments from Prince L. be preserved by one of you but let no quarrel result from this, so soon as they can serve you better purpose sell them, how glad will I be if I can still be helpful to you in my grave—with joy I hasten towards death—if it comes before I shall have had an opportunity to show all my artistic capacities it will still come too early for me despite my hard fate and I shall probably wish it had come later—but even then I am satisfied, will it not free me from my state of endless suffering? Come when thou will I shall meet thee bravely.—Farewell and do not wholly forget me when I am dead, I deserve this of you in having often in life thought of you how to make you happy, be so -

Heiligenstadt
October 6, 1802

Ludwig van Beethowen

Joseph Karl Stieler, *Portrait of Beethoven*

Franz Grillparzer: Oration at Beethoven's Funeral

When Beethoven died in 1827, the whole German nation mourned. Men openly wept, and editorials in newspapers lamented the great national loss. His funeral was a state event, attended by 20,000 people. All of Vienna's leading musicians were present; Schubert and Czerny were among the torch bearers.

It may seem unlikely today to imagine such an outpouring of grief at a musician's death. But we should not deceive ourselves; we have only to recall those occasions when a highly popular musician of our own time dies—Presley and Lennon come to mind—to see that things are really not much different today, and that musicians are far more significant in our national consciousness than we usually realize. Even now, years later, there is a powerful magnetism that draws visitors by the thousands to Presley's home each year, and Lennon is fondly recalled in countless writings, reminiscences, and speculations. Lest any classicists rise up at this comparison, let me quickly say that I am not trying to assert any equivalence between Beethoven and either Presley or Lennon, nor their gifts nor their respective contributions to art. But Presley was no less significant to the American population in the mid-twentieth century than Beethoven was to the German population in the early nineteenth. In each case, a musical figure died in mid-career, one who was revered by a very large number of his countrymen, and whose death was the occasion of a great public grief.

Beethoven's funeral oration was written by Franz Grillparzer, the brilliant Austrian dramatist (1791–1872).[37] In his early years, Grillparzer had made Beethoven's acquaintance, and was close to him throughout the 1820s. He appears often in the "conversation books," which record conversations between the deaf Beethoven and his visitors. At one point, Beethoven had hoped to work with Grillparzer on an opera, but the planned collaboration never came about.

It is interesting, from the vantage point of nearly two centuries, to note the centrality of Beethoven's great personal misfortune, observed here by Grillparzer and subsequently by almost every writer on Beethoven: almost apologetically, Grillparzer laments Beethoven's eventual isolation provoked by his deafness. And, in truth, it must have been an unknowable agony for Beethoven's intimates, Grillparzer among them, to watch him slide into his silent and self-contained universe.

---

[37] Although Grillparzer wrote the oration, it was delivered at the funeral by the Austrian actor Heinrich Anschutz.

As a whole, the text of the funeral oration is ornate, and perhaps too stilted for contemporary taste. However, the final paragraph is beautiful and compelling; often in the midst of a performance of one of Beethoven's symphonies, these words come back to me, and Grillparzer's prediction rings out as profoundly and eternally true. Grillparzer probably did not know Ben Jonson's memorial poem to Shakespeare. But like Jonson, Grillparzer was deeply and fundamentally aware that the man whose death he mourned was of surpassing greatness, and there are echoes between the two memorials. When Jonson says of Shakespeare: "He was not of an age, but for all time," these words find their parallel in Grillparzer's line "Thus he was, thus he dies, thus will he live for all time."

The oration has some references that may not be familiar. The "hero of German poetry" is Goethe, who died five years later. The reference to "Freude schöner Götterfunken" is the opening line of Schiller's "An die Freude" (Ode to Joy) which became the text in the famous choral movement of Beethoven's last symphony. Adelaide was a song for solo voice and piano composed in about 1795; the text is a poem in German by Friedrich von Matthisson (1761–1831), and Leonore is the heroine of Beethoven's opera Fidelio.

Beethoven's Gravestone

We who stand here at the grave of the deceased are in a sense the representatives of an entire nation, the whole German people, come to mourn the passing of one celebrated half of that which remained to us from the vanished brilliance of the art of our homeland, of the spiritual efflorescence of the fatherland. The hero of poetry in the German language and tongue still lives—and long may he live. But the last master of resounding song, the gracious mouth by which music spoke, the man who inherited and increased the immortal fame of Handel and Bach, of Haydn and Mozart, has ceased to be; and we stand weeping over the broken strings of an instrument now stilled.

An instrument now stilled. Let me call him that! For he was an artist, and what he was, he was only through art. The thorns of life had wounded him deeply, and as the shipwrecked man clutches to the saving shore, he flew to your arms, oh wondrous sister of the good and true, comforter in affliction, the art that comes from on high! He held fast to you, and even when the gate through which you had entered was shut, you spoke through a deafened ear to him who could no longer discern you; and he carried your image in his heart, and when he died it still lay on his breast.

He was an artist, and who shall stand beside him? As the behemoth sweeps through the seas, he swept across the boundaries of his art. From the cooing of the dove to the thunder's roll, from the subtlest interweaving of willful artifices to that awesome point at which the fabric passes over into the lawlessness of clashing natural forces—he traversed all, he comprehended everything. He who follows him cannot continue, he must begin anew, for his predecessor ended only where art ends.

Adelaide and Leonore! Commemorations of the heroes of Vittoria and humble tones of the Mass! Offspring of three and four-part voices. Resounding symphony, "Freude, schoner Gotterfunken," the swansong. Muses of song and strings, gather at his grave and strew it with laurel!

He was an artist, but also a man, a man in every sense, in the highest sense. Because he shut himself off from the world, they called him hostile; and callous because he shunned feelings. Oh, he who knows he is hardened does not flee! (It is the most delicate point that is most easily blunted, that bends or breaks.)

The excess of feeling avoids feelings. He fled the world because he did not find, in the whole compass of his loving nature, a weapon with which he could resist it. He withdrew from his fellow men after he had given them everything and received nothing in return. He remained alone because he found no second self. But until his death he preserved a human heart for all men, a father's heart for his own people, the whole world.

Thus he was, thus he dies, thus will he live for all time!

And you who have followed our escort to this place, hold your sorrow in sway. You have not lost him but you have won him. No living man enters the halls of immortality. The body must die before the gates are opened. He whom you mourn is now among the greatest men of all time, unassailable forever. Return to your homes, then, distressed but composed. And whenever, during your lives, the power of his works overwhelms you like a coming storm; when your rapture pours out in the midst of a generation yet unborn; then remember this hour and think: we were there when they buried him, and when he died, we wept!

Franz Stöber, *Beethoven's Funeral*

F. T. Marinetti: The Futurist Manifesto

The following Page is a rather curious item; not quite of the same historical interest as the other Pages in this book, but with a strong resonance for contemporary culture now, as we enter the third decade of the Millennium.

Filippo Tommaso Marinetti was an Italian writer who lived from 1876 to 1944. He wrote poetry, plays, translations, and journal pieces. In his early work he came under the literary influence of Mallarmé and the Symbolists. By the turn of the century, however, he had embraced a rather brutal modernism. In 1902, for instance, in "Fanfare of the Waves," he uses such images as:

> O Sorceresses of the impossible! Stars! Promisers of nothing! There you are, before me within reach of my vengeance! Oh my joy! Oh! that I may savor the unbridled drunkenness of spitting on your majestic faces!

Marinetti's best-known effort, the following Page, was a "Manifesto of Futurism," which appeared in *Le Figaro* on February 20, 1909. In this rather unpleasant work, Marinetti defines the values for the generation of Italian poets then coming of age in the new century, whom Marinetti dubbed "Futurists." Those values are destruction and violence; Marinetti's heroes are machines, speed, and dynamism.

In publishing a "manifesto" for a new literary movement, Marinetti was imitating the example of Jean Moréas, who had published the "Symbolist Manifesto" a quarter century earlier, also in *Le Figaro*. And Marinetti's Manifesto itself had several imitators; another "Futurist Manifesto" was published a year later by a group of Italian painters. A group of Russian artists and poets followed suit, publishing another manifesto "A Slap in the Face of Public Taste" in 1922.

Futurism attracted considerable celebrity, but had only moderate lasting effect. There was a limited influence on some avant-garde composers; Leo Ornstein, at that time a well-known modernist composer, gave a recital in London that included several of his own Futurist pieces as well as works by Schoenberg. It did not please the London audience; one reviewer wrote "We have never suffered from such insufferable hideousness, expressed in terms of so-called music."

The Futurist painters did have an impact on Cubism, as well as on the Surrealist and Dadaist painters. Sarah Newmeyer describes the basic techniques of the Futurist painters:

> In its most elementary form, Futurism depicts simple forward motion by a multiplicity of nearly similar, slightly overlapping images.

and suggests Duchamp's famous "Nude Descending a Staircase" as an example that combines Futurist and Cubist elements. But the Futurist poets had no similar success; in spite of early notoriety, they produced no works of importance comparable to the Futurist painters. By the following decade the movement had largely disappeared.[38]

The interesting point, however, is the remarkable currency for today of the images that Marinetti invokes. These images—aggression, the celebration of metal, the joy of destruction—are in fact comparable to the same images that are resurfacing now in much of the popular culture that surrounds us. In music, in cinema, and especially in the vast world of comic books (a genre largely unknown to many beyond the age of 50), these same images are rapidly becoming the symbols of a younger generation. Like Marinetti's Futurists, that generation will come of age as a new century matures. It is interesting to wonder what the members of this young generation might think of their century-old

---

[38] But the impulses that drove the Futurists—total rejection of the artistic values of the past—never quite died out. Similar outbreaks of violent obliteration of past art appeared every now and then throughout the century. Probably the most notable was that of composer Pierre Boulez in 1971: "It is not enough to deface the Mona Lisa because that does not kill the Mona Lisa. All the art of the past must be destroyed."

forebear.

Marcel Duchamp, *Nude Descending a Staircase, No.2*

One note about the text. The Manifesto consists of eleven statements that define the goals and ideals of the Futurist poets. But Marinetti embedded the Manifesto in a longer essay, where he first describes a dreamlike automobile ride with some friends, a ride that ends in a ditch. The description is filled with unpleasant images: his automobile is a snorting beast, upon which he stretches like a corpse on a bier; the steering wheel is like a guillotine blade poised at his stomach. The ride is chaotic, as they hurl themselves through the night, racing after Death. And finally:

> ... I spun my car around with the frenzy of a dog trying to bite its tail, and there, suddenly, were two cyclists coming toward me, shaking their fists, wobbling like two equally convincing but nevertheless contradictory arguments. Their stupid dilemma was blocking my way—damn! Ouch! ... I stopped short and to my disgust rolled over into a ditch with my wheels in the air ... Oh! Maternal ditch, almost full of muddy water! Fair factory drain! I gulped down your nourishing sludge and I remembered the blessed black breast of my Sudanese nurse.... When I came up—torn, filthy and stinking from under the capsized car, I felt the while-hot iron of joy deliciously pass through my heart!

The essay ends with a series of affirmations, challenges, and predictions of which the last line, often quoted, is the stunning moment when Marinetti shakes his fist at the heavens:

> We don't want to understand ... Woe to anyone who says those infamous words to us again!

> Lift up your head! Erect on the summit of the world, once again we hurl defiance to the stars!

A bitter and angry statement; it is perhaps prophetic that Marinetti wrote it only five years before the world plunged into the Great War.

We have no comparable statement for our time, no "manifesto" that purports to describe our own tomorrow. And that may be a blessing. For though I think that Marinetti's harsh vision is an apt description of the culture that surrounds us now, the two worlds are really not the same. In spite of our nuclear arsenals, in spite of rampant brutalization and the near-constant presence of conflict in the world, we today do not seem to be on the same brink of chaos that was apparent to most observers in 1909. So perhaps we will avoid a catastrophe like 1914. Thus, at least, shall we hope.

F.T. Marinetti

MANIFESTO OF FUTURISM

We intend to sing the love of danger, the habit of energy and fearlessness.
Courage, audacity, and revolt will be the essential elements of our poetry.

Up to now literature has exalted a pensive immobility, ecstasy and sleep. We intend to exalt aggressive action, a feverish insomnia, the racer's stride, the mortal leap, the punch and the slap.

We say that the world's magnificence has been enriched by a new beauty; the beauty of speed. A racing car whose hood is adorned with great pipes, like serpents of explosive breath—a roaring car that seems to ride on grapeshot—is more beautiful than the Victory of Samothrace.

We want to hymn the man at the wheel, who hurls the lance of his spirit across the Earth, along the circle of its orbit.

The poet must spend himself with ardor, splendor, and generosity, to swell the enthusiastic fervor of the primordial elements.

Except in struggle, there is no more beauty. No work without an aggressive character can be a masterpiece. Poetry must be conceived as a violent attack on unknown forces, to reduce and prostrate them before man.

We are on the last promontory of the centuries! . . . Why should we look back, when what we want is to break down the mysterious doors of the Impossible! Time and Space died yesterday. We live in the absolute, because we have created eternal, omnipresent speed.

We will glorify war—the world's only hygiene—militarism, patriotism, the destructive gesture of freedom-bringers, beautiful ideas worth dying for, and scorn for woman.

We will destroy the museums, libraries, academies of every kind, will fight moralism, feminism, every opportunistic or utilitarian cowardice.

We will sing of great crowds excited by work, by pleasure, and by riot; we will sing of the multicolored, polyphonic tides of revolution in the modern capitals; we will sing of the vibrant nightly fervor of arsenals and shipyards blazing with violent electric moons; greedy railway stations that devour smoke-plumed serpents; factories hung on the clouds by the crooked lines of their smoke; bridges that stride the rivers like giant gymnasts, flashing in the sun with a glitter of knives; adventurous steamers that sniff the horizon; deep-chested locomotives whose wheels paw the tracks like the hooves of enormous steel horses bridled by tubing; and the sleek flight of planes whose propellers chatter in the wind like banners and seem to cheer like an enthusiastic crowd.

Albert Einstein: Letter to President Roosevelt

Of all the technologies that have changed our lives so profoundly in the twentieth century—television, the automobile, the computer—the one that has entered our consciousness most deeply, and even given its name to the age, stems from a weapon. For when the bomb fell on Hiroshima on the morning of August 6, 1945, the Atomic Age was most definitely born. Preceding this painful birth, as happens with all births, there was a period of gestation and even before that a moment of conception. This Page is a part of that conceiving moment: it is Einstein's letter to Roosevelt urging that work should begin on developing the atomic bomb.

The story of that letter has some curious twists. In the popular imagination, Einstein, the father of the famous $E = mc^2$ equation, is the bomb's mastermind. He wrote a letter to the President that apparently opened Roosevelt's eyes to the potentials of nuclear fission and started the avalanche that led to the Manhattan Project, Little Boy, and Fat Man.[39]

But Einstein himself downplayed his own role. He was a lifelong pacifist and was horrified to be thought the progenitor of such a terrible weapon. He insisted that "My participation in the production of the atomic bomb consisted of one single act: I signed a letter to President Roosevelt." Other observers supported Einstein's view, and even disparaged his influence (though probably for reasons unrelated to pacifism). J. Robert Oppenheimer, head of the Manhattan Project, insisted that Einstein's letter had "very little effect." Vannevar Bush, Director of the Office of Scientific Research and Development, seconded that opinion, stating that "the show was going on before that letter was even written."

The full story is buried a little more deeply, as befits an event so primal as the explosion in Hiroshima. Certainly, Einstein was only one, albeit the most famous one, of many key players. But neither was he just a bit player, as his protestation might indicate. It is even more certain that the full story centers not on Einstein at all, but on the Hungarian physicist Leo Szilard, who really wrote (or co-wrote) the famous letter, and who was the true mastermind of those events that Einstein is commonly thought to be.

The tale begins with the developments in nuclear physics around the turn of the century. After Becquerel's discovery in 1896 that uranium emitted radiation, many of the world's greatest physicists struggled with the question of whether, and under what circumstances, nuclear fission could be harnessed. If Einstein's Theory of Relativity was correct, it suggested that fission would be accompanied by a huge release of energy. (More precisely, the energy-mass equation is a

---

[39] These were the names given to the bombs that fell on Hiroshima and Nagasaki, They were derived from different methods of originating each bomb's chain reaction.

derivation from the Theory of Relativity, one that Einstein made as early as 1909, at a lecture in Salzburg.) By 1930, research had clarified many important aspects of atomic behavior, but how atoms could actually be coerced into giving up their energy was still unknown. In 1934, Enrico Fermi experimented with bombarding uranium with neutrons, trying to force disintegration of the nucleus. His experiments were repeated by Joliet-Curie in France and Otto Hahn in Germany. By 1938, Hahn managed to split the uranium nucleus in two, releasing a large quantity of energy just as Einstein's theories had predicted. It was Hahn's work that led to the realization, in Germany and elsewhere, that nuclear weapons were not only theoretically possible, but might well be manufactured, and very soon.

Fermi and Szilard, both now refugees in America were among those who drew the same conclusion. Szilard was a physicist with a long interest in the weapons potential of fission. In 1933 he had formulated one of the key principles in understanding how a chain reaction could be sustained long enough for an explosive device to function. Together, Fermi and Szilard began actively warning against a German bomb. Fermi wrote to the Navy Department, but with no success. Szilard tried a different tack. Knowing that the Belgian Congo was the major source of raw uranium, and also knowing of Einstein's friendship with Queen Elizabeth of Belgium,[40] Szilard guessed that a warning from Einstein might convince Belgium to ban sales of uranium to Germany. In July 1939, therefore, Szilard approached Einstein, now a refugee in America as well, hoping to enlist Einstein's agreement.

Einstein had been remote from all of the recent research in fission. His own field of interest was the search for a unified field theory that would relate the laws of gravitation and electromagnetism. He also doubted that it would be practical to build a nuclear bomb, at least in the near future. But he shared Szilard's fear of Germany. Years later, even as he regretted that bombs had been built, he noted: "... there was some justification—the danger that the Germans would make them." So Einstein agreed to lend his name to the efforts of Fermi and Szilard.

After their meeting, Szilard made a sudden change of course. Alexander Sachs, a close friend of President Roosevelt, had indicated to Szilard a willingness to personally convey a message from Einstein to the President; this would obviously be a more direct path to action than the Queen Mother of Belgium. So Szilard made another visit to Einstein,[41] this time with a draft of a letter to Roosevelt. Einstein suggested a few small changes, and agreed to sign the final copy. On August 2, Szilard sent Einstein the final copy in two versions, one longer, more detailed one, and a shorter one.

---

[40] She was actually the Queen Mother at that point. They had become close friends in 1929, when she was Queen.
[41] On the first visit, Szilard had been accompanied by Eugene Wigner, another refugee physicist then working at Princeton. On the second visit, Szilard was accompanied by Edward Teller, later to become the "father of the H-bomb."

Einstein signed both and sent them back to Szilard, who sent the longer of the two to Sachs. Sachs was not able to see Roosevelt until October 11, after war had broken out in Europe. But he managed to convince Roosevelt that some action must be taken. (Roosevelt: "Alex, what you are after is to see the Nazis don't blow us up.") As a result of this meeting, a committee was established, headed by Lyman Briggs of the U.S. Bureau of Standards, and including Szilard, Wigner, Teller, General E. W. Watson (Roosevelt's secretary), but not Einstein. This committee was intended to coordinate all of the diverse nuclear research currently underway at Columbia, Princeton, Chicago, and elsewhere.

However, while Einstein did not participate in this activity, he was not inactive otherwise. As Ronald Clark, in his biography of Einstein notes: "Einstein, far from writing only the first letter to Roosevelt . . . did very much more." He met with Szilard on several occasions; a major result of these continued meetings was Einstein's explicit recommendation that the research path being pursued at Columbia was superior to the other efforts. This is embedded in a second letter, addressed to Sachs, but certainly intended for Roosevelt. Dated March 7, 1940, this letter expressed Einstein's recommendation to follow the Columbia approach (which was the one favored by Szilard). And yet a third letter from Einstein, ghostwritten by Szilard on April 19, 1940, stated the following:

> I am convinced as to the wisdom and the urgency of creating the conditions under which [nuclear research] can be carried out with greater speed and on a larger scale than hitherto . . . a nonprofit organization . . . given . . . the necessary funds . . . large-scale experiments and exploration of practical applications could be carried out much faster than through a loose cooperation of university laboratories and government departments.

"The conditions for carrying out research" and "an organization given enough funds" are an unmistakable description of what was to become the Manhattan Project in 1942; it is really this third letter rather than the first that was the actual first step in building the Bomb.

Through all of these events, Szilard was obviously the grey eminence. About the letter of April 19, Clark states it very strongly:

> As usual, Szilard had the situation well in hand . . . Szilard emerges as a combination of stage manager and producer, organizing into their correct places not only Sachs, Briggs, and Watson, but also Albert Einstein.

This may well be so. But Einstein is still the heavyweight among these players, one whose prestige lent massive authority not only to the words of Szilard, but also to the urgings of Fermi, Wigner, and all the other physicists doing this mighty research. Subject to the manipulations of others Einstein may have been; a purely naive victim of Szilard's machinations, probably not. Somewhere between mastermind and pawn, he was a pacifist who feared the enormity of the Nazi menace, and took a pragmatic step to defeat it. That the Bomb dominated the remainder of the century was perhaps a painful fact. But that Einstein had a significant role in its creation cannot be doubted. And his letter is a worthy Page with which to end our journey.

Albert Einstein

Einstein's Letter to Roosevelt

Sir:

Some recent work by E. Fermi and L. Szilard, which has been communicated to me in manuscript, leads me to expect that the element uranium may be turned into a new and important source of energy in the immediate future. Certain aspects of the situation seem to call for watchfulness and, if necessary, quick action on the part of the administration. I believe, therefore, that it is my duty to bring to your attention the following facts and recommendations.

In the course of the last four months it has been made probable—through the work of Joliot in France as well as Fermi and Szilard in America—that it may become possible to set up nuclear chain reactions in a large mass of uranium, by which vast amounts of power and large quantities of new radium-like elements would be generated. Now it appears almost certain that this could be achieved in the immediate future.

This new phenomenon would also lead to the construction of bombs, and it is conceivable—though much less certain—that extremely powerful bombs of a new type may thus be constructed. A single bomb of this type, carried by a boat or exploded in a port, might well destroy the whole port together with some of the surrounding territory. However, such bombs might very well prove to be too heavy for transportation by air.

The United States has only very poor ores of uranium in moderate quantities. There is some good ore in Canada and the former Czechoslovakia, while the most important source of uranium is the Belgian Congo.

In view of this situation you may think it desirable to have some permanent contact maintained between the administration and the group of physicists working on chain reaction in America. One possible way of achieving this might be for you to entrust with this task a person who has your confidence and who could perhaps serve in an unofficial capacity. His task might comprise the following:

To approach government departments, keep them informed of further developments, and put forward recommendations for government action, giving particular attention to the problem of securing a supply of uranium ore for the United States.

To speed up the experimental work which is at present being carried on within the limits of the budget of the university laboratories, by providing funds, if such funds be required, through his contacts with private persons who are willing to make contributions for this cause, and perhaps also by obtaining the cooperation of industrial laboratories which have the necessary equipment.

I understand that Germany has actually stopped the sale of uranium from the Czechoslovakian mines which she has taken over. That she should have taken such an early action might perhaps be understood on the ground that the son of the German Undersecretary of State, von Weizsäcker, is attached to the Kaiser Wilhelm Institute of Berlin, where some of the American work on uranium is now being repeated.

Yours very truly, A. Einstein.

Afterword

Having found our way to Einstein's letter, we have come to the end of this little journey. In the course of getting this volume ready for publication, several friendly reviewers suggested other documents that could be added to this collection, and though I had to deny them for the present book, it may be the case that another similar volume could appear in the future.

If so, then such Pages of History as the Declaration of Arbroath (from 1320, the Scottish appeal to the Pope during the First War of Scottish Independence), the Declaration of Sentiments (from 1848, among the earliest demands for women's rights), or the discovery of the structure of DNA (from 1953, leading to a revolution in molecular biology) would be ideal candidates for inclusion.

But whether or not that project ever takes flight, the present exercise has been an enormous pleasure for me. I sincerely hope that pleasure was shared by my Readers.

David Carney
Palm Springs, CA
November 10, 2020
Djc717@gmail.com

Acknowledgements

The author would like to thank the following persons who made significant and useful comments as this book was being written:

Kurt Wallnau and Fred Long saw many of the earliest drafts and made valuable comments that steered the document in its present direction. Patrick Place was a continuing and welcome critic over a number of years, most recently with regard to parts of the document that needed to be removed. James Fusco and Ronald Isetti read these pages, each with the eye of a professional historian, and helped me see with an historian's vision; Ron was also the generous author of the Foreword. Bill Wengeler played a comparable role by helping me see with a scientist's vision. Owen Korsmo provided fine-tuning of the text, and kept me from making some painful grammatical errors. Helen English, Michael Popcock and Jeffrey Goldberg provided useful information on many of the illustrations in the document. My brother and sister, John Carney and Margaret Steele, were constant cheerleaders for the book, particularly when I was on the verge of giving it all up. Another sister, Eido Frances Carney, and good friend David Ponder, gave the manuscript a phenomenal and much-needed scouring; it is their vigilance that removed an unconscionable number of typographical and grammatical errors from these pages; I am deeply in their debt.

And Jennifer Geist gave magisterial assistance in securing the appropriate rights and permissions for all of the illustrations, and was the principal reason that this document is now seeing the light of day. I am truly grateful for her contribution to this volume.

Bibliography and Sources of Texts

NB: Sources of text indicated by an asterisk

Section One: American Statesmen

Johnston, Alexander, and James Woodburn. *American Orations*. New York: G. Putnam, 1927.*

Wirt, William. *Sketches of the Life and Character of Patrick Henry*. Philadelphia, 1836, as reproduced in *The World's Greatest Speeches*. New York: Copland and Lamm, 1973.

Alden, John R. *A History of the American Revolution*. New York: Knopf, 1969.

Miller, John C., *Origins of the American Revolution*. Stanford, CA: Stanford University Press, 1943.

Selby, John E. *The Revolution in Virginia, 1775-1883*. Williamsburg, VA: The Colonial Williamsburg Foundation, 1988.

The Avalon Project at the Yale Law School: 19th Century. https://avalon.law.yale.edu/subject_menus/19th.asp.*

Leone, Bruno. *The American Revolution: Opposing Viewpoints*. American History Series, 1992.

Ross, George E., ed. *Perspectives on the American Revolution*. Carbondale, IL: Southern Illinois University Press, 1877.

Morris, Richard, *Great Presidential Decisions: State Papers that Changed the Course of History*. New York: J.B. Lippincott, 1960.*

Fite, Gilbert Courtland, John Samuel Ezell, and Rudolph Leopold Biesele, eds. *Readings in American History, Vol I*. Boston: Houghton Mifflin, 1956.*

Swann, Brian, and Arnold Krupat, eds. *Essays on Native American Literature*. Berkeley: University of California Press, 1987.*

Nevins, Allan, ed. *Lincoln and the Gettysburg Address: Commemorative Papers*. University of Illinois Press, 1964.

Wills, Garry, *Lincoln at Gettysburg*. New York: Simon & Schuster, 1992.

Commager, Henry Steele, ed. *Living Ideas in American History*. New York: Harper & Row, 1951.

Morison, Samuel Eliot, Henry Steele Commager, and William E. Leuchtenburg. *The Growth of the American Republic*. New York: Oxford University Press, 1950.

Whitman, Alden. *Portrait, Adlai Stevenson, Vol III, Governor of Illinois, 1949-1953*. Boston: Little, Brown & Co., 1947.

Johnson, Walter, ed. *The Papers of Adlai Stevenson, Vol III*. Boston: Little Brown & Co., 1974.*

Broadwater, Jeff. *Adlai Stevenson and American Politics*. New York: Twane Publishers, 1994.

Schlesinger Jr., Arthur M. *Robert Kennedy and His Times*. Boston: Houghton Mifflin, 1978.

Thomas, Evan. *Robert Kennedy: His Life*. New York: Simon and Schuster, 2000.

Margolick, David. *The Promise and the Dream: The Untold Story of Martin Luther King, Jr. And Robert F. Kennedy*. New York: Rosetta Books, 2018.

Klein, Joe. *Politics Lost: How American Democracy was Trivialized by People Who Think You're Stupid*. New York: Doubleday, 2006.

Wikisource contributors, "Speech on the Assassination of Martin Luther King, Jr.," Wikisource, https://en.wikisource.org/w/index.php?title=Speech_on_the_Assassination_of_Martin_Luther_King,_Jr.&oldid=6413772 (accessed November 10, 2020).*

Section Two: Freedom and the Human Spirit

Browning, Andrew, ed. *English Historical Documents, Volume VIII, 1660–1714*. New York: Oxford University Press. 1953.

The Avalon Project at the Yale Law School: 17th Century. https://avalon.law.yale.edu/subject_menus/17th.asp.*

The Avalon Project at the Yale Law School: 18th Century. https://avalon.law.yale.edu/subject_menus/18th.asp.*

Kenyon, J. P., ed. *The Stuart Constitution, 1603–1688: Documents and Commentary*. New York: Cambridge University Press, 1966.

Williams, E. Neville. *The Eighteenth Century Constitution, 1688–1815. Documents and Commentary*. New York: Cambridge University Press, 1960.

Costin, W. C. and Watson, J., *The Law and Working of the Constitution: Documents 1660 – 1914*. London: Steven, Adam and Charles Black, 1952.

Jones, J. R., *Country and Court: England, 1658-1714*. Cambridge: Harvard University Press, 1978.

Parrington, Vernon L. *The Colonial Mind 1620 – 1800*. Harvest Books, 1927.

Kramer, Lloyd. *Lafayette in Two Worlds*. Chapel Hill: University of North Carolina Press, 1996.

Cocks, Charles, and Jules Michelet, trans. *History of the French Revolution*. Chicago: University of Chicago Press, 1967.

Gottschalk, Louis Reichenthal, and Margaret Maddox. *Lafayette in the French Revolution*. Chicago: University of Chicago Press, 1969.

Wilson, Vincent Jr., ed. *The Book of Great American Documents*. Brookville: American History Research Associates, 1982.

McIver, R.M., ed. *Great Expression of Human Rights*. New York: Institute for Religious and Social Studies, Jewish Theological Seminary of America, 1950.*

Riasanovsky, Nicholas V. *A History of Russia*. New York: Oxford University Press, 1963.

Buehr, Wendy, ed. *The Horizon History of Russia*. New York: American Heritage Publishing Co, 1970.

"October Manifesto," Emerson Kent, http://www.emersonkent.com/wars_and_battles_in_history/russian_revolution_of_1905.htm#October_Manifesto.*

Section Three: The World Wars of the 20th Century

The Avalon Project at the Yale Law School: 20th Century. https://avalon.law.yale.edu/subject_menus/20th.asp.

Cooper, J. M., ed. *Causes and Consequences of World War I*. New York: Quadrangle Books, 1972.

Taylor, A.J.P. *The Origins of the Second World War*. New York: Athenaeum, 1966.

Great Britain Parliamentary Papers, Treaty Series, 1911.*

WWI Document Archive: Official Papers. "The Austro-Hungarian Ultimatum to Serbia." https://wwi.lib.byu.edu/index.php/The_Austro-Hungarian_Ultimatum_to_Serbia_(English_Translation).*

Schmitt, Bernadotte E. *Triple Alliance and Triple Entente*. Henry Holt & Co., 1934.

Berghahn, V. R. *Germany and the Approach of War in 1914*. New York: St. Martin's Press, 1973.

Seton-Watson, R.W. *Sarajevo*. London: Hutchinson & Co., 1925.

Taylor, A.J.P. *The Origins of the Second World War*. New York: Athenaeum, 1966.

Gauss, Christian. *The German Emperor as Shown in his Public Utterances*. New York: Charles Scribner's Sons, 1961.*

Address by the President of the United States. The Congressional Record, January 8, 1918.*

Watt, Richard. *The Kings Depart: The Tragedy of Germany, Versailles, and the German Revolution*. New York: Simon & Schuster, 1968.

Radek, Karl. *The Winding-up of the Versailles Treaty: Report to the IV Congress of the Communist International*. Hamburg, 1922.

Stevenson, D. *French War Aims against Germany*. Oxford: Clarendon Press, 1982.

Bailey, Thomas A. *Woodrow Wilson and the Lost Peace*. Quadrangle Books, 1944.

Eyre, Howard Elcock. *Portrait of a Decision: The Council of Four and the Treaty of Versailles*. Methuen, Ltd, 1972.

Massie, Robert K. *Dreadnaught: Britain, Germany, and the Coming of the Great War*. New York: Ballatine, Books, 1992.

Albrecht-Carrié, René. *A Diplomatic History of Europe since the Congress of Vienna*. New York: Harper & Row, 1958.

Ease, Charles, comp. *The War Speeches of the Rt. Hon. Winston S. Churchill, Vol I*. London: Cassell & Co., 1951.*

"Address to Congress. Requesting a Declaration of War with Japan. December 8, 1941." FDR Library & Museum. http://docs.fdrlibrary.marist.edu/tmirhdee.html.*

Kase, Toshokasu. *Journey to the Missouri*. New Haven: Yale University Press, 1950.*

Feis, Herbert, *Japan Subdued*. Princeton: Princeton University Press, 1950.

Wainstock, Dennis, *The Decision to Drop the Atomic Bomb*. Westport: Praeger, 1996.

Terkel, Studs, and Paul Tibbets, "One Hell of a Big Bang." *The Guardian*, August 2, 2002. https://www.theguardian.com/world/2002/aug/06/nuclear.japan.

Funabashi, Yoichi, "The Third Atomic Bomb," *The Asia-Pacific Journal*, August 9, 2003.

Section Four: Faith and Religion

Brown, Raymond E., Joseph A. Fitzmeyer SJ, Rolans E. Murphy, and O. Carm, eds. *The Jerome Biblical Commentary*. Englewood Cliffs, NJ: Prentice-Hall, 1968.

Smith, Huston. *The Religions of Man*. New York: Harper & Row, 1958.

Jungmann, Josef A. *The Early Liturgy to the time of Gregory the Great*. Francis A. Brunner, trans. University of Notre Dame Press, Notre Dame, 1954.

"Roman Martyrology, Complete, December: December 25." *Boston Catholic Journal*. http://www.boston-catholic-journal.com/roman-martrylogy-in-english/roman-martyrology-december-in-english.htm#December_25th.

Gevbels, Thomas. *The Roman Martyrology,* St. Omers, 1667.

The New Catholic Encyclopedia. New York: McGraw-Hill, 1967.

Thatcher, Oliver, and Edgar Holmes McNeal, eds. *A Source Book for Medieval History*. New York: Scribners, 1005.*

Southern, R.W. *The Making of the Middle Ages*. New Haven: Yale University Press, 1953.

Tierney, Brian. *The Middle Ages, Vol I: Sources of Medieval History*. New York: Alfred A. Knopf, 1970.

Hayes, Carleton, Marshall Baldwin, and Charles Cole. *History of Europe*. New York: The Macmillan Company, 1956.

Dickens, A. G. *The English Reformation*. New York: Knopf Doubleday, 1946.

"The Act of Supremacy, 1534. Catalogue reference: C 65/143, m. 5, nos. 8 and 9." *The National Archives*. https://webarchive.nationalarchives.gov.uk/+/https://www.nationalarchives.gov.uk/pathways/citizenship/rise_parliament/transcripts/henry_supremacy.htm.*

Elton, G. R., ed. *Renaissance and Reformation.* London: The Macmillan Company, 1968.

Bindoff, S. T. *Tudor England.* Baltimore: Penguin Books, 1963.

Powicke, Sir Maurice. *The Reformation in England.* London: Oxford University Press, 1961.

Wikisource contributors, "Bible (King James)/Preface" *Wikisource,* https://en.wikisource.org/wiki/Bible_(King_James)/Preface (accessed November 10, 2020).*

Grant, Frederick C. *Translating the Bible.* London: Thomas Nelson & Sons, 1961.

Hammond, Gerald. *The Making of the English Bible.* New York: Philosophical Library, 1983.

Daiches, David. *The King James Version of the English Bible.* Chicago: University of Chicago Press, 1941.

Jones, Alexander, ed. *The Jerusalem Bible.* New York: Doubleday & Co., 1966.*

Section Five: Art and Science, Wisdom and Understanding

Miles, Steven H. *The Hippocratic Oath and the Ethics of Medicine.* Oxford: Oxford University Press, 2004.

Roth, Gottfried, "The protection of human life as reflected in medical vows," in: Johannes Bökmann, ed., *Liberation from the objective good?* Vallendar-Schoenstatt, 1982, 221-233.

"The Oath, *"Hippocrates of Cos.* Loeb Classical Library, 1923.

Grahan, David. "Revisiting Hippocrates," in *Journal of the American Medical Association,* Dec. 2000.

Wikipedia contributors, "Hippocratic Oath," *Wikipedia, The Free Encyclopedia,* https://en.wikipedia.org/w/index.php?title=Hippocratic_Oath&oldid=986471411 (accessed November 10, 2020).*

Drake, Stillman, trans., *Discoveries and Opinions of Galileo.* Garden City: Doubleday & Co., 1957.*

Campanella, Thomas, trans. by Richard J. Blackwell. *A Defense of Galileo.* Notre Dame: University of Notre Dame Press, 1994.

Segre, Michael. *In the Wake of Galileo.* New Brunswick: Rutgers University Press, 1991.

Langford, Jerome J. *Galileo, Science, and the Church*. Ann Arbor: University of Michigan Press, 1992.

Ciyne, G. V., M. Heller, and J. Zycinski, eds. *The Galileo Affair*. Vatican City: Specola Vaticana, 1985.

Santillana, Giorgio de. *The Crime of Galileo*. Chicago: University of Chicago Press, 1955.

Eliot, Charles, ed. *Prefaces and Prologues to Famous Books*. New York: P.F. Collier & Son, 1938.*

Hinman, Charlton K. *The Printing and Proof-Reading of the First Folio of Shakespeare*. Oxford Clarendon Press, 1963.

Mosten, Doug, ed. *The First Folio of Shakespeare*. New York: Applause Books, 1995.

David, Hans T. *J.S. Bach's Musical Offering*. New York: G. Schirmer, Inc., 1945.

Davison, Archibald T. *Bach and Handel*. Cambridge: Harvard University Press, 1951.

Brown, Nicholas A. "Pondering Bach's Brandenburg Concertos" *Library of Congress Blog*, https://blogs.loc.gov/music/2014/02/pondering-bachs-brandenburg-concertos/* (accessed November 10, 2020).*

Spitta, Phillip. Clara Bell & J. A. Fuller-Maitland, trans. *Johann Sebastian Bach*. London, Novello & Co., 1951.

David, Hans T., and Arthur Mendel, eds. *The Bach Reader*. New York: W. W. Norton & Co., 1945.

David, Hans T., Christoph Wolff, and Arthur Mendel, eds. *The New Bach Reader*. New York: W. W. Norton & Co., 1999.*

Landon, H.C. Robbins, ed. *Beethoven: A Documentary Study*. New York: Collier Books, 1975.*

Thayer, Alexander. *The Life of Ludwig van Beethoven Vol. I*, 1921.

Lockwood, Lewis. *Beethoven: The Music and the Life*. New York: W. W. Norton & Company, 2003.

Lang, Peter, ed. *Stung by Salt and Water: Creative Texts of the Italian Avant-Gardist F. T. Marinetti*. New York: Peter Lang, 1987.

Collins, Joseph. *Idling in Italy: Studies of Literature and Life*. New York, Charles Scribner's Sons, 1920.

Newmeyer, Sarah. *Enjoying Modern Art*. New York: Reinhold, 1955.

Hazelton, Claire Kohda. "Boulez in his own words," in *The Guardian*, Thu 26 Mar 2015.
https://www.theguardian.com/music/musicblog/2015/mar/26/boulez-in-his-own-words.

Morris, Richard B., ed. *Significant Documents in American History*, Vol. II 1888-1968. Van Nostrand, Reinhold Co., New York, 1969.*

Frank, Philip. "Einstein's Philosophy of Science." *Reviews of Modern Physics,* Vol. 21, 1949.

Clark, Ronald W. *Einstein*. World Publishing Co., 1971.

Sources of Illustrations

Section One: American Statesmen

Alvesgaspar. Washington Monument in Washington DC. Photograph. *Wikimedia Commons*. CC BY-SA 4.0, October 5, 2016. https://commons.wikimedia.org/wiki/File:Washington_October_2016-6_(cropped)_(cropped).jpg.

Skyring. Saint John's Church, Richmond. Photograph. *Wikimedia Commons*. CC BY-SA 3.0, September 27, 2010. https://commons.wikimedia.org/wiki/File:StJohnsRichmond.JPG.

Jones, Alfred, Engraver, and Peter Frederick Rothermel. *Patrick Henry before the Virginia House of Burgesses.* United States Virginia Williamsburg, 1852. Photograph. https://www.loc.gov/item/2006691555/.

Peale, Rembrandt. *Thomas Jefferson. Wikimedia Commons*. 1800. https://commons.wikimedia.org/wiki/File:Official_Presidential_portrait_of_Thomas_Jefferson_(by_Rembrandt_Peale,_1800).jpg.

David, Jacques-Louis. *Napoleon Crossing the Alps. Wikimedia Commons*, 1801-1803. lent to Belvedere by Kunsthistorisches Museum.

Morse, Samuel. *Portrait of James Monroe Wikimedia Commons*, c. 1819. https://commons.wikimedia.org/wiki/File:James_Monroe_White_House_portrait_1819.jpg.

Sammis, E. M. Seattle (v. 1786-1866), Chef De Six Tribus Indiennes Établies Dans L'actuel État De Washington, Dont Les Dumawish Et Suquamish. 1864. Photograph. *Wikimedia Commons*. https://commons.wikimedia.org/wiki/File:Chief_seattle.jpg.

Raul654. Photograph of the Abraham Lincoln Statue by [Attilio Piccirilli for Daniel Chester French] (1920) in the Lincoln Memorial. August 12, 2002. Photograph. *Wikimedia Commons*. https://commons.wikimedia.org/wiki/File:Lincoln_statue,_Lincoln_Memorial.jpg

President Harding snaped i.e., snapped at the dedication ceremonies of the Lincoln Memorial today. Washington D.C, May 30, 1922. Photograph. https://www.loc.gov/item/94503006/. Cropped version from https://commons.wikimedia.org/wiki/File:Lincoln_Memorial_Dedication_with_President_Harding_crop.jpg.

Leffler, Warren K, photographer. White House: head shots of Amb. Adlai Stevenson / WKL. 1961. Photograph. https://www.loc.gov/item/2009632123/.

Photographer unknown. Photograph, John F. Kennedy. ca. 1960. Photograph. Papers of John F. Kennedy. Presidential Papers. President's Office Files. John F. Kennedy Presidential Library and Museum, Boston. https://www.jfklibrary.org/asset-viewer/archives/JFKPOF/007/JFKPOF-007-008?image_identifier=JFKPOF-007-008-p0080

Leffler, Warren K, photographer. *Martin Luther King, Jr., head-and-shoulders portrait, facing right, at microphones, after? meeting with President Johnson to discuss civil rights, at the White House,/ WKL.* Washington D.C, 1963. Dec. 3. Photograph. https://www.loc.gov/item/2011648312/.

Leffler, Warren K, photographer. Attorney General Robert Kennedy testifying before a Senate subcommittee hearing on crime. Washington D.C, 1963. Photograph. https://www.loc.gov/item/2011648827/.

Section Two: Freedom and the Human Spirit

King John of England. Charter of King John of England (1199–1216), granting liberties to the English people ('Magna Carta'): Runnymede, 15 June 1215 § (1215).
https://commons.wikimedia.org/wiki/File:Magna_Carta_(British_Library_Cotton_MS_Augustus_II.106).jpg. This document is held at the British Library and is identified as "British Library Cotton MS Augustus II.106."

Wale, Samuel; engraved by "Carey" (possibly J. Cary). *The Bill of Rights Ratified at the Revolution by King William, and Queen Mary, Previous to their Coronation.* London, 1783. Engraving.
https://en.wikipedia.org/wiki/File:Samuel_Wale,_The_Bill_of_Rights_Ratified_at_the_Revolution_by_King_William,_and_Queen_Mary,_Previous_to_their_Coronation_(1783).jpg.

Second Continental Congress, reproduction: William Stone, Declaration of Independence § (1776). *Wikimedia Commons*. July 4, 1776.
https://commons.wikimedia.org/wiki/File:United_States_Declaration_of_Independence.jpg

Madison, James, Bill of Rights § (1789). https://catalog.archives.gov/id/1408042.

Peale, Charles Willson. "Marie Joseph Paul Yves Roch Gilbert Motier, Marquis De Lafayette." Independence National Historical Park, National Park Service, 1779. INDE 14080. http://www.nps.gov/museum/exhibits/revwar/image_gal/indeimg/lafayette.html.

Lincoln, Abraham. Emancipation Proclamation, 1862. https://www.wdl.org/en/item/2714/.

Lipgart, Earnest. Nicholas II of Russia. 1900s. Painting. *Wikimedia Commons*. https://commons.wikimedia.org/wiki/File:Nicholas_II_of_Russia_painted_by_Earnest_Lipgart.jpg.

Unknown. Crowd Facing Armed Soldiers in Moscow, an Event That Led to the Revolution of 1905, in Russia. 1905. Photograph. *Wikimedia*. https://en.wikipedia.org/wiki/File:Gapon_crowd_1905.jpg.

Section Three: The World Wars of the 20th Century

"Europe, 1914 - Lines Drawn." n.d. Map. United States Military Academy West Point. https://www.westpoint.edu/sites/default/files/inline-images/academics/academic_departments/history/WWI/WWOne02.pdf. Map courtesy of the United States Military Academy Department of History.

Fildes, Luke. Portrait of King Edward VII, 1902. 1902. Painting. *Wikimedia Commons*. National Portrait Gallery. https://commons.wikimedia.org/wiki/File:King_Edward_VII_portrait.jpg.

Bain News Service, Publisher. Delcasse. [No Date Recorded on Caption Card] Photograph. https://www.loc.gov/item/2014685739/.

Bain News Service, Publisher. Franz Ferdinand & family. ca. 1910. [Between and Ca. 1915] Photograph. https://www.loc.gov/item/2014695529/.

Cassowary Colorizations, ed. Gavrilo Princip in His Prison Cell at the Terezín Fortress, 1914. 1914. Photograph. Flickr. https://www.flickr.com/photos/150300783@N07/27324412597.

Bain News Service, Publisher. Kaiser Wilhelm. [Between c. 1910 and c. 1915]. Photograph. https://www.loc.gov/item/2014691940/.

Woodrow Wilson and wife riding in backseat of a carriage to second inauguration, March 5th. Washington D.C, 1917. Photograph. https://www.loc.gov/item/96522409/.

Jackson, Edward N. Council of Four at the WWI Paris peace conference, May 27, 1919 (candid photo) (L - R) Prime Minister David Lloyd George (Great Britain), Premier Vittorio Orlando (Italy), Premier Georges Clemenceau (France), President Woodrow Wilson (USA). May 27, 1919. Photograph. https://commons.wikimedia.org/wiki/File:Big_four.jpg

Unknown. Nchener Abkommen, Staatschefs. September 29, 1938. Photograph. Das Bundesarchiv. https://www.bild.bundesarchiv.de/dba/de/search/?query=Bild+183-R69173.

Karsh, Yousuf. The Roaring Lion. December 30, 1941. Photograph. *Wikimedia Commons*. Library and Archives Canada. https://commons.wikimedia.org/wiki/File:Sir_Winston_Churchill_-_19086236948.jpg.

US Navy Photo, 80-G-26848. Atlantic Charter, August 1941. August 10, 1941. Photograph. National Museum of the U.S. Navy. https://www.history.navy.mil/content/history/museums/nmusn/explore/photography/wwii/wwii-conferences/atlantic-charter/80-g-26848.html.

Maritime Quest. https://www.maritimequest.com/warship_directory/great_britain/battleships/prince_of_wales/hms_prince_of_wales_page_2.htm.

USS *Arizona*, at height of fire, following Japanese aerial attack on Pearl Harbor, Hawaii. Hawaii Pearl Harbor. December 7, 1941. Photograph. https://www.loc.gov/item/92500933/.

US Government. FDR Addresses Congress. December 8, 1941. Photograph. National Archives Catalog. https://prologue.blogs.archives.gov/2016/12/08/the-day-of-infamy-speech-well-remembered-but-still-missing/.

United States Navy, photographer. Signing of the Japanese surrender document aboard the U.S.S. *Missouri* in Tokyo Bay, Sept. 2, 1945. Gen. Douglas MacArthur is shown broadcasting the ceremonies as Japanese Foreign Minister Mamoru Shigemitsu signed for the emperor Hirohito. Japan Tokyo Bay, September 2, 1945. Photograph. https://www.loc.gov/item/2013648116/.

Joint Chiefs of Staff 2/9/1942-9/17/1947. Instrument of Surrender of Japanese Forces in New Guinea New Britain New Ireland Bouganville and Adjacent Islands. September 6, 1945. Nate D. Sanders. https://natedsanders.com/original_draft_of_the_wwii_japanese_instrument_of_-lot57567.aspx. Courtesy Nate D. Sanders Auctions.

Section Four: Faith and Religion

Michelangelo. "The Last Judgment." Created from 1536 to 1541. *Wikimedia Commons*, August 18, 2011. Photograph. https://commons.wikimedia.org/wiki/File:Last_Judgement_(Michelangelo).jpg.

Doré, Gustave. "Moses Coming Down From Mt. Sinai." La Grande Bible De Tours. Tours, France: Mame, 1866. Pixabay. https://pixabay.com/vectors/moses-ten-commandments-mount-sinai-4914546/.

Botticelli, Sandro. "Madonna of the Eucharist." *Wikimedia Commons*, 1470. Isabella Stewart Gardner Museum. Long Gallery, P27w73. https://commons.wikimedia.org/wiki/File:Botticelli_-_Madone_de_l%27Eucharistie.jpg.

Colombe, Jean. "Miniature: Pope Urban II Preaching at the Council of Clermont. Sébastien Mamerot, Les Passages D'outremer." *Wikimedia Commons*, c. 1474. https://en.wikipedia.org/wiki/File:CouncilofClermont.jpg.

Holbein the Younger, Hans. "Portrait of Henry VIII." *Wikimedia Commons*, after 1537. https://commons.wikimedia.org/wiki/File:After_Hans_Holbein_the_Younger_-_Portrait_of_Henry_VIII_-_Google_Art_Project.jpg.

Church of England. Frontispiece to the King James' Bible, 1611. *Wikimedia Commons*, 1611. Uploaded on November 5, 2016. https://commons.wikimedia.org/wiki/File:King-James-Version-Bible-first-edition-title-page-1611.png.

Section Five: Art and Science, Wisdom and Understanding

Rembrandt. "Aristotle with a Bust of Homer." *Wikimedia Commons*, 1653. Metropolitan Museum of Art. Room 637, 61.198.

https://commons.wikimedia.org/wiki/File:Rembrandt_-_Aristotle_with_a_Bust_of_Homer_-_WGA19232.jpg. Purchase, special contributions and funds given or bequeathed by friends of the Museum, 1961.

Pontius, Paulus, after Peter Paul Rubens. "Portrait of Hippocrates." 1638. *Wikimedia Commons*, from Welcome Images. Engraving. https://commons.wikimedia.org/wiki/File:Engraving;_portrait_of_Hippocrates,_Wellcome_L0016239.jpg.

Unknown, from Hippocrates. Ms. *Twelfth-Century Byzantine Manuscript the Oath Was Written out in the Form of a Cross, Relating It Visually to Christian Ideas, 12AD*. https://commons.wikimedia.org/wiki/File:HippocraticOath.jpg.

Villamoena, F. Galileo Galilei, 1564-1642. 1623. Engraving. https://www.loc.gov/item/2002710468/.

Galilei, Galileo. "Frontispiece (by Stefan Della Bella) and title page." Dialogue Concerning the Two Chief World Systems. Florence, Italy: Giovanni Battista Landin, 1632. *Wikimedia Commons*. https://commons.wikimedia.org/wiki/File:Galileos_Dialogue_Title_Page.png

Galilei, Galileo. Galileo offering his telescope to three women possibly Urania and attendants seated on a throne; he is pointing toward the sky where some of his astronomical discoveries are depicted. 1655. Engraving. https://www.loc.gov/item/2006690469/.

William, Shakespeare. "Title page." Mr. William Shakespeares Comedies, Histories, & Tragedies. London, England: Edward Blount and William and Isaac Jaggard, 1623. *Wikimedia Commons*. https://commons.wikimedia.org/wiki/File:William_Shakespeare_-_First_Folio_1623.jpg.

Shakspeare sic performing before Queen Elizabeth and her court. [Between 1780 and 1850]. Engraving. https://www.loc.gov/item/96506570/.

Haussmann, Elias Gottlob. "Portrait of Johann Sebastian Bach." *Wikimedia Commons*, 1746 (copy from 1748). https://commons.wikimedia.org/wiki/File:Johann_Sebastian_Bach.jpg.

Bach, Johann Sebastian. [Title Page], The Brandenburg Concertos. 1721. Pen on paper. Bridgeman Images. https://www.bridgemanimages.us/en-US/asset/308429/.

A.Savin. Ensemble of Sanssouci Neues Palais in Potsdam (Germany). July 18, 2017. Photograph. *Wikimedia Commons*. https://commons.wikimedia.org/wiki/File:Potsdam_Sanssouci_07-2017_img4.jpg.

Stieler, Joseph Karl. "Portrait Beethovens Mit Der Partitur Zur Missa Solemnis." *Wikimedia Commons*, 1820. https://commons.wikimedia.org/wiki/File:Beethoven.jpg.

Beethoven, Ludwig van. "Heiligenstadt Testament." *Wikimedia Commons*, October 6, 1802 to October 10, 1802. https://commons.wikimedia.org/wiki/File:Beethoven_Heiligenstaedter_Testament.jpg.

Prater, Ethan. Beethoven Grave - Vienna Central Cemetery. April 10, 2009. Photograph. Flickr. https://www.flickr.com/photos/eprater/3806101585/in/photostream/.

Stober, Franz: "Beethoven Funeral." Retrieved from https://commons.wikimedia.org/wiki/File:Beethoven_Funerals.jpg

Duchamp, Marcel. "Nude Descending a Staircase, No. 2," 1912. Philadelphia Museum of Art. https://en.wikipedia.org/wiki/File:Duchamp_-_Nude_Descending_a_Staircase.jpg.

Sommariva, Emilio. Italian Poet Filippo Tommaso Marinetti. 1913. Photograph. *Wikimedia Commons*. https://commons.wikimedia.org/wiki/File:Marinetti5.jpg.

Turner, Orren Jack, photographer. Albert Einstein, 1879-1955. c. 1947. Photograph. https://www.loc.gov/item/2004671908/.

Einstein, Albert. Letter to F. D. Roosevelt. "Einstein-Szilárd-Brief." Franklin D. Roosevelt Presidential Library and Museum, August 2, 1939. https://www.fdrlibrary.org/documents/356632/390886/document007.pdf/3483329d-7b68-442d-953d-eb91e0c5c9b1

Department of Defense. Department of the Air Force. 9/26/1947-, retouched by Mmxx. First atomic bombing of Hiroshima, Japan by B-29 superfortresses on August 6. American Hiroshima Japan, August 6, 1945. Photograph. *Wikimedia Commons*. https://commons.wikimedia.org/wiki/File:Atomic_cloud_over_Hiroshima_-_NARA_542192_-_Edit.jpg Original from https://catalog.archives.gov/id/542192.

www.ingramcontent.com/pod-product-compliance
Lightning Source LLC
Chambersburg PA
CBHW080637170426
43200CB00015B/2870